...lkans,
...our in the SAS
...where he conducted devastating,
...dercover operations against cocaine cartels. Since leaving the SAS as a Warrant Officer he has been involved in security work in the Congo, Nigeria, Eastern Europe and the Middle East. He now runs a company training personnel mainly for security work in Iraq and Afghanistan.

Praise for Highway to Hell

'A remarkable look at Iraq's invisible army . . . without whom no Western civilian could stay alive for more than a few hours'   Frederick Forsyth

'An eye-opening book'   *Daily Mail*

'A gripping and honest story which provides an unusual take on the war memoir'   *The Good Book Guide*

Also available by John Geddes

Spearhead Assault

JOHN GEDDES

HIGHWAY TO HELL

arrow books

Published in the United Kingdom by Arrow Books in 2007

3 5 7 9 10 8 6 4

Copyright © John Geddes and Alun Rees 2006

John Geddes and Alun Rees have asserted their right under the Copyright, Designs and Patents Act, 1988 to be identified as the authors of this work.

First published in the United Kingdom in 2006 by Century

Arrow Books
The Random House Group Limited
20 Vauxhall Bridge Road, London, SW1V 2SA

Addresses for companies within The Random House Group Limited can be found at:
www.randomhouse.co.uk/offices.htm

The Random House Group Limited Reg. No. 954009

A CIP catalogue record for this book is available from the British Library

ISBN 9780099499466

The Random House Group Limited makes every effort to ensure that the papers used in its books are made from trees that have been legally sourced from well-managed and credibly certified forests. Our paper procurement policy can be found at:
www.randomhouse.co.uk/paper.htm

Typeset in Sabon by Palimpsest Book Production Limited, Grangemouth, Stirlingshire
Printed and bound in Great Britain by
CPI Bookmarque, Croydon, CR0 4TD

Dedication

To all the PMCs who have died in the name of protection . . .

1

CONTACT!

I first saw them on the slip road. They were trapped in a muddle of traffic, jostling to get through, eager, anxious, impatient; the mood of the driver transmitted down through the steering wheel and the throttle into the jerking, pushy movements of the car. I'd watched them as we drove past and now they were behind us framed in my observer's mirror, kicking up a plume of road dust as they weaved through the morning traffic on the highway through Fallujah. Pickups loaded with workers on the open backs, loose-fitting robes snapping in the milky warm slipstream, moved to let the black BMW 7 series charge through. They were like members of a herd making way for a big predator which had earmarked its prey further into the throng.

I knew what was coming now just as the herd, watching from their pickups and battered saloons, did. They simply watched the pursuit with relieved interest, glad not to be the ones pursued and hoping above all not to be noticed. To be honest I'd known what was coming from the moment I'd seen the BMW, with its blacked-out windows, stuck temporarily on the slip road. It was typical, too typical, of the motors used by gangs of insurgents in Iraq, and as the car loomed up in my mirror I knew with utter certainty they were about to strike. But the difference was that I am not one of the herd.

My name is John Geddes. I used to be a warrant officer in the SAS and now I'm a soldier of fortune. I'm a hired gun, a mercenary if you like, and I was trying to keep the other guys in the car alive on the drive from Jordan to Baghdad along the most dangerous road in the world, down the Fallujah bypass and round the Ramadi ring road. It's a route they call the Highway to Hell.

There were four others in the car, a TV crew from a major UK network and a Jordanian driver, and as I watched that BMW gaining on us all my senses combined to help me stay focused on keeping my clients and myself alive. I barely took my eyes off the mirror, leaving my peripheral senses to tell me if other predators had joined the chase, but as events unfolded it was to be just us and them. Ahmed my driver had seen them too and I didn't have to tell him who they were. He started to mutter and jabber under his breath and I couldn't tell whether he was praying or cursing, only that he was terrified. He never usually perspired but within seconds beads of sweat were running down his forehead and the sides of his neck.

The BMW was cruising behind us closely matching our speed, and that's a real giveaway. They call it a combat indicator in the military but I didn't need any indicators; I'd had a shit feeling about it ever since I'd spotted the 7 series.

Then they began moving up on us and I weighed the AK-47 lying on my lap in my hands for a moment before resting it back there again. I had my window open but now closed it to hide behind its tinted glass. The BMW came up alongside and the black window in the front came down like a theatre curtain to reveal the driver and a guy who had the air of the man in charge sitting beside him.

They cruised past us at a good speed, nice and steady though; after all they'd got nothing to worry about. It was their backyard; they were the top predator in the chain and they were going to take their time. I guess they were thinking that maybe we were rich Iraqis or Kuwaitis. Japanese tourists would be nice and yes, believe it or not, they do come sightseeing from Tokyo. The guys in the BMW would have loved the three-man Western TV crew I'd actually got on board – all that hostage money and whatever happened they'd have the camera kit and three satellite phones to sell. A real steal and just for good measure Ahmed would be slotted like a dog.

Ahmed kept on muttering under his breath and they were in no hurry to put him out of his suspense as I watched them drop back alongside us a second time. Then they fell behind us to spurt forward and come back alongside yet again. Maybe they were enjoying their game of cat and mouse. My clients were sleeping off hangovers. No need to wake them, I thought. Nothing they can do about it.

Anyway I had one advantage – our big GMC four-wheel drive gave me a view down onto the gunmen – and as I looked their back windows were lowered and I saw three armed men on the rear passenger seat. In the front the driver was wearing a sick smile behind a *shemag* which had partly fallen away from his face; the guy beside him had his *shemag* wrapped around his features as he leant halfway across the driver to gesticulate with his AK-47. I've got one of them too, I was thinking, but I'm not showing it. His eyes were burning with hatred and disdain and he obviously wanted us to pull in. I couldn't believe it when I felt our bonnet come back towards me as Ahmed, the man with most to lose if you count his life, actually began to obey.

'Fucking drive, Ahmed,' I snarled at him. His foot went down again and we temporarily spoilt the synchronised driving display of the scumbags in the 7 series, but they were soon back with us.

Terrified, Ahmed was gibbering out loud in Arabic in a continuous flow as I looked through my tinted window at the four armed men in the car. Years of experience told me that their demeanour and the way they were holding their weapons meant that the last thing they were expecting was a real fight. They must have believed they'd got all the cards and that sooner rather than later we would be pulling in to the side of the road to deliver them their prize. I decided to keep my ace well hidden, on my lap and out of sight.

They forged ahead once more and the boss leaned across again but this time he shoved the AK in front of the driver and out of the window and let go a burst across our bonnet to encourage us to pull over. I fought hard with any idea of dropping my window and lifting the AK off my lap and into sight. Ace under the table was my mantra at that moment, ace under the table. I pushed everything else out of my mind but the gunmen and the thought of the card I would play. I knew what I had to do because the next time he fired the burst would be aimed into our vehicle and that would be a very bad thing.

I stared through my tinted window across the three feet of door metal and swirling, dusty air that separated us and I could clearly see that the scowling gunman next to the driver was trying to eyeball me.

I lowered my window and looked back at him. I looked straight through him and then I did it. I played my ace but even then I didn't lay it on the table; they never even saw the card. I just pressured my finger onto the trigger of the Kalashnikov still resting on my lap and let go a long burst of fire.

The familiar metallic clattering of an AK was amplified inside the car into the most terrible, deafening cacophony of sound. *Clat! Clat! Clat!* It seemed to go on and on, filling my world with an awful fanfare of destruction. *Clat! Clat! Clat!*

The armour-piercing assault rounds tore through our door and into theirs in a microsecond, ripping metal and flesh without discrimination in the 7 series. I watched the driver's head explode as the height difference of the two vehicles laid it on the line. The gunman next to him screamed, open-mouthed in horror, all hatred and disdain wiped from his eyes by disbelief, as the assault rounds sliced into him too and tracked through his body.

Clat! Clat! Clat! My finger still pressured the trigger and rounds kept tearing across that three-foot space for another couple of seconds until the BMW suddenly faded and fell back. I followed it in the observer's mirror and saw steam and black smoke billowing from under the bonnet, and I knew the end of my burst had smashed their engine block.

In mirror image I watched the BMW start to

fishtail and skid. We were still in traffic but cars and trucks were now evaporating away from the scene of the high-speed shoot-out with practised ease. But my interest wasn't in traffic flow; the critical thing was my certainty that the driver was dead and his boss beside him probably dead too. As for the three gunmen behind them, they hadn't even had time to spit let alone respond and they were helpless as the BMW spun out of control.

'Drive, fucking drive,' I screamed at Ahmed, and he maxed out at 120 kph as I turned to the correspondent and his crew, who were now sitting transfixed and deafened after the rudest awakening of their lives.

'Okay, guys?" I asked, barely able to hear my own voice. They nodded rigidly through the haze of acrid cordite that filled the car. I watched as their eyes kept wandering away from mine towards the gun still resting on my lap and then to the door beside me and then back again. They were trying to work out why I hadn't fired through the window, why the door wasn't a mangled mess, just pierced by a series of neat holes marked out by flash burns. They were trying to work out why they were still alive.

'Welcome to Fallujah,' I said, but they looked very pale and not another word was spoken until Baghdad.

Our journey had begun at dawn that day as light welled up over the city, still cooling from the heat of the day before like a giant concrete radiator, and the haunting wail of the call to prayer floated down from a minaret over downtown Amman.

That chant of the muezzin to the faithful, the clichéd soundtrack to every documentary ever made on the Middle East – you know exactly what to expect but it still gets to you every time and never fails to raise the hairs on the back of your neck. These days it never fails to set me on edge. It's become the theme tune for death and mayhem and starts the day with an unwelcome reminder that a religion founded on a philosophy of order and mutual respect has been twisted into an alibi for murder and bombing.

I'd already showered and shaved and my kit had been checked, rechecked and checked again; it was ready to go so there was nothing to do but get on with it. The checking of kit is an abiding theme in my life and has become such a routine that I almost find myself looking into the mirror to check I'm taking the right bloke on the job. I grabbed my small day sack with a survival kit in it, checked I had my ID and passport and then went downstairs to join the others in the hotel foyer. The correspondent was a regular, his cameraman an experienced guy who knew the ropes, and the soundman-cum-fixer was the third member of the crew. Ahmed was a veteran on the run.

I went through the drill with them. It always begins with the briefing, the 'actions on' as the military call it, when I cover what they've got to do in the event of a road traffic accident, an ambush or a hijack. I stood there feeling like cabin crew going through the pre-flight emergency drill while, sprawled out on the hotel's leather sofas, my clients looked just as bored as the average business passenger.

They smiled wanly when I got to the bit where I tell them, 'Remember, we don't stop at service areas, we piss on the side of the road; and we don't look at our dicks while we're doing it, we keep aware and look about us.' There were no women on that trip but it would have been just the same for them, with a biological variation of course, and the guys knew that I was serious when I told them, 'There are service areas but they're a no-no since a CNN crew stopped at one for a cuppa and got rumbled by insurgents. They were followed and a few rounds were fired through the back of the vehicle. The driver was killed and they were very lucky to get away.'

It was time to go and they hauled themselves out of their seats and joined the pile of aluminium boxes stacked under the front awning of the hotel along-side the big GMC. 'Hard cases up against the back seats, please,' I told them, and the camera boxes were packed where they would afford at least some protection from any incoming rounds to our rear. The soft luggage, rucksacks and holdalls of clothing were piled against the boxes. While the kit was being packed the correspondent paced nervously up and down as though he was rehearsing a piece to camera. He'd been up drinking with the cameraman into the early hours and all they wanted to do was to get into the vehicle and go to sleep.

Meanwhile, Ahmed dragged on a foul-smelling cigarette. I placed myself upwind of him, carefully watching the unfolding scene as the rising sun glinted off my mirrored shades. He's a nice guy, Ahmed, a family man who knows only too well that captured Jordanian drivers are always killed by insurgents. Why? Because they're not worth a bean on the hostage market and anyway they've betrayed Islam by chauffeuring the infidel invaders. Like all the Jordanians who daily risk their lives on the Baghdad run, Ahmed's either very broke or very brave or, I suspect, both.

I pointed towards the car bonnet and he lifted it so that I could personally check the oil and radiator levels. I even looked at the screen wash. Check and recheck; it's attention to detail that keeps you alive. I glanced at the tyres too just to make sure they had some tread on them, then Ahmed turned the key in the ignition and I watched the needle on the fuel gauge rise to full.

'Thanks,' I told him. 'You happy with everything?'

Ahmed smiled in reply and I turned to the TV crew. 'All aboard, guys, time to roll. Just make sure you've got everything you need.'

It takes three hours to get to the Iraqi border and there wasn't a great deal of chat in the car once they'd discussed a few arrangements, who they'd be meeting and the first story they hoped to get in the can. The correspondent and the cameraman soon nodded off, heads occasionally lolling from side to side with the movement of the car. It wasn't long before the soundman joined them.

That first leg of the journey is always unrelentingly boring with mile after mile of yellowy-grey rock and sand, and I knew that we wouldn't see a scrap of vegetation until we got to Iraq. The civil service mandarin in Britain who drew the lines on the map, demarcating the boundaries of the two countries nearly a century ago, gave the Jordanians the short straw. They got a lunar landscape with not a drop of oil beneath it while the Iraqis got two rivers and a bit of greenery sitting on top of a gigantic oil well. I spotted the change in landscape just before I spotted the border post itself, a nondescript collection of buildings with a small US Army stockade situated at arm's length from the local administration. The sight of the border galvanised me out of the wheel-drumming monotony of the past three hours and I knew that the mood would now be very different.

The Jordanian checkpoint is always a flurry of activity: waiting in a queue of fifty, visas stamped, and of course the obligatory payment to lay off any more border bureaucracy. The Iraqi border patrol just waves you through most of the time only occasionally taking a look at credentials, but there's never a lot of fuss and we soon pulled up outside the US guardhouse for the really important part of the proceedings.

'You guys put your flak jackets on while I collect my tools,' I told them, and then I vanished into the guardhouse.

When I first arrived in Iraq I learnt that a lot of the security teams bury their weapons in caches on the Iraqi side, take a GPS bearing on the spot and just dig them up when they cross back over the frontier on their next run in. I didn't like the sound of that at all. What if there's a pair of unsympathetic eyes out there watching as you make your cache? When you return you might just find yourself digging into a booby trap or walking onto a small anti-personnel mine laid as a welcome mat by insurgents. No, I didn't think that was the way for me so I pondered the problem for a while until my natural affection and admiration for the Americans and their way of doing business led me to a direct approach. I visited the US border detachment on my first run and spoke to the big Louisiana-born master sergeant in charge.

'Do you know those Western movies where the

sheriff takes the weapons off the cowboys when they arrive in town?' I asked him when the introductions were over.

'Sure do,' he said.

'Well, I'm not a cowboy and you're not the sheriff but I wondered if you could do the same sort of thing for me but in reverse and take my guns off me when I leave town, so to speak, and go back to Jordan?'

'Why hell, yes, it'd be our pleasure,' he told me, and that's the way it panned out. I just handed them in and got a receipt and they locked them up until I returned. No fear of landmines or a nasty ambush, no sweaty digging in the scrub. In fact no burial party of any sort at all.

This civilised transaction had another key benefit and that was the chance to chat to the Yanks in the guardhouse and get any intelligence on insurgent activity that had come back down the line to them. There were very few problems close to the Jordanian border but the guys in the guardhouse always knew about anything going on further up the road and liked to shoot the breeze with people passing through. Information can mean survival in Iraq.

The master sergeant and I sealed the deal that day with a case of beer, which the Yanks are always grateful to receive as the poor suckers fight in a dry army, and then I showed them a couple of special shooting range drills with an AK and gave them a bit of instruction on the finer points of fighting with my Russian friend. They were chuffed and I was pleased to leave a unit of the US Army with a little bit of Hereford polish on its troops.

So it was that I stepped into the guardhouse as usual and handed over my gun chitty then waited for my weapons to be brought out from the armoury and handed over to me.

'Here you go, sir.' The young GI counted out my private arsenal. 'One AK-47 serial number—'

'No need for the number thanks; I'm sure it's the right one.'

'Sure thing, sir. So that's one AK-47 assault rifle plus six thirty-round mags, one Glock pistol, plus four twelve-round mags. Serial number?' He looked up enquiringly.

'No, thanks.'

'Okay, so here we go. Two NS L2 grenades and one white phos' grenade. That's everything sir, so if you just sign here you can take your weapons. Anything else I can help you with, sir?'

'Not really, thanks very much.' I scrawled my name across the bottom of the chit. 'Nothing going on up the road, is there?'

'All quiet as far as we know, sir. Now you all have a safe journey.'

'Thanks, old son. See you on the way back.'

I transferred the weapons to the vehicle where the crew studiously avoided mentioning them because officially the guns were not supposed to exist at all, let alone the grenades.

The British and other European networks mostly work on the principle that once weapons are involved journalistic impartiality and neutrality are lost and their crews will then be open to hostage-taking and the unthinkable possibility of execution. Paradoxically, it's argued, the absence of weapons will protect correspondents and crews from those fates as this tangibly demonstrates their non-combatant status. If only, if only. You can be fairly sure that people like the infamous Musab al Zarqawi, al Qaeda's man in Iraq, have not taken the trouble to read the editorial handbooks of the TV stations but their actions spell out clearly their views on the issue. It's quite simple. The word 'neutrality' does not exist in their dictionary and all that matters to them is their own twisted interpretation of the word of the Almighty embodied in the Holy Koran. That boils down to a rule of thumb that absolutely no one at all is entitled to safe passage through their lands, a stance which goes against the deeply ingrained traditions of hospitality in the Arab world. In today's Iraq you're more likely to be exploited for your propaganda value on a few pleading video appeals then have your head chopped off.

The US networks have been quick to recognise the realities in the region and tend to travel with more than enough firepower to take on the average gang of insurgents. No one can legislate for sniper shots or a lucky hit with a rocket-propelled grenade and no one can insulate himself against a suicide bomber intent on hell, but if less than the worst happens they reckon to have enough to protect and maintain the convoy until help arrives. There are certainly arguments for and against their strategy, which you might characterise as heavy-handed, but there are absolutely no sane arguments for moving around Iraq without any weapons at all. None.

Anyway I'd already had a free and frank exchange of views with my clients about the issues and had told them that they could certainly instruct me not to carry a weapon. I, however, would ignore their instructions and would be carrying a weapon unless they absolutely did not want me to, in which case they'd have to find someone else. Therein of course lay their dilemma because finding someone willing to drive the Highway without a weapon is a bit like looking for a free beer in a brothel. Like quite a few others on the security circuit out there I had been persuaded to travel the Highway unarmed on a score or more occasions but the number of close shaves I had had left me feeling like Kojak and I had resolved to travel armed or not at all. If people didn't like it they didn't have to travel with me.

'Look,' I told the correspondent, 'just tell the news desk that you're travelling with a bodyguard who has been told not to carry a weapon. When you've done that just pretend you haven't seen the weapon I'm carrying. It's simple. You didn't see it so if it goes pear-shaped then I'm the one to blame.'

'That's all very well, John, but I could get the sack for travelling with an armed bodyguard,' he replied.

'Of course you could and that would be terrible, but you could just as easily get yourself dead if I don't carry a weapon. Besides, the only way your bosses will find out that the rules have been broken is if we get captured, at which point it won't matter anyway.'

'What you say is all very well, John, but what if—'

'No what ifs, mate. I'll tell you what. If a band of insurgents decides to take us hostage because I am carrying a weapon it will be because I haven't used the weapon. Therefore, if we are taken then either way it's my fault so you can sack me before they sack you. In the meantime pretend I'm the man with the invisible gun. Agreed?'

'Okay but—'

'No buts. Deal?'

'Deal.'

That's the way it went yet I know full well that he could still face the sack today if his news desk – sitting safely back in the London studio – found out that he'd broken their standing orders on war coverage. Crazy.

Anyway the deal was done and I had sealed it by retrieving my weapons from the US armoury, so I went back to organising the trip. The crew had put on their body armour, the bulky type you commonly see on TV reports, which provides maximum protection but is crap for moving about in. I use my own high-spec 'restricted entry' body armour designed for fighting in tight spots, which is very expensive but in the words of the brochure an 'effective compromise between total protection and mobility'. Don't know about that but I certainly feel more comfortable in it.

The tension in the car had shifted up a couple of gears by then and there was a tangible sense of apprehension even though it would be another hour and a half before the really high-voltage ride through Fallujah and Ramadi began. The start of the roller coaster is the point known as Feature 127. It's just a stone waymark at the side of the road in the middle of nowhere erected to tell the weary traveller that there are 127 kilometres to go to Baghdad but it has taken on great significance for those who travel the

Highway. That's because for some reason nothing ever seems to happen to the west of Feature 127 and all hell can, and often does, break loose on the other side of it. Now it's a common rendezvous point and a place to stop, consider and compose oneself before the ride begins.

I recognised the landscape around 127 before we reached the waymark itself and told Ahmed to pull in for a pit stop. I reminded everyone on board to have that heads-up piss before we continued because there would be no stopping on the road from then on unless we were absolutely forced to pull up. The correspondent yawned and looked a bit fed up at being woken from a kip that might have seen him sleep untroubled by the stresses and dangers of the Highway until he arrived at his hotel in Baghdad.

Unscrewing a bottle of water I took a swig then set about arranging the cabin space for the rest of the run. At the same time I was tuning myself up mentally for whatever might come with a routine that clearly signals a watershed in the journey and the need for a more focused mindset. 'Right, fellas, get your helmets on and keep them on for the rest of the trip, please. If there's anything you want out of your kit get it now if you would, and please don't mention it to me once we've set off again. I won't be interested. Whatever it is.'

They strapped their helmets on and I looked at them

carefully. They all had the expression of incipient fear of someone about to take a white-knuckle ride. Their eyes were flat, almost glazed by a sheen of adrenalin waiting to be used. They didn't want to do it but they were going to do it anyway and they were becoming increasingly aware of the thumping of their hearts and the dryness in their mouths as they fought the demons within to remain outwardly composed.

Ahmed fingered his worry beads and unconsciously chewed on his lip as he waited anxiously to take the wheel again. I was busy hanging spare body armour onto the door furniture inside the car to create a barrier between the passengers and small-arms fire. It's an effective precaution that has saved many lives. The check reflex kicked in again and I looked at the oil, water and fuel. Just in case. When we were all loaded up I cradled the AK in my lap, covering it with my green and black *shemag* head-dress to hide it from any prying eyes, and I handed Ahmed the Glock pistol. I knew he could use it because I'd shown him how. He stuffed it between his leg and the seat and nodded to me.

'Let's roll,' I said, and Ahmed did just that, accelerating down the road as if he was trying to lift a jet off a runway, pushing it and pushing it. He'd push the car like that all the way to Baghdad, keeping the speedo at 100 klicks as if a cart full of demons was tailing him – and perhaps it was.

The traffic began to thicken a little as we approached Fallujah, a town that straddles the Highway like a piece of malevolent lagging, bombed, battered and shot up but largely unyielding. And that's when I spotted them jostling to find a way through the constipated traffic on the slip road. And then the black BMW was framed in the observer's mirror as it charged up behind us . . .

2

FROM DRAMA
INTO CRISIS

'Half a league, half a league,
Half a league onward,
All in the valley of Death
Rode the six hundred . . .'

I strained to keep my voice strong and clear while at the same time I frantically tried to stop it erupting into a strangled shout as I rendered the best version I could of Tennyson's epic poem 'The Charge of the Light Brigade'. My nerves were stretched taut with the effort so that the palms of my hands and my forehead were covered with a film of perspiration. Somehow I kept on going, struggling to remember the words and staring past the glare of a spotlight at faces I couldn't make out. I kept going, just like the Light Brigade, and gratefully sucked in a lungful of air as the words of the poem faded away.

Was I was reciting poetry as a way of shutting out

the brutal bellowing of interrogators, hell-bent on breaking me down, during one of the notorious sensory disorientation exercises in the SAS? No, it was worse than that by far; I was performing in a drama school show at the tender age of seventeen at a time when my burning ambition was to be a film star.

My screen heroes Lee Marvin and Steve McQueen had been the inspiration when I'd gone to my school careers adviser, got a list of acting academies and left home in Newcastle upon Tyne to head off for the bright lights of the Birmingham School of Speech and Drama. I didn't have a single decent academic qualification to my name because I'd preferred boxing to books and in those days I'd been a promising amateur fighter, but I did have the utter conviction of youth that I was destined to become a cinema great. As it turned out my exam results weren't a stumbling block and a panel of two women and a cool, laid-back bloke decided to give me an audition. After I'd read a piece out loud they gave me a frank appraisal of my gifts.

'Well, you've certainly got the looks,' I was told, 'but you haven't got any talent at all. Not that that matters these days because a lot of film stars don't have any real acting talent either. We'll give you a place and see how you get on.'

I wasn't surprised to be accepted by the school; after all it was my destiny, wasn't it? Nor was I put

off by the judgement that I was completely devoid
of talent. So I went back home to Newcastle to break
the good news to my mum – Dad had died when I
was thirteen – and I was soon back in Birmingham
sharing a room in the YMCA with a Jimi Hendrix
lookalike who was a native of the city and knew
every club, pub and most of the girls in the city centre.

Of course the panel had been right about my lack
of talent and the principal of the school, a formidable lady called Mary Richards, homed in on me
within days of my arrival. She hadn't been at the
audition and was obviously appalled that I'd slipped
through the net and got into her establishment in any
role other than mopping the floors. A friend of
Laurence Olivier and very much of the theatrical old
school, Miss Richards made it her mission in life to
constantly shout at me and make me go back over
practically every word I uttered, and as the weeks
went by it was clear she believed I had been inflicted
on her as a practical joke by her staff. Needless to
say it wasn't a happy relationship and I lived in terror
of her haughty looks, her imperious stares and the
razor-sharp edge of her tongue. Things weren't
helped by my rendition of the song 'We have all the
time in the world' during one of the shows we regularly had to put on. I can tell you it wasn't Fame
Academy. My singing was so appalling that when it
was over the audience of fellow students was silent

for several seconds before a faint ripple of applause relieved the embarrassment, but I noticed the principal remained too shocked to put her hands together at all.

I could see I was going nowhere in the college and I knew I had to leave before Mary Richards booted me out but I was still determined to become a screen idol and, obviously, a potent sex symbol too. There were no thoughts of going back to Tyneside to look for a shipyard apprenticeship but I did come to the conclusion that I needed a new strategy to reach my goal. I decided to follow the example of my heroes Steve and Lee, who had both served in the US Marine Corps and seen action. I reasoned that if I left the Birmingham School of Speech and Drama and enlisted in the army I would get the experience that would turn me from a mere player into a convincing hero who could draw on his combat experience to make the action leap off the screen. The army would become my drama school and I would rehearse for my movie career in battle. At the time I thought my plan had the beauty of simplicity on its side.

Then fate intervened as we were given a new project to rehearse for the end-of-term show. We were told to take a piece of military history famous in literature, study the work in question and prepare a recitation based on it. Of course lots of people turned straight to Shakespeare and waded into Agincourt and Bosworth and soon the sounds of 'Once more unto the breach' and 'A horse! a horse! my kingdom for a horse!' reverberated around the college as we prepared to put on our military medley before an audience of students and invited guests. For the first time we had been given a piece of work that I relished and I wanted to do something different, so after careful thought I chose the Crimean War and the awesome charge of the Light Brigade as my subject. I worked hard at it and tried to put as much expression into Lord Tennyson's poem as I possibly could as I prepared for the show.

Meanwhile the principal had put the arm on one of her old acting chums and grandly announced that the guest of honour would be the great Dirk Bogarde himself. This sent a wave of nervous anticipation through the college but I kept cool. No sweat, I thought. I'll just give it my all on the night. I did just that, pouring heart and soul into my recitation knowing that a real screen hero was out there among the silhouettes beyond the footlights listening to me.

It was the best thing I'd ever done at the college and I got my first and last spontaneous round of applause from an audience. Afterwards Dirk Bogarde himself came up to me, accompanied by the principal. Her face was locked in a smile that suggested even mild success for her pupil from hell had brought

on a case of tetanus. But Dirk gave me a critical acco-
lade I'll never forget.

'Bloody good effort that,' he said. 'Difficult to get
that poem right – got to weigh and balance it properly.'

'Thanks,' I said, then rather lamely, 'I just gave it
my best shot.'

He laughed at my accidental pun then told me
he'd been a soldier himself during the Second World
War.

'I was in the Parachute Regiment,' he said. 'Fought
in Normandy at Plimsoll Bridge. Unforgettable
experiences, you know.'

That settled it. It was obvious I'd been right and
the military was the place to learn about acting. If the
army was good enough for Dirk it was good enough
for me. Term ended a couple of days later and as
soon as I got back to Newcastle I was hammering at
the door of the army recruiting office to sign up for
the Parachute Regiment and begin the long journey
from Birmingham to Baghdad in a military career
unwittingly launched by the great Dirk Bogarde.

I'm sure the army was in me anyway, just masked
by my teenage obsession with being a matinee idol.
After all I was the son of a wartime Desert Rat – my
father had fought at the battle of El Alamein – and
I'm certain the fact that I was born in Rhodesia, as
Zimbabwe was then known, and brought from Africa

to Tyneside at the age of three gave me a bit of a soldier's wanderlust too. So a few weeks later I found myself in Aldershot at the Parachute Regiment Depot and enlisted with 2 Para after successfully completing the gruelling P Company selection process. I was now in the drama school of my choice but what a different world it turned out to be.

The depot staff knew I'd come to them straight from drama college so as you might imagine there was a lot of ribbing and they called me Duke after another of my screen heroes, John Wayne. As luck would have it though I turned out to be a reasonably good crow – Para slang for a rookie – and they didn't give me too much grief over my foray into the world of luvviedom.

After five years in 2 Para and several tours of duty in Northern Ireland I'd already had my fair share of enemy contacts and I'd survived the massacre at Warrenpoint on 27 August 1979 when eighteen soldiers, mostly paratroopers, lost their lives. Warrenpoint was the biggest single success against the army of the IRA's cowardly campaign. I was lucky that day – lucky not to be with the main party when a huge bomb was detonated on the road, and lucky to have had the instinct to take cover on dead ground as the cottage next to me erupted in a second explosion. It galls me to say it but that was a good ambush the IRA laid on. However, I believe it was our own failings that allowed it to happen because, as I understand it, Special Branch had warned the IRA were planning a spectacular in the area. Someone in the military or intelligence hierarchy either didn't take it in properly or worse ignored the warnings.

I'd been fortunate that day when the IRA struck but nothing was to prepare me for what followed when we got the call to liberate the Falkland Islands. It's a war that's been written up in many books and I've actually been mentioned in two or three of them and it changed my life profoundly. When we sailed for the South Atlantic I was a corporal and patrol commander in C Company, which specialised in reconnaissance and was charged with getting as close as possible to enemy lines to report on their deployment in detail, a mission that's known in the jargon as CTR or close target reconnaissance. I didn't like the Falklands much. It was colder and wetter than a YMCA shower and the landscape was as bleak and unyielding as the Brecon Beacons in winter, only five times as big. Tabbing across the terrain was a nightmare because the boggy ground was littered with large balls of moss that squelched and gave way underfoot – the lads christened them babies' heads with that peculiar brand of gallows humour that the British soldier delights in. It was the perfect landscape for a very hard war.

Eventually my patrol was tasked to do the CTRs on the enemy lines at Goose Green in the run-up to the decisive battle in that stark, unyielding place. We got so close to the enemy in the mist that we used the stench from their makeshift toilets to prevent us from stumbling into their slit trenches as we followed the smell of crap on our side of their positions, where those young Argentine conscripts habitually went to the toilet. If the smell was too strong, we knew we were right on top of them.

We were to report on numbers of troops, machine-gun positions and their tactical deployment, the enemy's morale, their state of readiness, who was asleep and who was awake. We discovered one position where most of them were asleep with only the occasional word of Spanish heard in the mist; they later paid with their lives when our information led to them being bayoneted in their sleeping bags in a silent attack. When our work was done we went back to the start line to hold it until the rifle companies came up to wreak their havoc and suffer the consequences. The battle for Goose Green, in which Colonel H. Jones gave his life and won a posthumous VC, was the fiercest and most dreadful struggle of the Falklands conflict and two defining episodes in that day's combat have remained with me ever since.

The first was the death of my close friend Steve Prior, who was as brave and decent a man as you could hope to meet. On the ship to the South Atlantic one of the younger guys was obviously very scared of what was to come, as indeed were most of us, but Steve took it upon himself to give the youngster some support: he simply and starkly told him, 'Don't worry. If it comes to it I'll die so that you can live.' On the approach to Goose Green that's exactly what happened. Several members of A Company lay wounded out in the open on the forward slopes of Darwin Hill and four corporals including Steve dropped their gear and ran out over the wickedly exposed terrain to bring those lads back. One of them was the youngster on the boat. He was brought to safety while Steve was shot in the head by Argentine fire as he laid down his life for his mates.

I'll never forget Steve or the prophetic words he spoke on his way to his death. For men and women who have seen combat those Cenotaph thoughts are not annual Remembrance Day reflections but real memories of friends left on the battlefield and a constant backdrop to the way we live and act.

The second enduring image I brought with me out of the Falklands came during the vicious battle for the School House at Goose Green, a heavily fortified Argentine position. It was an L-shaped building and eight of us manoeuvred our way up the re-entrant before assaulting the building with rifles and grenades under the cover of smoke. Just a few minutes before

the assault our two patrols had given our heavy gear
– light machine guns, M79 grenade launchers and
several 66 millimetre anti-tank rockets – to the
forward element of D Company, who were low on
kit after fighting all day. They gave us covering fire
and the timing of their support team commander
Corporal Tom Harley was impeccable as a ferocious
weight of lead was unleashed to slam into the building
with devastating effect, lifting only as we assaulted
from the left flank.

We had matchsticks jammed into the sears of our
SLR rifle mechanisms so they would fire in bursts
instead of single rounds and a mate called Nick W.
and I fought furthest forward on the apex of the
building posting grenades through the shot-out
windows. I worked my way to the front door, which
was already burning and falling apart, kicked it in
and emptied a magazine into the building. Burning
shadows which will haunt me for the rest of my life
crumpled to the floor. For a split second across the
hall I spotted through the acrid smoke one of those
wooden platforms you often see in schools, used as
a stage for the children's performances. It was at the
far end of the room and I only glimpsed it as I stum-
bled back into the open to take cover behind the
school wall as incoming fire hailed down on us from
deeper Argentine positions. But I had a weird flash-
back and heard Mary Richards' voice telling me I'd

never be an actor, *'not in a thousand years'*. I finally got it: the army wasn't a rehearsal and I wasn't going to be a film star. I was a soldier.

From then on I became increasingly proficient and professional and I focused my every fibre on becoming a member of the SAS. I'd seen those guys operating in the Falklands – men apart, deadly wraiths who came and went in the mist and left the enemy smashed behind them. I wanted to be one of them and eventually I was.

I passed selection in 1984 and became a member of D Squadron. I specialised in HALO – high altitude, low opening covert parachute entry into combat zones. During my career with the Regiment I was involved in many highly classified operations around the world:

I fought terrorists in Northern Ireland but I'd rather consign those memories to history where I hope that conflict will remain for ever; I operated against cocaine cartels in South America in a secret war in the jungles and the foothills of the Andes; I went on top-secret missions in Africa and Asia; and with other SAS soldiers I became the eyes and ears of NATO in the Balkans. Then as a staff sergeant with 22 SAS there was one more operation in the Middle East.

It was a strange one that. The operation itself was straightforward but I was kicking my heels on gardening leave in the run-up to my retirement date from the army when I got the call. I'd already handed my kit in and I thought I'd 'beaten the clock' but the Regiment was short of bodies and I had to go. For those of you who don't know, the names of those who die fighting in the SAS are inscribed around the base of a large clock on the Regiment's parade ground and those of us who survive our service are said to have beaten the clock. The expression comes from the title of one of the first TV quiz shows called *Beat the Clock*. You can imagine the banter as I queued up to get my kit with some of the fresh entry guys going on their first mission. Anyway, the job went smoothly and in the end I obviously did beat the clock even if I'd been one of the few who'd had to undergo a rewind.

Special Air Service and special forces are titles that confer a very real exclusivity and military pre-eminence on those who are part of them. These formations are special in a very real sense and not just in terms of the skills, the knowledge and the courage deployed by their members. I believe what's really special about the SAS are the friendships and comradeships found in its ranks. They are often born out of hardship and usually forged in the dangers of live covert operations, and that makes for strong and lasting loyalties. It follows that most of my close friends are fellow blades; that's the name we give ourselves, taken from the winged dagger of our regimental emblem. Perhaps it seems a bit of a cliché but it's men and women who have endured those experiences and survived those dangers that we can most easily relate to.

One of the lasting friendships I made is with a formidable Welsh warrior called Mike Curtis. We fought together at Goose Green and then served in the SAS, where Mike and I were on many operations together before we joined the Regiment's unpublicised war against the cocaine cartels in Bolivia. Since leaving the Regiment I've worked on many dangerous jobs as a security consultant, bodyguard and mercenary fighter, often alongside Mike Curtis, but one of the most unusual experiences, and one strangely relevant to my story, is an incident Mike and I call the Near Death of a Princess.

It happened in the penthouse suite of a very smart London hotel and the princess in question was a member of one of the most powerful royal families in the Middle East. She was a charming and lovely person who was really easy to get on with and she relied on our advice quite closely. Mike and I were the heavies in the entourage but we tried to be as discreet as we could and make her feel comfortable and safe as she moved around London on a carousel of shopping expeditions – she appreciated that. There was one other vital member of her staff always nearby and that was a nurse because our princess, and she was our princess while she was in our charge, suffered quite badly from diabetes and her doting parents could afford to have medical help at hand twenty-four hours a day.

After a particularly gruelling day tabbing around the West End on a seriously tactical shopping expedition we got back to the hotel and I was just settling down to the evening routine of meal and bed when Mike banged on my door. As I recall he'd been to the gym; we'd take it in turns to work out while the other was on standby.

'John, we're needed! Room service found her in a coma! They've gone for the nurse! Let's go.'

I can remember my heart pounding as I ran down the thickly carpeted corridor after Mike. I was praying she was going to be all right. We really liked her and I was truly worried, but to be honest a part of me didn't want 'lost a princess' stamped across my CV either. We arrived at the princess's bedroom just after the nurse and the hotel manager, who'd been called too. I'm a trained patrol medic and I could see that our princess was in bad shape and rapidly slipping away into a hypoglycaemic coma.

That was bad enough but I could also see the nurse was frozen to the spot. I don't know where the family had found her but I quickly realised she had not experienced any life-or-death admissions at A & E for a very long time and she had a critical situation right there in front of her. She had all the kit with her – the glucose drip, the adrenalin, everything she needed – but she just wasn't physically able to move, petrified by the gravity of what was happening.

'For Christ's sake, she's hypo. Do something,' I hissed. No movement. I knew it was going to be down to me so I grabbed the gear off her and got to work while I gave Mike the strangest order he'd ever had. 'Get on the bed with her and keep her warm! Cuddle her!'

It was vital we didn't let her body temperature drop if we could help it but for a fraction of a second Mike's eyes met mine and I could read every word of his thoughts: She's a princess. She's a devout Muslim. She's not allowed to have blokes anywhere near her. I'd get stoned to death for this in her country. But he could see I meant it so he shrugged, wrapped her in a cover then dived onto the bed to hold her close to his body and give her what he assured me was a brotherly hug called a *cwtch* in Wales. The glucose and Mike's body heat did the trick and we saved her life. We never saw the nurse again but I swear I'll never forget the sight of one of the toughest men ever to serve in the SAS cuddling the life back into an Arabian princess.

There's a very eerie postscript to that incident because on that very night Princess Diana was killed

in a Paris underpass in the very same model of
Mercedes 500 that we were using to drive our princess
around. Mike and I experienced some spooky feelings about the lottery of fate that gave one princess
life and took it from another on the same day. It over-
laid our genuine sadness over Di's death.

Now for those of you who thought this was a book
about my life in the SAS, it's not; it's about my work
as a private military contractor in Iraq and the huge
mercenary army that has been employed to protect
the businessmen and engineers flooding into the
country to work on multi-billion-dollar projects to
regenerate the country.

I'll be describing the private military contractors
and how they work, emphasising the difference
between American and British tactics on the Highway
to Hell. The insurgents too will come under my focus
as I describe the roots and causes of the insurgency
and the qualities of the men who fight for it.

I'll be describing the extraordinary exploits of
some of the British PMC heroes and my own contacts
with the enemy during the eighteen months I worked
in Iraq. There were some very low points for me
personally after months of working the Fallujah road
as a lone bodyguard and I'll be telling you how stress
and drunken nights with TV crews nearly sent me
over the edge. I'll be telling you too about the women

who have joined the mercenary army and the love affairs and marriages that take place in the midst of the nightmare insurgency.

I still visit Iraq and the Middle East but in the spring of 2005 I stopped working the highways of Iraq as a security guard and now I run a familiarisation course for other soldiers who want to work there. They include my own son Kurt and a lot of his mates from the Paras so I have been kept up to the minute on all that goes on in the mercenary army and some of the extraordinary fire-fights with the insurgents that have happened since.

Obviously my background is part of the story but I've deliberately avoided describing in any detail my experiences while I was actually in the SAS. I want to respect the secret nature of my service with the Regiment and plenty has been said and written about its operations.

During my SAS service I was involved in operations that were designed to thwart paramilitary activities on all sides in the Bosnian conflict and to preserve innocent, unarmed civilians from ethnic cleansing and murder.

Obviously I can't talk about those operations, but I can say that lives were saved on all sides, although because of the balance of ethnic power in the country that inevitably meant that most of the people protected were Bosnian Muslims.

The important thing is that innocent civilian lives were saved and the fact that they were Muslim lives is neither here nor there. Does what I did make me a mujahid fighting for Islam in a war where fatwas were certainly proclaimed? Does it make me a traitor to the Christian Serbs, who had saved Europe from a Muslim invasion 400 years ago and believed they were doing the same thing again in the twentieth century?

Does the fact that Mike and I saved the life of a Muslim princess whose family actually propagated and spread the fundamentalism that has swept through the Islamic world make us heroes of Islam? I don't think so. I refuse to ally myself to credos, labels and religions. I wasn't concerned about the religions of those people in that country; I was just concerned that one side were paramilitaries with guns intent on malleting unarmed civilians. I was concerned that it was unfair and inhuman.

It took the West too long to react to ethnic cleansing, rape and murder in the Balkans and there were some shameful episodes, like the failure of Dutch UN soldiers to protect the enclave at Bihać. But in the end many Christian soldiers and airmen risked their lives to end the wholesale slaughter of countless followers of Islam. In the final act of the Balkan conflict we bombed Belgrade, a Christian capital, to oust the Milošević regime and end a

shameful war which hindsight tells us was probably
ignited by a Kosovo Liberation Army largely funded
by Osama bin Laden as he made his global mischief.

I know of an SAS soldier, a friend of mine, who
was observing a Serb column about to fall like wolves
on a town full of unarmed Muslim men in Kosovo.
He was hidden in an observation post just fifty metres
from the advancing Serbs when he called in an air
strike on them. In a breathtakingly unselfish action
he gave the coordinates of his own position to make
sure the strike would hit the Serbian column with
maximum impact. That cool, utterly courageous man
later joked that he felt completely safe because the air
force never achieves direct hits on targets, especially
with smart bombs, but he put his life on the line for
total strangers of a religious persuasion and culture
alien to his own. He did it out of a sense of humanity.

I've never heard a word of acknowledgement or
thanks from the world of Islam for what was done
for their brothers and sisters in the Balkans, and I
won't mind if I never do, but when years later I drove
along the Highway to Hell I knew that I could look
anyone from any community in the eye. I believe I
am no man's enemy unless he chooses to make me
one. For me it's humanity that counts, not the words
written in the book of any religion.

3

THE BREAKING STORM

DESOLATE, traumatised people, their eyes hollow with fatigue, their minds nearly broken after nights of bombing, were performing a ghastly mime of normal life. Many simply stood and watched as we drove through the shattered outskirts of Baghdad, where buildings reduced to rubble were the only milestones and the broken sticks of electricity poles, draped in a spaghetti of useless cable, pointed accusingly to the sky. Bridges were buckled into the water like toys which had been stamped on and a thin layer of bomb dust lay over the city, the freshly milled flour of modern warfare.

It had been a mind-numbing five-hour drive from Kuwait on a road that runs like a black ribbon through the barren rock-strewn landscape and most of us had dozed off for half the journey. Highway Tampa the Americans call it, and it's haunted by the ghosts of the First Gulf War a decade or so earlier, when a convoy of thousands of Iraqi conscripts fleeing from Desert Storm had been consigned to oblivion by US Apache helicopters and A-10 Thunderbolt aircraft.

There were thirty-five of us on the road, all ex-British special forces, mostly former SAS blades, and we were the vanguard of the massive private army that would follow, the first private military contractors to go into Iraq at the end of a war that we all hoped had been decisive. Usual rules applied: stubble on our faces and a steely indifference to the jet lag that comes from travelling halfway round the world to go to work. Official hostilities had ended just a few days earlier and we were travelling in a convoy of seven soft-skinned vehicles. We didn't have a solitary weapon between us but we didn't feel threatened. Not then.

'Most of them are pretty fucked up, John,' said Bungo, the guy sitting next to me. 'They've had the shit kicked out of them.'

'Hope so, mate,' I replied, ever the practical man. 'Let's face it, life's going to be a lot easier if there's no fight left in them, and that's for sure.'

'There's nothing in their eyes, John; they're just empty. Thirty years of Saddam then twenty-odd days of air strikes followed by an invasion. They didn't ask for any of it.'

'True enough, pal; they just happened to be in the way. You know how it works as well as I do. If you can't move out of the way you get caught up in it, and this lot had nowhere to go. Anyway, it's early days yet. The people who might cause real problems are probably regrouping right now.'

'Yeah, the next couple of months will tell which way it's going to go,' he replied.

If anything kicked off in Iraq the threat would come from soldiers who had dispersed from key units like the Republican Guard and Saddam's fedayeen, who'd been indoctrinated to lay down their lives for him. They'd be unleashed and directed by those men whose faces featured on the US Army's famous deck of cards, with the fugitive Saddam at the top of the pack handing out wads of cash he'd conned out of the UN in the oil for food programme. Yet most of the people we saw as we drove into Baghdad had simply been caught up in the squeeze. Fight or flight hadn't been options for them so they'd hunkered down and taken their chances; all around us we saw a shell-shocked population tired of it all. The euphoria they'd felt at the fall of Saddam and his hated Ba'ath party had been short-lived as the reality of hour-by-hour living took hold again. They had children to feed and lives to salvage from the rubble. What did they care about elections? What use was democracy to them when they needed food, water and power to keep their children alive?

I shook those thoughts aside and focused on what

we needed. No matter how cowed and desolate the Iraqi people appeared, basic common sense told us that this was not a place to be British and unarmed. We were soldiers and the first thing we wanted to do was get ourselves properly armed.

We'd been recruited as private military contractors (PMCs) by a big security corporation to carry out an 'in-country survey' of Iraq, which basically meant we had to fan out into key areas like the oilfields, the ports and Baghdad on fact-finding missions to assess the stability of those areas and any threat to the safety of the army of specialist engineers, surveyors and businessmen which would soon be pouring into Iraq to work on contracts for the multi-billion-dollar reconstruction programme of the country funded by the US. We weren't entirely on our own in the country; a team of Americans from a corporation called Blackwater had arrived at about the same time on a similar task. Blackwater is one of the huge private military companies that dominate the world of modern mercenary warfare. Owned by the Halliburton group, which in turn was run by US Vice President Dick Cheney from 1995 to 2000, they had contracts to guard State Department officials in Iraq and Afghanistan as well. That prime listing meant they could ride on the shirt-tails of the US military when they arrived in-country.

We on the other hand were flying by the seat of

our pants in the finest British tradition. We were billeted in a huddle of hastily erected Portakabins, grandly called a pioneer camp by the Yanks. It just happened to be on the front lawn of a palace once owned by Saddam's son Uday, and there was a US tank on the lawn too. No sooner had we dumped our kit than we were out foraging for weapons.

Bungo had been in Iraq throughout the war, embedded with a TV crew in Baghdad, and he'd only spent a couple of days at home before he'd signed up for this new job and was back in-country. He's a bald stocky barrel of a man with a big moustache, but what he carries in the barrel is all muscle and he's a severe close combat man, or Jap slapper as it's known in the trade. Naturally enough, the time he'd spent in Baghdad meant that Bungo knew the lie of the land and we were soon chatting to an ex-US ranger captain in an admin post with the Office of the Coalition Provisional Authority, as it was known then. There's a kind of brotherhood of special forces soldiers and we tuned right into the ranger. In a few minutes he understood our needs completely and responded with the unique sympathy many Americans have for a bloke without a gun. To him we appeared naked and he wanted to see us properly clothed.

'No problem, guys,' he said. 'There's an arms dump in the compound at the airport and it just happens that a friend of mine is in charge of it. I'll call him and tell him to expect you.'

We shook hands and left him with our heartfelt thanks and a case of beer and wasted no time in driving out to Baghdad International along a route that is now a closely guarded corridor and the gruesome scene of many suicide car bombings. Then it was a free road but we spotted the first hint of things to come in the shape of a wasted Humvee, the broad-nosed vehicles now used by the US military in place of jeeps. Some poor bastard had found his smoking hole. The vehicle was a burnt-out shell and the incident was post op – all over bar the clean-up. We heard it was an improvised explosive device (IED) which had just looked like a bag of shit on the road; the Hummer went over it and boom! We drove on to meet our man feeling a little bit grimmer with every passing minute.

There were 12,000 troops at Baghdad International Airport in those early days and it was a military city on the grand American scale. It had everything you could want from comfortable beds to hot showers and there was a nightclub, a cinema and even a small duty-free shopping mall. We quickly navigated our way around the giant camp and found the officer we needed to meet. He drove us out to a building on the airport perimeter which from the outside looked like an ordinary house but inside it was packed to the rafters with weapons and explosives. Our scrounging was about to pay off big time.

'Take what you like,' the officer said with a broad smile. So we did.

We were like kids in a sweet shop as we grabbed thirty AK-47s all in good nick and a similar number of Heckler & Koch G3 assault rifles and assorted pistols; we took boxes of grenades, boxes of ammunition. The guns were all well greased and unused and the ammunition was dry and fresh – the casings hadn't gone that blue-green verdigris colour that comes with age and dampness. We took a fair amount of demolition material too in the form of explosives and mines, and finally we found several M79 grenade launchers in nice condition, then loaded the lot into our Tahoe 4 x 4s, which sank onto their springs. When we got back to the pioneer camp the other lads had found bits and pieces but they knew we'd hit the jackpot when they saw the grins on our faces and the weight on our tyres.

Around the same time, according to intelligence reports that have since been leaked in the US, Saddam and a couple of the faces featured on the deck of cards held a meeting in a car in a Baghdad park. They were there to play their own hand and activate the insurrection against the Coalition. What none of us realised then was that the allies had overlooked a minor detail in the run-up to the invasion when someone somewhere in the infrared glow of a computerised ops room had forgotten to designate Saddam's huge arsenals as priority targets. Tragically that left his supporters and the chaotic insurgency of a hundred terrorist groups that followed with the biggest free weapons arcade the world has ever seen. In a strange irony we'd just armed ourselves with guns and explosives from basically the same sources the insurgents were using. Soon we'd be turning those weapons on each other.

Each security vehicle was now allocated its own radio call sign and Bungo and I distributed the gear among the call signs so that every team we deployed would have enough weaponry and kit to mount anything from a surveillance operation, through a hostage release mission to close protection. I'll never forget leaving the camp the following day to go up to Mosul when a young black US ranger – he was no more than eighteen – waved us down and put his head through the window to have a look inside. He saw two privateers armed to the teeth with AKs, pistols and a grenade launcher stashed around the compartment.

He gave a low whistle, put his hand out to shake mine and said, 'Man, you guys are rigged for combat!'

I hope that kid got home safe and well to his family because things were changing by the hour and over the next few weeks more and more of his comrades would be going home in body bags. We couldn't have been there for much more than a fortnight when Bungo and I started exchanging knowing glances as the US body count quickly racked up from one a week to one a day.

Combat awareness, developed in Northern Ireland and perfected in the Balkans, was telling us a shit-storm was about to break. On the streets there were more and more incidents, although US soldiers were still allowed downtown on a 'semi-operational' basis, in other words they could go shopping and sight-seeing as long as they carried their weapons. You'd see them taking photos of each other at one of the toppled statues or against the backdrop of one of Saddam's palaces but now the empty looks of a shell-shocked population were being replaced by more and more stares of open hostility. I imagine German soldiers got the same treatment from the citizens of Paris as they went sightseeing down the Champs-Elysées. The isolated incidents culminated in a GI being shot in the head when an insurgent stuck the barrel of his pistol under the back of his helmet and fired. That's when the sightseeing jaunts ended. That in my view marked the beginning of the insurgency, which from then on began to run rampant.

After six weeks in Iraq our job ended. We'd done the assessment but then we were sidelined as our firm lost the protection contract to a US-owned company based in London called Armourgroup. It was all political of course; that's the way things are in the PMC business, shifting contracts and new bosses every few weeks or sometimes every few days.

Our company rep, a young ex-army captain with all the gear and no idea who'd arrived to organise a smooth changeover, gave us our instructions: 'Right, men. Their team are going to arrive from Kuwait in the morning and then they'll be taking your weapons, vehicles and call signs. You'll be boarding a coach and they'll escort you out of Iraq and back into Kuwait . . .'

He took one look at our faces and saw that his words had fallen on deaf ears. The rep, who looked a bit like Clark Kent but without the glasses and red underpants, tried to say something more but was told to shut the fuck up. Who exactly did they think we were? They wanted us to hand over our gear to a load of comparative amateurs who were taking our jobs off us. By then we had three times as much weaponry and we had cached our spare guns and ammo safely away for a rainy day, but that wasn't the point.

'You're having a fucking laugh,' said Bungo. 'These aren't company weapons, mate; they were honestly scrounged and we're not giving them to anyone. We might sell them to the company but then again we might not, and as for being escorted out of Iraq you can forget it. At least eight of the blokes here drove out of Iraq in their pinkies after blowing up Scud missiles the last time they visited and they aren't going home in a fucking bus.'

The bosses knew that we had no intention of singing from any song sheet but our own, so they came up with a new plan, which was to do more or less exactly as we said. We drove halfway to Kuwait and met the incoming crows at an RV point in the desert. I don't know whether their company had paid due diligence to their CVs but what we saw was a weird bunch of odds and sods. They were mostly midlife-crisis ex-army dickheads who hadn't done a day's soldiering in years, moonlighting from various mundane security jobs or building sites – soldier civvies, we called them – looking for a thrill and to make some serious dollars. There are a lot of them in Iraq. There were a few old has-beens with them too and most of them looked so pathetic that in the end we decided to take pity on them and hand over a couple of our second-division weapons so they could defend themselves as they drove into the Wild East in their shiny new 4 x 4s.

We drove on to Kuwait City and got our flights home knowing that we'd been the vanguard of the PMCs that would follow but as it panned out I was back in Baghdad within a week, protecting a media team from a London TV network. Those six weeks were to prove invaluable during the eighteen months I was to work in Iraq. They weren't eventful in terms of shoot-outs or attacks because then the insurgency wasn't happening so we travelled extensively around Baghdad and along the main routes around the country without hindrance. I also met a lot of decent Iraqi people who just wanted to get on with their lives. Those weeks of in-country familiarisation probably helped keep me alive when I returned.

When we left Iraq that day Bungo and I knew in our bones that a storm was about to break and when it did it would be a bastard. What we could never have guessed was the awesome size of the mercenary swarm that was already stirring and on the move to Iraq.

To understand the way the swarm gathers you've got to leave the battlefield for the boardroom because it's in the plush London and Washington offices of the security companies that the life-or-death deals of the PMC business are done.

For the first half of the last century during two world wars and up to the end of the cold war there had been no room for private soldiers in a world of huge national standing armies. Mercenary was a dirty word in those days – and still is to many people – but how things have changed. As the cold war first thawed then melted in a global warming of super-power relations, fresh challenges were presenting themselves and a new business took root in the UK and South Africa, where special forces officers from units like the SAS and the Selous Scouts – a regiment of the Rhodesian Army who fought in the Bush War of 1965–79 – saw opportunities to offer sophisticated security, military and intelligence services to wealthy governments.

Jim Johnson, an ex-SAS officer, among others, had the foresight to see the way the wind was blowing and helped found one of the first of the new PMC outfits, a company called KMS (Keany Meany Services). Jim is a real character, a posh ex-Guards officer who was one of the ops team on the famous Iranian embassy siege. KMS clients were mostly oil sheiks and KMS personnel were exclusively blades employed to train local troops and provide personal security for the rulers and their families. Every now and then when a client had a particularly thorny problem on his doorstep the lads would be asked to go out in full gear and do a 'special', which true to form would be pulled off with the least possible fuss.

Others eyed KMS and decided to cash in on this new business opportunity. A succession of companies came and then went as they were taken over by rivals in lucrative deals or simply vanished off the radar as their directors moved on to new ventures.

All the while the companies were growing both in number and size at a steady rate as Middle Eastern rulers in particular continued to use their highly specialised services to beef up their own forces and to watch their backs. Given that a number of energetic South African and Rhodesian soldiers had entered the fray it wasn't surprising that some of the companies were soon involved in African wars from Angola to Zaire, and some less scrupulous outfits got in far too deep with a few very nasty sub-Saharan heads of state.

Watching all this unfold through the 1980s were some US special forces officers who also recognised the potential and set up their own companies – firms like DynCorp and Kellog Brown and Root (KBR), the latter being acquired by Haliburton in 1962 but only really expanding its business in the late 1980s. While the European and South African companies were growing they were growing too, and all the time all these companies were building up relationships with the British and US intelligence services and, crucially, with the Pentagon. They were natural bedfellows and an unofficial understanding developed between the spooks of MI6 and the CIA, the American top brass and the new private military contractors.

Over the years there have been periodic complaints from the political left in the UK and USA about the growth of these companies and their involvement in

Third World conflicts but the protests had little effect given that the Soviets, Chinese and Cubans were up to their waists in the mire of African politics themselves. But then suddenly and dramatically the map of world politics changed with the implosion of the Warsaw Pact and the fall of the wall in Berlin. Within the space of a few years literally millions of soldiers were stood down and cashiered from armies around the world. Some estimates put the figure as high as 6,000,000. At the same time the new high-tech armies of the West, particularly those of the USA and Britain, who'd been at the forefront of the forty-year stand-off in Germany, found themselves chronically short of manpower.

Unlike in make-do-and-mend Britain, the five-star generals in the Pentagon simply got the chequebook out and picked up the phone to their old buddies in the PMCs and that's when the business really started to rock and roll. Last year it encompassed around 900 companies based in more than a hundred countries on every continent but the Antarctic, earning a global income of over $100 billion.

Private military contractors come in three basic varieties. Some offer upfront fighters, hard-core on-the-ground troops. A few offer a gaggle of ex-generals as consultants to advise small states on strategy and long-term military planning. Then there are the military support firms, MSFs; they provide behind-the-lines logistics like transport, cooks, helicopter and aircraft maintenance, and whatever else the client army wants to pay for.

At the last count there were 30,000 of these non-combatant camp followers working in Iraq on top of the estimated 30,000 fighting men. MSFs are huge and mainly employ cheap unarmed labour from Third World countries with low health and safety standards to do an army's dirty work. A lot of MSF employees in Iraq come from the Philippines, Pakistan or Turkey and a few of them have been killed in mortar attacks on military bases. But it's the truck drivers, known locally as jundhis, who take the most hits and nearly a hundred of them have been bombed or pulled out of their cabs and summarily executed at the roadside by insurgents. At the other end of the spectrum MSFs also provide technicians to service tanks and helicopters; they maintain B-2 stealth bombers and one company actually hires out the drones that fly spying missions over the Sunni Triangle. They even forecast the weather for the military.

Private military intelligence specialists were involved in running the Abu Ghraib prison and some were investigated over allegations of torture and abuse during the interrogation of prisoners. Interestingly it wasn't thought a good idea to arrest any PMCs and it was GIs who ended up taking the rap.

Because the US Army is the biggest employer of

PMCs US private military companies like KBR, Blackwater and DynCorps are the big providers, offering services across the whole spectrum from combat to behind-the-line workers. During the Second Gulf War private contractors made big bucks and one in every hundred members of the US forces in Kuwait was a private contractor. They've earned a mountain since as a third of the entire US fighting budget in Iraq, around $30 billion, is paid out in contracts with one in ten of the US presence in the country a civilian contractor. KBR is the largest PMC in Iraq with an army of 50,000 employees. Some of them are armed fighters but most are the cooks, bottle washers and truck drivers that supply and feed the US Army. KBR has a staggering $11. 84 billion Iraq contract with the Pentagon.

UK companies haven't been left out although they're almost exclusively in the business of providing ex-British soldiers for upfront protection. Erinys is a British outfit with a formidable and highly trained warforce and contracts to protect the US Corps of Engineers, which unlike the British Royal Engineers, is only semi-military. It also had contracts to distribute the new Iraqi currency to banks and others to guard oil installations. All this has seen them grow to a 14,000-strong armed force in Iraq with deals worth $100 million.

In September 2005 the new power of the PMCs

was starkly demonstrated by the British company Global Strategies, who closed down Baghdad International Airport. The reason? They had the contract to secure it and they hadn't been paid by the Iraqi government for seven months. The Iraqis sent police and militia to take control of the airport but when they arrived they found US marines in tanks standing alongside their British pals and they had to stump up at least some of the money. While that was going on other changes were taking place too. In the early days when I first arrived companies would issue their own permits to carry weapons but in August 2005 the Iraqis issued new laws to regulate the PMCs and their weapons.

All of this is part of a growing trend towards the legitimisation of PMCs. The huge scale of the industry and the fact that the US finds them increasingly vital mean that after hundreds of years mercenaries are coming in out of the cold.

A quiet moment in early 2005 and Jim, one of my ex-Royal Marine friends, showed the other guys in his call sign a photograph of his wife. He passed it round and one of the guys took it. This bloke, who'd been getting on well with Jim, looked at the picture, handed it back and never spoke a word to Jim again. Jim's wife is beautiful but she's Asian. Why do I say 'but'? She's just Asian and beautiful but the guy who'd looked at the picture is a white South African. He is a Boer and a racist. Uncomfortable to live with but true.

There are thousands of South Africans working as PMCs in Iraq and as I've said some of the major PMC corporations were founded by South Africans and Zimbabweans. These people are extremely tough and not afraid to fight; they'll also look for a fight. The other thing about them is that they're nearly all white. A lot of Brits don't like working with them; they find South Africans introspective and difficult to get on with. Perhaps there's a bit of history at work too. We fought the Boers for possession of South Africa at the end of the nineteenth century. We won but you'd never know it.

I don't generally enjoy working with them either and perhaps I'm as prejudiced as some of them. But I'm a southern African myself – born in Zimbabwe when it was Southern Rhodesia. I've worked there on and off until one day my Arab client, a great buddy of President Mugabe, got a letter stating that his 'bodyguard' was an MI6 agent, was not welcome in the country any more and should leave forthwith. So I've got a background in southern Africa and I sort of know where they're coming from. You might call it an affinity or just an instinctive understanding.

It's also true that a lot of the South Africans in the business are ex-apartheid people. Some worked in special forces units like Koevoet, which used highly questionable and brutal methods in the dirty war in Namibia, or Vlakplass, a secret police organisation used to suppress the black majority. Others seem to be genuine citizens of the rainbow nation founded by Nelson Mandela. They're a different generation, very tough but clean-cut young men whose only real prejudice is against anyone who shoots at them.

No surprises then that South Africa is one state that still hates mercenaries. In the autumn of 2005 the ANC government threatened to seize the property of any citizen involved in operations in Iraq. South Africa had already passed the Foreign Military Assistance Act in 1998 banning its citizens from any involvement in conflicts abroad without government permission. A review of the act in 2004 was precipitated by the number of South Africans working as PMCs in occupied Iraq and also by the plot involving ex-SAS officer Simon Mann to overthrow the government of Equatorial Guinea. That's the plot Maggie Thatcher's son Mark was implicated in.

However, even ordinary South African PMC foot soldiers are going home rand millionaires after a year in Iraq and they're spending it in South Africa so why aren't the ANC pleased about all those dollars pouring into the country? Is it inverted racism? Are they jealous of the success of their white compatriots?

I think I know why. Look at the equation. On one side we have the most powerful country in Africa sliding towards instability because of Aids. We know how many of its citizens are dying of the disease – millions – but we don't know how many of its soldiers and police officers are HIV positive. I imagine the figure is a state secret but it is perhaps relevant that fifteen years ago 75 per cent of the Malawi police and armed forces were HIV positive.

On the other side we have a white minority which is very significant in terms of economic power and know-how if not in numbers. Several thousand of them are making large amounts of money in operations that keep them militarily current and well connected to large companies with huge military resources. It's not totally far-fetched to imagine the military whites biding their time and making their plans. Then, when the black military is incapacitated by Aids what's to stop them regaining power in one of the most beautiful, fertile and mineral rich countries on the African continent?

Certainly Zimbabwe is already in such desperate straits under Mugabe that if a mercenary army of any colour marched in to relieve the people of their suffering and give them a fair election then I can't see anyone objecting. Except of course South Africa, which has sat on its hands and watched a country that was bountiful descend into misery.

I believe it's this underlying possibility of a coalition of white PMCs in southern Africa that's got the ANC into a sweat. It's the spectre of resurgent white power not some moral revulsion against the trade of the mercenary. I don't blame them; I'd be looking over my shoulder too. But maybe if they acted to bring down the murderous thieving regime in Zimbabwe they'd take the heat out of the political situation in their sphere of influence. They could do worse than to hire their very effective white PMCs to go and sort out that excuse for a man called Mugabe.

Ten in the morning at the post of the resettlement officer in Hereford and a long-serving permanent-cadre SAS soldier has popped his head round the door to discuss his options on leaving the Regiment. The guy in resettlement has heard it all in his time and seen the lads go into the law, tree surgery and in one famous case the Church of England as a vicar. Typically though the guys stick to what they know best and this one's no different. He just hands the officer his CV and a form he's completed for a resettlement grant and asks, 'Could you push my details around the security companies for me?'

It's routine and soon twenty or thirty companies will have details of a fresh, ex-Regiment face; it's their database of former soldiers which is definitely the most valuable asset of any PMC. Our soldier will use his resettlement money to go on serious hostile environment refresher training and familiarisation courses for Iraq – I run one myself – and then he'll wait for the job offers to come in. He won't have long to wait because the companies are gagging for operators and a blade will be snapped up in no time. Of course all those high-powered business deals I've talked about don't matter a lot to the guy on the ground. His own deal will be what's on his mind and his first question will be 'How much?' There's nothing wrong with that. If a bloke is going to put his life on the line he'd be mad not to ask how much he's going to be paid to do it.

The same process is happening in the rest of the British Army as more and more blokes tipping out of a wide range of units are deciding on the free-lance route to maximise the cash potential from their hard-earned military skills. Not surprisingly lots of ex-Paras are lining up for the big pay day but the rest come from a broad spectrum of regiments and corps. Don't get the idea that the 'ordinary' soldiers from regiments the SAS and the Paras derisively call crap hats are not wanted. Far from it. Most ordinary British soldiers are highly skilled, hard-fighting men by any world standard. So if you get a guy from REME that's good news because these days we like to balance the skills of a call sign. It's ideal if you can put a couple of shooters from, say, the Paras with the bloke from REME, who can mend the engine if it goes bang in the back of beyond while they're out on a risk assessment. Chances are he'll be quite handy with a rifle too.

The pool of special forces men ran out pretty early on in the Iraq crisis and now they usually find themselves in ops managers jobs running the show from Baghdad, so these days relatively few SAS men go out on daily protection runs but they're quite often leaping into their vehicles to race off and give some hard-edged support when there's a contact with the enemy.

JY is one exception – he still escorts clients around Iraq clocking up hundreds of sorties, which through his consummate skills in moving through a hostile environment have attracted relatively few contacts. There've been enough though and despite the fact that JY now runs his own company he's a registered war junkie and insists on making the runs – 'John, the guys need somebody on the ground they can respect.' I think he's got a point.

Although ex-blades like JY and me are now rare out there we did leave a great legacy from those early days three years ago: a superb set of good working practices for the people that followed. We call them standard operating procedures or SOPs. They are the ways of moving through country, the ways of responding to attack, drills for regrouping – a whole set of life-saving rules that have become a survival manual in a forest of terror.

I've described the way most British PMCs make the transition from national soldier to international freelance but there are obviously as many stories as there are men in Iraq and as many variations on the theme as there are countries involved. But it's not just ex-soldiers who find their way into the privatised firing line and a surprising number of wannabes turn up in Iraq simply by applying for a job through one of the many PMC websites. They pluck a credible CV out of thin air and then con their way onto the flight. Some of the less scrupulous firms don't even bother to check the credentials of applicants, who if they look the part are likely to get the job. A few of them have done dodgy bodyguard courses; others have fed their egos on right-wing survivalist magazines and on websites that glorify guns and knives in a very unhealthy way. I met a couple of them in Iraq and thought they'd have been quite at home having a pint with Michael Ryan, the weirdo responsible for the Hungerford Massacre.

I've seen men from that sort of background spin round and leave the country in a matter of days when reality gives them a terrifying kick in the crotch. Others stay on and present a very real threat to themselves and any clients entrusted to them, but the professionals can spot them from a hundred paces by the way they carry themselves, their obvious lack of awareness and weapon carriage and the way they duck when a car backfires. They just stand out like the idiots they are and, once spotted, they are unceremoniously booted the fuck out of the country.

It was the same story around the world. Websites and resettlement officers in a host of armies directed men to Iraq so that within a year of the invasion in 2003 the number of PMC operatives had swollen to over 20,000 and by the summer of 2005 it was estimated there were an incredible 30,000 combatant private military operatives in Iraq. Combined they formed an unsung unofficial army in Iraq that dwarfed the 8,500 troops of the British contingent and was second only in size to the US Army presence itself.

It's now a huge and disparate army of men and a few extraordinary women earning an average of £600 a day to provide security for the businessmen, surveyors, building contractors, oil experts, aid workers and of course TV crews who flocked to the country to pick over the carcass of Saddam's regime and help Iraq rebuild. Without doubt it's the biggest mercenary army the world has seen for over two centuries since those distant days when the British East India Company used soldiers of fortune to depose the fabulously wealthy maharajas and conquer

India and King George hired Hessian soldiers from Germany to fight against George Washington's Continental Army and lose America for Great Britain. Since the dawn of military history such men have been called freelances, mercenaries, soldiers of fortune or dogs of war, but today they are known as PMCs, the new politically correct label added to the lexicon of war.

Among them are the so-called hard men from a score of countries, the nightclub bouncers and bare-knuckle boxers who found their way to the action foolishly believing that courage would compensate for a lack of weapons training and tactical aware-ness. Many of the trained guys are regulars on the circuit, registered with big multinational contractors, and take to the road bristling with weaponry and armour-plated vehicles; others come as one-man bands equipped with little more than a beaten up 4 x 4 truck, an AK-47 and a holdall full of luck, but just like professional soldiers through the ages they come for one thing, in this case a share of the estimated £30 million a day being spent on private security in Iraq.

They come from across the globe: former special forces soldiers from Britain, the US, Australia, Canada, New Zealand and every country on the European mainland. There are Gurkhas from the Himalayan foothills and Fijians from the South Sea islands. There are men who learnt their skills with the Japanese anti-terrorist paramilitaries and many as we have seen from southern Africa. There was even one guy who'd served in the Chinese People's Army before heading off to earn a dangerous fortune in Iraq. Chilean commandos and Sri Lankan anti-terrorist experts who fought the Tamil Tigers for years have joined the mercenary gold rush to Iraq as well.

They don't share a common ideology or a common loyalty but what they do share is a thirst for adventure and a hunger for big bucks; Iraq is the one place they are certain to find both. Some of them pay the ultimate price for their appetite for adventure and as far as I can tell between two and three hundred PMCs have been killed in contacts with insurgents. There's no way of knowing exactly how many because it's not in the interests of the companies who hire them to advertise their body count, and back home dead men don't matter if they aren't wearing the uniform of their country.

4

LOW PROFILE

No one took a blind bit of notice as a battered old tipper truck loaded with tons of building rubble trundled out of Baghdad on the Mosul road grinding through the gears. The driver was a lean muscular young man dressed insurgent-style in a loose-fitting blue and grey robe over baggy Ali Baba trousers and a pair of Nike trainers. The fit-looking guy with his arm resting on the passenger window wore a cheap brown leather jacket with his baggy trousers and had a *shemag* wrapped round his neck. Between the two of them, jammed on the occasional seat behind the gear lever, was an older guy in his fifties, heavily jowled and very nervous as he clutched a large leather holdall on his lap, his face hidden by the hood of an old Iraqi army-surplus parka.

A suffocating hour later the lorry turned off the main road and drove two or three miles through goat scrub then turned into the gates of an oil installation compound south of Kirkuk. The guard on gate duty looked at their load manifest. It was all properly signed by the manager so he waved them on.

They pulled to a halt around the back of the site office with a hiss of air brakes out of sight of the bored security guard on the front door who'd watched their arrival. The driver dropped to the ground like a cat and circled the truck as if he was checking out the tyres but a closer look showed that he was carefully observing the scene around him. Then a flourish of warm desert wind snapped his gown against his side for a moment and briefly outlined the shape of the automatic rifle concealed beneath it. At that moment the second young man jumped down from the passenger side of the lorry and had a good look round too; the older guy stayed in the cab still clinging to the holdall as if his life depended on it. The driver quietly ordered him to get out and he climbed ponderously to the ground, the holdall heavy and awkward, then he looked intently at the oil pipeline about thirty metres to his left. His bag could easily have been packed with explosives but this was no insurgent attack on a vital installation. Far from it. In fact it was a scheduled run by a British PMC whose policy is to go deep undercover when they ferry their clients around Iraq.

'All right, it's all clear.' The driver had spoken English not Arabic and he quickly ushered the engineer with his bag full of blueprints and technical specifications

through the back door of the site office. It was vital
that not even the local security guards witnessed him
slipping into the building. Careless talk back in the
village could see them under attack on their next run
and a guard could easily be a spy for the insurgency.

This company uses old cars and pickups as well
as trucks, sometimes travelling with a load of fruit
or vegetables on board. Occasionally a goat or a
couple of sheep are tethered to a flat bed as living
camouflage. Attention to detail is everything. They're
careful with their number plates as each region in
Iraq has a distinctive plate; they change them if they
leave Baghdad for Basra with a meticulous emphasis
on preparation that comes from the ex-blade leadership of the company. I know these guys well; I trained
most of them on my course, and like me they never
wear shades when they're on a job. Why? Because
the Iraqis simply don't wear sunglasses, or at least
very few of them do. If you do wear them it's a dead
giveaway that you're a white eye – so-called from the
pale, un-tanned ring left by the shades.

While I usually go low profile, or jingly jangly as
we call it, these guys go deeply covert and I admire
them for that. The guy who runs the company is an
ex-D Squadron SAS warrant officer and one of an
increasing number of ex-NCOs who are putting the
noses of former officers out of joint by setting up
successful PMCs and, as the officers see it, taking their

turf. But his way of doing things mirrors my own philosophy: if you can't be seen, you can't be hit.

I asked one of the guys if he felt vulnerable in a ponderous vehicle like a tipper truck bumping along the highways and byways of Iraq.

'Not really,' he said with a broad grin. 'The body-work's crap but the engine's really sound and we've got a strategy if we're rumbled.'

'Which is?'

'If we're in town we head for a narrow road between houses and tip the load to block the way. If we're on the highway we still tip the load then one of us gets in the back with some heavy kit and gives them all we've got as we head off. It'll do seventy when it's empty, you know, but the thing is we never get sussed.'

In fact they're so good at going covert that it's proven a double-edged sword as a totally unexpected enemy has emerged in the form of our American friends. Those guys who look for all the world like Iraqis going about their business are more likely to get whacked by the Yanks than insurgents.

Now don't get me wrong. I love the Americans and I consider the USA my second home; I've spent a lot of time out there over the years training with Delta Force soldiers, whom I admire and like immensely. I think they're a wonderful people but they do have a couple of serious attitude problems that come out like a rash when they're in a conflict. Their biggest problem is communication with anyone who doesn't speak English. Outside the USA a lot of Americans can be quite insular, arrogant and very paranoid, relaxing only when accosted in a familiar language, especially if the accent is British. They are the new empire but they just don't know how to deal with it. The Brits on the other hand, with hundreds of years of imperial and colonial experience behind them, have learnt that you might be able to conquer a people but you'll never suppress them. Instead you just get on and do business with them.

While the British PMC philosophy in Iraq is, roughly speaking, you won't get hit if no one sees you, the Americans go more for something more like, 'Here's my head; my arse will follow.' And that's the way they move their clients across the warscape in Iraq, head first in large convoys with as many as twenty armed guards, an armoured scout car front and back and sometimes top cover in the form of a helicopter gunship. They treat all Iraqis as potential insurgents and I've seen their PMC convoys strafe junctions with machine-gun fire if they don't like the look of the vehicles on the road ahead.

Some British companies involved with US clients are contractually obliged to move in high profile and like their American counterparts they regularly get whacked by insurgents because an offensive posture while engaged in an essentially defensive role is playing right into the hands of the enemy. Tactically it's a crock of shit and it inevitably draws the Americans into a wagon train situation when they're attacked, where all they can do is form a circle and fire like fuck. The helicopter cover doesn't really help because the helo is hanging there like a buzzard vulnerable to a malleting itself if it gets too close.

Tragically a chopper leased by Blackwater was shot down by a ground-to-air missile fired by the Islamic Army of Iraq in May 2003. It wasn't guarding a convoy but the Russian built MI-8 was apparently being used to transport US officials from Baghdad to Tikrit when it was hit over a deserted piece of countryside. Six Americans died along with the three-man Bulgarian crew and two Fijian security contractors hired by Blackwater. In a cold-blooded and typically filthy piece of work the insurgents found one of the crew who'd been thrown clear on impact and made the shocked middle-aged man stand and walk away so that they could shoot him in the back. True to form they videoed the whole thing from the downing of the helicopter to the execution of the crewman in blue overalls.

But you've got to ask yourself why a team of insurgents armed with Stinger missiles and video cameras just happened to find itself under the flight plan of a helicopter in the middle of nowhere. I refuse to believe it was an accident and either they were tipped off by a supporter at the airbase with access to flight plans or the answer might be complacency on the part of the contractors. Avoid routine is the number-one rule in any secure movement operation. It was most likely an established route compromised by followers of the cause at a high level. It could have been an opportunistic attack but that strikes me as being just too lucky to be feasible. We'll probably never know the truth of it.

The much-publicised murder of four Blackwater operators in Fallujah was another example of what happens when it all goes wrong. Blackwater took over a contract from British rivals Control Risks, who gave them a full rundown of the safest operational routes. In other words they were told precisely where to go and where not to go. But, soon after, four Blackwater operatives, one ex-Delta Force, three former US Rangers, were tasked to go up the Fallujah road towards a forward operating base (FOB), which are always at covert locations. They were on a route I know well travelling in two soft-skinned 4 x 4s with two men in each vehicle, and I'm told they were actually carrying kitchen utilities in flat packs to furnish the base. They weren't even on a hard-core protection run.

For some inexplicable reason they went down a road that took them into town and onto a street near the River Euphrates, where they were ambushed by half a dozen insurgents with AKs and machine guns. Then grenades were posted through the windows to finish the job and they were dragged through the street burning and dismembered before being hung off a bridge over the river. It was videoed of course and the film records grim scenes of crowds mutilating the corpses.

Some say they were off route and orientating themselves special forces-style and ended up in the wrong place at the wrong time – hard to believe considering that elements of the call sign were ex-Delta Force and rangers. I think they were just dicked – set up and malleted. That's how it works on the Highway. This incident has been portrayed as the catalyst for the huge US marine assault on Fallujah that followed but I think it unlikely that the US command would risk the political shit storm that would follow dozens of regular marines being sacrificed because a few PMCs carrying flat-pack kitchens were slaughtered in the city. I also think it unlikely that the US Marine Corps would get the go-ahead to attack in such a short time. No, that assault was calculated, planned in advance and executed perfectly. Maybe the military thought those four deaths were as good a starter flag for the assault on Fallujah as any.

So the American way is not my way. I don't mind a scrap but I draw the line at mooning the enemy and inviting him to shoot at my backside, and that's virtually what the Yanks are doing. I'm also convinced that many Americans hate the Iraqis, not just the insurgents but all Iraqis, and I've had conversations with many PMCs and regular US soldiers who are evangelical Christians and see themselves as in a crusade against the Muslim hordes. In my view they're not much different to the Iraqi militiamen and foreign fighters who see themselves at the heart of a jihad against the Christian crusaders. What a mess.

The Yank PMCs feel no qualms at all about infuriating ordinary Iraqis by setting up roadblocks to give their convoys priority. It's not just roadblocks either; they make a habit of forcing other vehicles off the road by ramming them from behind or forcing them over from the side. This is especially true in Baghdad, where they will actually fire at any vehicle that they feel is in the least bit suspicious. I know it's suicide bomb central but I believe such behaviour has alienated moderate Iraqi citizens, who aren't interested in jihad but just want to get on with their lives.

To be fair to the US military they do not behave in the same way and have tried to introduce some hearts and minds stuff into their daily operations, being careful whenever possible not to get up the noses of ordinary Iraqis. They've got a lot of top professional troops, who have been on the world's steepest learning curve and have adapted well. That's not true of many of the American PMCs, who seem to have watched too many movies and think that

intimidating the locals is the way to make your mark.
The US PMCs have alienated a lot of their international colleagues too. Like me, my son Kurt works
as a security contractor in Iraq, and he and his mates
are in constant scrapes with American columns and
convoys. More than once I've heard him mutter, 'I
hate those bastards more than the scumbag insurgents.'

Now if a Brit who's had several vicious contacts
with insurgents can say something like that how much
more galling must it be for the Iraqis, who feel dumped
on in their own country? I find the Iraqis charming
and open but they are a very proud people living in
a country where weapons are freely available. I'm
certain that a fair percentage of attacks on Yank
contractors in Baghdad have been made by locals fired
up with road rage. They may not be part of an armed
cell or network of insurgents but nor do they appre-
ciate having their car bashed by some foreigner, and
if they're angry enough they've got guns to make their
point.

I've been very pissed off by the behaviour of
American PMCs myself when I've been operating low
profile and found myself bounced off the road by big
fuck-off US armoured cars driven by contractors with
too much attitude. Once an American contractor's
scout car scraped half the paint off the wing of my
car, which was really annoying until I realised they'd

done a good job of improving my camouflage. On another occasion I even had my car forced into a ditch by a British PMC armoured call sign. But that was nothing compared to Bungo's experience when he was travelling high profile on the outskirts of Baghdad, escorting an American client with his call signs all flying Union Jacks on their vehicles to clearly identify themselves against friendly fire.

'You wouldn't believe it, John,' he told me. 'We spotted a big column of Yank PMC vehicles coming towards us when suddenly they were firing at us out of the blue. About a dozen rounds hit the back end of my vehicle too close to the fuel tank for comfort and I swerved off the road and pulled up. We all piled out of the car including the American client, who was terrified and well hacked off after watching his tax dollars incoming in the form of machine-gun rounds that had nearly killed him.

'As they got closer we showed ourselves, arms outstretched, to clearly show them we weren't carrying. I can tell you I was crapping myself because they were so thick I thought they might let us have another burst. Anyway, they pulled up when they realised we were all white eyes. I was furious and I strode up to them and had a real ding-dong.

'I was yelling, "Don't you know the British flag when you fucking see it?" and do you know what the bloody hillbilly in the turret said? Unbelievable, John, he said, "Gee, I'm sorry. I thought they were Iraqi flags."

'Iraqi flags? I tried to explain to this muppet that in any event he was supposed to be on the side of the Iraqis who actually flew their flag, and the insurgents are the only fuckers who don't have any flags. I might as well have been talking to the wall. Some of those rednecks live in a parallel universe.'

Bungo was lucky to survive that encounter and even though he's a veteran SAS Scud buster and a man not prone to nerves I know the stupidity of that encounter left him quite shaken. He flies the Stars and Stripes now but still reckons the Americans are more dangerous than the insurgency.

Between these two extremes of very high profile and deeply covert a lot of the British and Commonwealth blokes travel low profile or jingly jangly. The general idea is to make yourself look as unappetising a target as possible to the big predators. You set your car up to look like a local vehicle. The bodywork should preferably be a bit beaten up but the engine and the working parts should be in top condition and souped up for a chicken run. Most of the guys add their own individual touches: worry beads hanging off the rear-view mirror, transfers with Islamic slogans stuck on the back window, anything to give the authentic Iraqi touch. The idea is not to become invisible like the deep covert boys but to avoid being offensive and confrontational. It's to match the wallpaper for a few seconds, even if you're going to be sussed on a second glance, because those few seconds get you down the street and onto the next hazard. You can travel in a fairly loose convoy in this way and nine times out of ten it'll get you through the day without a shot being fired in your direction, but beneath the rough exterior of the battered vehicles there has to be a tight tactical deployment in the event of an attack.

Typically we'd have four vehicles running low profile and obviously we wouldn't have a line-up of the same make of vehicle so that we looked like a row of ducks in a shooting gallery. We'd mix and match distinctly different vehicle types in an attempt to achieve the authentic Baghdad look. Front and back we'd have more heavily armed cars kitted out with machine guns, RPGs and any other sizeable ordnance we could get our hands on. They are there to cover the protection call sign in the middle which carries the client. Loosely shadowing these cars would be the gun vehicle or counter attack team. While the convoy was on the road travelling the CAT would wander up and down looking for trouble, which obviously can come from any direction. The moment it kicks off they aim to take the fight straight back into the enemy's face and seize the initiative away from him so that he is put on his back foot allowing the others to deploy and get the client away. Believe me it works.

You can't fight bombs; only luck can help you there, but all the cars would be ready to change role and transfer personnel or clients from one to another in an instant if there was an explosion. If a vehicle was disabled by a bomb or by heavy gunfire then the others would deploy for the transfer and extraction of the call sign that's been whacked and begin any first aid that's needed. The moment an attack began the CAT would start the fight while we simultaneously called for the cavalry in a radio contact to the Coalition. If the CAT team's vehicle was hit and disabled then it was time for a big boy's decision and you may have had to leave them to fight and make their own way out. Nothing is cut and dried out there on the Highway to Hell.

Iraq has been known for millennia as Mesopotamia, the land of two rivers, but now a third river flows, a river of blood. It follows that firepower is everything out there and I'll now explain the weapons of choice that the private military contractor carries.

Basically it cuts two ways. As I've said, the American companies are usually closely linked to the US military and so use standard GI weaponry. They carry the M4 rifle, a short-barrelled 5.56 millimetre piece which is compact and very accurate; on their vehicles they use Minimi light machine guns or 50 cal. inch heavy machine guns. The average British contractor, and here again I include Commonwealth blokes, had to scrounge their weapons when they first got to Iraq, just as Bungo and I did, but later a lot of the guys exchanged those weapons for properly imported gear.

Personally, I like the shooting kit we cadged and foraged in those early days. A lot of it is Soviet and it's immensely robust and durable with inbuilt service-ability. That means the mechanism of an AK-47 will still fire if you fill it with sand and leave a cleaning rag inside it. The AK is quite simply the best assault rifle in the world; it's accurate, it doesn't break and it doesn't stop. It's just what you need if you're going against the same weapon and remember the AK is universal among insurgents. Some operators carry Heckler & Koch MP5 carbines, which are lightweight, pretty and perfectly engineered, but the MP5's got no punch outside a room so you may as well stand there and throw the rounds at someone trying to shoot you up with an AK.

Perhaps most important in the context of Iraq is the fact that Warsaw Pact kit generally packs a heavier punch because the preferred Russian approach to warfare, developed in hellish campaigns against the Nazis, is not just to kill your enemy but to blow a hole through him so that you can see his mate behind him. So I've remained fond of my Kalashnikov and stayed loyal to the PKM machine gun. I'm keen on the Soviet built RPK-74 light machine gun too. It comes with a bipod stand, is essentially an AK with a longer stronger barrel and uses the same magazines. I also like to stash a Draganov sniper rifle in the vehicle simply because you never know when you're going to have to take a long shot. But it's the Soviet PPSh-41 submachine gun that we used for a really heavy punch. It's the one with a big drum magazine underneath that you always see in those Second World War films. That big magazine holds seventy heavy-hitting rounds and if you come under attack you can just hose your enemy with a drumful. At times we also had a huge 50 cal. Dushka mounted on a tripod at the end of hotel corridors just in case we got disturbed at night.

In the early days I carried a Walther PPK for personal protection or an Iraqi Tariq pistol which is good at close quarters, but the safety catches are dodgy and it has excessive trigger poundage / pressure to fire (basically, the amount of force required to pull on the trigger to engineer a discharge). Still it was better than nothing until we could get some superior Berettas, Glocks and Czech CZ pistols. More recently most British contractors have ensured they have a US or Belgian-made Minimi in their line-up of weapons because it really can pour out a tremendous weight of fire and well directed it will make most opponents think twice about standing their ground.

Weapons apart, PMCs have developed a dress code which suits the environment and the job at hand. They tend to wear light shirts with an element of ultra-violet proofing to protect the skin from sun, lightweight body armour and a kit vest worn over it. Most of the guys wear light fairly loose-fitting cargo pants with four or five patch pockets where they can stash a small survival kit, important ID documents and field dressings. I prefer blue jeans and tend to stash my survival kit and medical stuff in my vest. Desert boots or lightweight climbing boots are the favourite footwear.

In country we tend to eat a lot of US military rations (official designation Meals Ready to Eat, known universally as MREs), which became famous during the first Gulf War when they first made their appearance on the stage of world cuisine. They come in thick brown plastic wrappings and contain enough food for a day with dishes like beef stew and macaroni. The main reason for scoffing MREs is that you need to be careful about what you eat in a situation where for obvious reasons an upset stomach and a nasty case of the squits are not really the way forward if you're caught in an ambush.

Water is vital in the hot testing climate of Iraq although you shouldn't forget that winter in the uplands and parts of the desert at night can be absolutely freezing. Generally though it's hot and humid and mineral water in litre bottles is stashed all over the vehicles and everyone makes sure they get at least two bottles down their necks every day. Again, most people avoid drinking local water for the simple reason that the public supply in Iraq is not safe and no one wants to get a bug if he can avoid it. The dangers of dehydration are very real and if you neglect to drink plenty of water you'll quickly know that things are going wrong when your urine starts to go dark in colour and it stings when you piss. Believe me, that soon gets you reaching for the water bottle.

When it comes down to the wire, weapons and water are two of your best friends in the uncertain world of Iraq, but there's a third that's equally important. You may only call upon it for relatively short, frantic and intense periods of time but it may save your life. It's called situation awareness.

A pair of black kites wheeled and circled in the sky over the half-eaten corpse of a dead dog on the waste ground between Highway 6 heading north out of Baghdad and the main railway line to Mosul. As the convoy passed, the sun was rising and warming the air into tired snatches of wind which picked up scraps of paper from the heaps of rubbish then dropped them again. Ahead was the North Gate out of Baghdad, beyond it the open road.

There were three vehicles in the line with three men in the first two call signs and four in the gun truck bringing up the rear. It was a routine run with no clients on board, just a recce for a regular trip they'd be making with a paying customer over the next two or three weeks. That made things easier. Shepherding an unarmed civilian is a big responsibility and one that the guys take extremely seriously; after all his life and your life may depend on your actions. Life's a lot simpler when you've only got yourself and your mates to look after.

The 4 x 4s picked up speed as the open road beckoned. Only the gate to drive through then they'd really turn up the speed. The twin turrets of the gate, flanking an upended-tulip-shaped arch between them, loomed ahead. As they got closer random patches of ceramic tiles on the gate glinted in the sun. They had once been part of a mosaic portrait of Saddam, the rest of which had been etched away by machine-gun fire so that the face of the towers resembled a map of some distant archipelago.

Hal, the driver of the first vehicle, scanned the road ahead. Brad, the navigator and team leader, was distracted by a movement near the railway line but Hal was getting edgy and he wasn't sure why.

'This doesn't look right, mate,' he said, calling Brad's eyes back to the road ahead.

Brad took the scene in and immediately caught

the vibe. No one about, no one at all. No street
vendors, no rubbish scroungers, no people carriers
parked up and waiting to pick up relatives who'd got
a lift in from the country on a lorry. No cabbies and,
the big giveaway, no police.

'Stand by, here we fucking go.' Brad had spotted
the tiniest movement on the rampart over the arch
and called it on the radio. 'Heads up. Keep an eye
on the fucking gate arch!' Hal was about to turn the
wheel to start weaving but he didn't have time.

Bang! Bang! Bang! A burst of .50 calibre rounds
slammed into the engine block of their vehicle. It
stopped abruptly as if a huge invisible hand had
slapped the radiator grille. The engine screamed and
whined as bits of it chewed it up. Flashes and smoke
erupted on the North Gate as the big gun poured out
its venom. More horrific bangs. The bonnet of the
car was torn apart. The windscreen exploded as the
big rounds slammed into the cabin of the 4 x 4,
whistling right between Hal and Brad, perforating the
interior of the vehicle like a demented staple gun. The
other call signs reacted instinctively as Hal and Brad
abandoned their now burning hulk.

'COME ON! COME ON!' The guys in the second
truck screamed urgent encouragement as they rolled
out of their vehicle with weapons and radios intact.
The gun wagon was turning on its handbrake, leaving
half its tyres on the road to give the rear gunner a

Through the windscreen - a typical view driving down the Highway. Beaten-up vehicles, open back trucks and everyone desperate not to be noticed.

A smoking hole. An Improvised Explosive Device (IED) has knocked out a Private Military Contractor (PMC) vehicle and the guys are going through the post-op phase, picking up the pieces and watching each other's backs.

The Yanks are coming. Big, brash and all-powerful they may be, and the helicopter stunt flying is one thing, but the true picture on the Highway is of a gruelling war of attrition with a committed enemy.

Ships of the desert – the old and the new, as a PMC call sign kicks dust in the desert.

John Geddes under fire in the playground during the battle for the School House at Goose Green in 1982. You can see the playground swings behind him!

Mike Curtis, who wrote *CQB*, working as a PMC in the Serb Republic. A great friend and a superb advocate for the future of properly run and regulated private military companies.

This is the perceived image of an insurgent, but they rarely strike a pose like this. In reality they come in all shapes and sizes and all manner of disguises.

Another typical image of the insurgency - a staged propaganda video. Thankfully this time it features a captured US spy drone not somebody's beheading.

My son Kurt.
He fought in Iraq
with the Paras. Here
he's back in the country
as a civilian PMC.

PMC's deploying near an oil installation. These guys are probably local Iraqis who
risk everything to protect their country's interests.

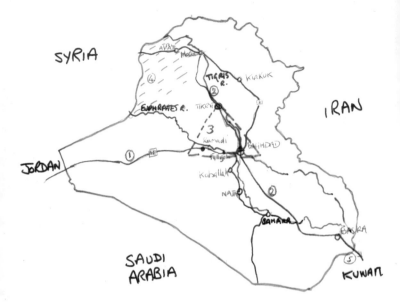

(1) Route 10 from Amman to Baghdad through Fallujah and Ramadi. For the first year to eighteen months after the war was officially declared over, this was the Highway to Hell. It's still a nightmare but Route Irish from the international zone in the city centre to Baghdad International Airport is now the most dangerous road since the airport opened to full capacity for Westerners entering Iraq.

(2) Route 1 from Mosul in the north through Baghdad and on to Basra in the south is a bastard of a road. Three hundred miles of dangerous and desperate insurgents. It got progressively worse when heads started rolling.

(3) All routes and roads within the Sunni Triangle (red dashed lines) are fraught with danger. Travel at your peril, this is pure orange boiler suit country.

(4) The whole western border with Syria from Tal afar in the north to the Euphrates River is bandit country, full of al-Qaeda and foreign fighters. It's a no-go area for most PMC's. Here be dragons!

5) The short haul from Basra to Kuwait City lulls many into a false sense of security. Many have been whacked on the quiet here and you need eyes like bulldogs, as Tak can testify.

The Angel of the Middle East. This statue is outside the entrance to the BIAP (Baghdad International Airport). When you spot this you've almost made it after driving along Route Irish, one of the most dangerous stretches of road in the world.

A room with a view. This one's from the Palestine Hotel in Baghdad across the city, showing the warren where insurgents can move with ease.

Behind the wire. This is the Interior Ministry in Baghdad, operating inside a highly-fortified enclave. Many PMC call signs travel to and from these security ghettoes.

The crazed windscreen tells the story. Rob wasn't close enough to an exploding IED to be badly smashed up, but close enough not to laugh about it.

clear field of fire on the gate with the wicked Minimi he had poking out of the back. Whining like an angry hornet the Minimi ripped more of Saddam's portrait off the wall of the gate and the ceramic map was again redrawn. As the team laid down covering fire Brad and Hal climbed into the middle wagon as the guys recovered them and left their vehicle for scrap.

Then silence. The 50 cal was gone. No more metal-rending rounds. The would-be assassins had been one-burst wonders and they'd carted their prized weapon off and out of the tower as soon as they'd had their fairground shot at the lads. No way were they going to risk losing their weapon or their lives; they'd fled in a car hidden behind the right-hand tower of the gate. Pursuit would be pointless and possibly fatal as they were probably covered by a second ambush waiting to mallet anyone who followed them.

It was luck which had sent those big rounds slamming down the middle of the car between Brad and Hal like a hot lead cheese wire from hell but it was situation awareness that had allowed them to suss that something was about to go down. It was the hairs on the back of Brad's neck that had given them the split-second edge so they'd been able to give the other call signs a heads up. That had allowed them to deploy in an instant and if they hadn't put that suppressing fire on the North Gate the 50 cal would certainly have claimed at least one of the team.

Then suddenly the battle had ended without resolution and the adrenalin they'd pumped round their bodies had nowhere to go. The guys stood for a moment and scanned the urban horizon around them, half hoping another terrorist would come along and have a go. Brad and Hal felt a liberating sense of relief after surviving the burst of cannon fire that had cut the air between them while the gun wagon guys felt cheated because the bastards hadn't stood their ground and fought it out. In fact, they all felt that way. It's an impotent, unresolved rage common on the Highway as time and again the guys watch hit-and-run killers evaporate back into the community without standing to fight.

Brad spoke for them all as he kicked the tyre of the burning truck and said, 'What the fuck was all that about?'

5

THE SHEIKH OF THE BEHEADERS

I'M lying in the corner of a brightly lit room dressed in an orange boiler suit that's too small and pulls at my arms and chest. Not that it matters because I'm trussed up like a turkey anyway, hands and feet tied together by nylon rope. I'm struggling, Christ, I'm struggling but I can't get free and across the room a small bearded figure with a false leg is leering at me with his black, shark eyes while he strokes the blade of a wicked-looking, scimitar-shaped knife. I know who he is. I know his face. He calls himself the Sheikh of the Beheaders. I scream with fury but my defiance comes through the gag in my mouth as a muffled gurgle. He's laughing. Someone standing next to him with a video camera in his hand has made a joke about me. Then the beheader starts to walk towards me with the knife. I know he wants to cut my head off but I'm going to live. I'm fucking well going to live. I brace myself and pull at the ropes that hold me with all my strength – and suddenly I'm free. With a single bound I leap across the room to meet my executioner full on and punch him as hard as I can. He falls to the floor and now he's the one gurgling as I leap on him, pulling the gag from my mouth. Then I bite at his nose and tear it off with my teeth before spitting it in his face.

'John, John, it's time to go.'

As I swam to the surface of consciousness through my retreating sleep I recognised the voice calling me. It was Ian, one of the cover team going with me to the meeting point that night.

'You all right, mate? You were thrashing around a bit.'

'Yeah, yeah. Fine thanks,' I said, 'Just a bad dream.'

I didn't tell him what I'd dreamt. There was no need; after all, everyone in Iraq has nightmares about Abu Musab al Zarqawi, head of al Qaeda in Iraq and the self-styled Sheikh of the Beheaders. Al Zarqawi, a Jordanian psychopath under sentence of death in his own country, has been responsible for organising most of the suicide bombings in Iraq. The al Qaeda network trawls for young men in the Islamic religious schools called madrasas around the world, who are then delivered to al Zarqawi along underground routes leading through Syria

and across the Iraqi border. Then Zarqawi arms
the human warheads and sends them on their one-
way missions into the streets and marketplaces of
Iraq. He's also been the evil inspiration behind the
tactic that has most terrorised Westerners in Iraq,
the kidnap and beheading of hostages. Al Zarqawi
dresses his victims in orange boiler suits, mimick-
ing the prison uniform in Guantanamo Bay, then
he executes them by beheading with a knife. He
transforms these horrifying murders into public
executions by videoing them and posting them on
Islamic websites.

Al Zarqawi is one of bin Laden's most loyal lieu-
tenants and no act is too savage or barbaric if it
furthers the cause of their twisted concept of a great
world religion. In short he is a nightmare, but in
the upside-down world of Iraq al Zarqawi inspires
other dreams among the thousands of private military contractors. These are dreams of great wealth
which stem from the fact that the Americans have
posted a $25 million reward on his head. We have all
imagined collecting it and buying the harbour-side
house in the Caribbean with a yacht tied up at the
private jetty.

As soon as the reward became public the whole
PMC community got very interested in al Zarqawi
and quite a number of serious-minded people have
put a lot of mental resources into dreaming up ways

of getting him. I seem to remember it was $10 million at first but he became such a huge pain in the arse that the State Department raised it to match the bounty on bin Laden himself. With $25 million on the table most people in the PMC trade memorised every feature on the wanted poster just in case they were lucky enough to come across him in the street, and for a few of us hunting him down became a serious if dangerous ambition.

You'd be in the crowded lounge of a hotel when the CNN news came on the television and no one would take a blind bit of notice of the latest suicide bombing, but the moment al Zarqawi was mentioned a hush would descend over the room and a number of steely eyes would focus their undivided attention on the screen. No one admitted what they were doing of course, not publicly anyway, but everyone kept an eye open for that opportunity that might present itself to capture al Zarqawi, and they didn't mind if it was dead or alive.

That's what I was doing that night: I was out to get al Zarqawi, dead or alive. Things are never simple though and this was to be my first step on the trail. I'd asked around discreetly and while I was on a visit to Dubai been introduced to a Kurdish businessman. We beat around the bush a bit and then I said, 'Everyone wants to find al Zarqawi. I wonder how that might be done.'

It would be very difficult indeed, he confided, but it so happened he had a sister who was married to a Sunni who happened to be a former Ba'ath Party member. It's always this way in the middle East: there's always a relative, a sister's husband or someone from my village you can trust. It's an endless game of family trees and complicated loyalties.

'So, your sister's husband. He knows what goes on in the Triangle?'

'Yes, of course. He is a very well-connected person.'

'How so?'

'Well,' he said, 'when my sister met him and fell in love with him he was running a small business in the Kurdish no-fly zone but I think he was a spy for Saddam. It was obvious to me that he was a spy for Saddam.'

'If he was an agent for the regime why was he tolerated?' I knew the answer as I posed the question.

'You understand, of course you do, that it is not impossible that one man's spy can be a different man's spy too. This is not a great problem.'

'Where is he now?'

'He is in the Triangle. He is helping those who want to fight the Americans. He has to do this or some of his family will be put into a very difficult position.'

'What about your sister? Is she with him?'

'No, of course not; we would not allow that. He comes and goes; his children are safe with her in Kurdistan. They would not come there; they would be killed very quickly.'

'So you think he might have information about the man I'm interested in?'

'Maybe not today, but he did before and that was not long ago. Maybe he will again another day soon. I think you should meet him and make a good arrangement to have the information you need quickly when it is available.'

'Fine, but why would he do this?' Again I knew the answer.

'For money, of course. He will have enough money to get his family out of Iraq and take my sister and their children to a safe country. Maybe Sweden or maybe America. There's enough money for everyone.'

'Including you?'

'Of course, including me. I am a businessman; I make my living by trading and by charging commissions. But we could not do this thing ourselves. It must be someone like you. They would know he had been sold by someone but you would be between us and them and you would never be named.'

'Too bloody right I wouldn't. Okay, can you arrange a meeting?'

It had taken nearly a month but my Kurdish friend

had done just that. The meeting with his brother-in-law would be in the morning but just in case me and the lads would be at the meeting place a long time before the appointment. That's why I'd been taking a kip in the early evening; it was going to be a long night. I checked my kit, rechecked it, took a look in the mirror then slipped my personal security card into my top pocket. Interesting thing, the card; it's the same dimensions as an ordinary credit card but twice as thick and hinged so it falls open into two flat sections. You never open it unless you're in real, al Zarqawi-style trouble. When you do it transmits a GPS signal which can be tracked from about a thousand metres. This is not very far in the middle of a desert but in a city a radius of a thousand metres covers two or three suburbs and hundreds of thousands of people. In other words it can find a human needle in a terrorist haystack. The hope is that even if you can't open it then an inquisitive captor will do so as he's searching you. Once it's open it can't be resealed and the signal keeps pulsing out.

We set off from our safe house with some friends just inside the Kurdish area and headed out in two vehicles to an RV – army jargon for a meeting point – in a remote area on the edge of the Sunni Triangle where we were to meet this guy, whom I'll call Zuhair.

You might think this was a bit barmy; after all, this bloke Zuhair could have been anyone at all. I agree. The fact is he could have been completely dodgy on a number of counts. He might have been a con man, although he wasn't going to get a penny from me until the target was in the bag. My real concern was that he was on a fishing expedition and that I was meant to become the trussed turkey in the orange boiler suit of my nightmare. That's why I was taking some of the lads with me, that's why I had my card and that's why we were going to look over the RV very carefully a good six hours before the meeting. And there was the small matter of $25 million. Even a thousand to one chance that I could meet someone who'd been anywhere near the Beheader of Baghdad and might give me a shot at that sort of reward money was worth a punt, and the lads thought so too.

We'd had a good look at the area on maps and seen some aerial photography too, then we'd had a drive-past recce ourselves earlier in the day, but this time we were going to carefully check out the ruined house where the RV was to take place and stake it out for the night. When we got close enough we killed the car lights and moved slowly into LUPs (Lay Up Position) we'd looked at earlier in the day with the two drivers, who put on precision night guidance headgear ready for the drop-off. They tucked the vehicles out of sight, rigged up the tracking devices for the card, set up the radios then settled down to wait. I walked off into the night towards the house.

About thirty yards from it I stopped and settled down behind a boulder to view the place through a light-intensifying monocular. I watched the half-collapsed walls glowing a ghostly green through the lens for a few minutes then I moved round to look at the house from another angle. Only when I'd viewed the RV carefully from all sides did I move in for a closer look and discovered after a thorough viewing that the property was clean. It was going to be a long night and I hid myself away in a spot with a good view of most approaches to the house. The others were covering any spots blind to me.

Five hours later and dawn rose after a night of mind-numbing boredom during which nothing had moved except a few scurrying rodents and some sort of fox. Half an hour later a 4 x 4 came up the track that led from the reasonably busy trunk route two miles away. It was covered in dust but quite a new vehicle and a short, slightly built Iraqi got out of the car and moved nervously around the building. He was a good-looking sort of bloke and when I saw his face clearly I recognised him from the family snaps my Kurdish friend had shown me. It was Zuhair; the cheeky bugger had arrived two hours early for the meeting.

He had only a cursory look about and although he came close to my hiding place didn't spot me, so I just stayed put while he stood around near his vehicle listening to Arab music on the radio and occasionally answering calls on his mobile. He smoked a few fags as the minutes dragged by and as the agreed time drew closer took a small pair of binoculars out of the car and began scanning the track back down to the road, obviously expecting to see my vehicle turn off the main drag. He nearly crapped himself when I walked lightly up behind him, right on time, and said, 'Morning, Zuhair.'

His face was ashen and his knees nearly buckled as he spun round. His hand seemed to move towards the inside of his jacket but if he was carrying he thought better of it and composed himself quickly when he saw my hands were empty.

'Hello, Mac,' he said. I'd not given him or his brother-in-law my real name. 'You surprised me.'

'Sorry about that; just being careful.'

'I think we should be quick about this,' he said, getting straight down to business.

I nodded in agreement and we cut to the chase. 'Can you help me and how much do you want?'

'Yes, I can help you and I want half,' he replied.

'You only have to point me in the right direction,' I said, 'but I have a great many things to do after that. There'll be a lot to arrange and other people to pay. Fifteen per cent for you.'

He shook his head, muttering, 'No, no.' Then he said, 'Twenty-five.'

'Agreed. Okay, so where do I find him?.'

'When I know I will contact you with the details.'

'Fair enough. I'll wait to hear from you.'

We made some contact arrangements using a system which for various reasons I'm not going to describe here. The meeting ended. He got into his car and drove back down the track towards the main drag. When he'd gone Ian and the others moved in to collect me.

'What d'you think, Johnny? Is it a runner?' asked Ian.

'Tell you what I think, mate. I think my arse in a sling would mean cash in the bank for that little bastard. I bet you he'll be wanting another meeting in a couple of weeks' time just to clear up a few details of the deal and I bet he'll want to meet quite close to al Qaeda's backyard. I also bet you a few of his mates will try to lift me, then sell me to al Zarqawi or someone similar.'

'Well, we thought it could be dodgy all along. The list of mates who know where al Zarqawi's going to be at any given moment must be shorter than your Christmas card list, John, and I can't see a Kurdish double agent being on it.'

I was wrong about one thing though: it was only a week, not two, before Zuhair contacted me. He needed to talk to me about the arrangements; he had to have assurances about his safety; he needed more money because so many of his family would have to be moved out of Iraq; he wanted to explain some details to me. Could I meet him in—'

I cut him off mid-flow and my reply was to the point. 'Zuhair, if I ever see you again I will kill you.'

This was not an honest threat, more of a message that I believed he was trying to line me up for a kidnap and that if I did see him I would assume that was about to happen. My mission to get al Zarqawi hadn't even got off the runway and my visions of wealth were just dreams again but, as they say, if you don't try you don't get. I know that variations on my particular experience are still going on as the bounty on offer continues to tempt soldiers of fortune in Iraq, but November 2004 I had a call from another old Regiment boy.

After catching up on old times Danny said, 'John, I'm trying to put a team together for a special job. It's got to be all ex-Blades, Delta or similar, and I reckon I'll need five or six teams. Trying to muster so many guys when Iraq's giving everyone full employment is a hell of a job but I know you're in the swim and you may know who's available. I'm also hoping you'll want to get in on it yourself.'

'What's the job, Dan?' I asked.

He told me straight off because ex-SAS men don't go into all that need-to-know bullshit with each other. If an old Blade takes you into his loop you keep your mouth shut and that's that. It's an accepted fact of life. Danny was trying to cook up his own scheme to get al Zarqawi and his plan made my attempt to track down the al Qaeda chief look pretty lame. His idea came after a bit of light reading. Danny's always looking through journals like *New Scientist* and *Nature* to keep up on technological advances, hoping he'll spot some new development or a piece of kit he can use. One day he found a short article about microchips which can be implanted under the skin and can hold an individual's medical history and other personal details so that they can be read in case of death or injury. Apparently some scientists in the US and Britain are working towards a chip that holds all this info but also has an integral GPS capability not unlike my security card, and they've produced prototypes.

'It can be implanted with a simple medical procedure, John, and it's virtually undetectable,' he told me.

'So. You've got a chip under your skin. My dog's got a chip under his skin in case he runs off,' I said.

'Precisely, mate. Your dog's got a chip so you can identify him if he's found. Our chip has GPS so we can find lost or stolen humans; I'm thinking of having our clients chipped for additional security. But the big idea is to chip one of the lads and stake him out for capture like a tethered goat for a tiger.'

'You're having a fucking laugh,' I said.

'No. One of the boys says he'll do it for ten million bucks, which is fair enough, but we'd have to have a big backup operation as well and that would take a lot of blokes. In a nutshell, we get him kidnapped and then we follow the signal, burst in on the Beheader and his team and waste them, rescuing our bloke as we go.'

'I suppose it could work in principle, Danny, but there are so many variables involved it's bound to end in a fuck-up.'

'Obviously we'll have to make sure the chip is up to scratch – no one's going to literally put their head on the block with dodgy kit – but there's one thing that's not variable in this equation, John.'

'What's that?'

'The reward.'

'Fair point, mate. It's definitely worth a go.'

Danny and I agreed that he'd come back to me when he'd further investigated the microchip. However, he dropped the venture because of technical difficulties – not, you'll note, because he couldn't find a lad with balls enough to do it. We've since learnt that around the time Danny was planning Operation Tethered Goat, al Zarqawi had actually been arrested by the Iraqi police and held overnight in a cell. Despite the fact he has only one leg, following a US air strike on his chemical warfare training camp in Afghanistan during the war against the Taliban, the police failed to identify al Zarqawi and released him. This only came out when one of his team was arrested in the summer of 2005 and told US intelligence officers the story. They made enquiries but the IP just shrugged and claimed they knew nothing. It's generally believed that the police involved that night weighed up the reward money against the almost certain slaughter of all of their families and opted to let him go after a good breakfast.

The night of 7 June 2005 was clear and the pilot of the US Air Force F-16 could see every detail of his target as he dropped a big, fuck-off 500 lb bomb onto the farmhouse thirty miles north of Baghdad. Just in case that hadn't done the trick his wingman dropped another 500-pounder right on the nose as well.

The next day the Yanks called a press conference in Baghdad and announced that the Sheik of the Beheaders had been malleted. They paraded before and after pictures of the most wanted man in Iraq.

Before – the smirking, arrogant psychopath, certain in the power that his terror endowed on him; after – a bloated cadaver with plugs of blood in his nose from the massive brain haemorrhage caused by the blast.

There's no doubt he was betrayed for the $25m bounty on his head and I'm pretty certain that it was an inside job. I don't believe that any PMC was lucky enough to get onto his case but even so we were all looking for signs of anyone who'd left Iraq to live a lottery-win lifestyle.

Someone from inside al Qaeda's Iraq operation put the Americans onto Zarqawi's spiritual adviser, the Muslim equivalent of a confessor, and tracked him with everything from surveillance teams to satellites until he led them to the man himself.

The bogey man is dead, but his nightmare continues as the sectarian holocaust he brewed develops into near civil war. And there are still rewards to be earned for catching insurgents on the US wanted list and as long as there are, we'll be looking for them.

I'll never forget the words of a Kuwaiti businessman at the end of the Iraq War in 2003 when he told me, 'Yes, the Iraqis have been liberated from Saddam but now they're free to kill each other, and that's just what they'll do.'

Well he was bang on and in my view his statement gets to the nub of the problem. I'm no historian and I don't pretend to be a political analyst but I'm a soldier and fighting men have their own common-sense approach to working out why all hell has broken loose. I'm going to try to give you a practical, down-to-earth soldier's briefing on the roots and causes of the insurgency in Iraq.

One thing I can't emphasise too strongly is just how violent and bloody the insurgency is. It's a hundred times worse than Northern Ireland. In my view it's significantly worse than the ethnic cleansing in the former Yugoslavia, although that's a purely subjective judgement, as most of the time in Yugoslavia, we weren't the ones being directly shot at. You tend to modify your opinion when bullets start whizzing past your ear. Another thing you've got to get your head round is that there was always going to be chaos in Iraq. The truth is it didn't matter whether it was the Coalition or an internal revolution that got rid of Saddam Hussein; the ingredients for mayhem already existed in the country and more was bound to follow as Iraq cracked along racial, tribal and religious fracture lines there long before the US brought him down.

When a dictator falls the rest scrap for power in the vacuum and there are telling parallels between Iraq and the former Yugoslavia. Marshal Tito was a strongman able to hold together Croatia, Macedonia, Slovenia, Bosnia–Herzogovenia and Serbia, but Yugoslavia lasted only months after his state funeral before nationality, tribe and religion exploded to the surface and years of civil war followed. In Iraq the arithmetic says it all. A Sunni minority of 20 per cent of the population sitting on zero per cent of the oil wealth was able to suppress and rule the rest of the Iraqis – who had lots of oil – for over forty years. In the south were the Shias, 60 per cent of the population, while up in the north were the Kurds (20 per cent). The Sunnis did this through a dynamic and ruthless instrument of power called the Ba'ath Party, which held to some notion of Arab brotherhood – as long as the Arabs in question were Sunni.

Saddam took the party over nearly thirty years ago and held it in his vice-like grip through repeated ruthless culls of all who opposed him. He crushed the Shias and declared war on the Shia Muslim state of Iran in a conflict which killed a million men, and in between turned his attention to the Kurds in the north, destroying whole villages and dropping nerve agents on innocent communities. Full of bravado he then invaded Kuwait and got booted out by the coalition put together by the first President Bush, but he was able to claim a phoney victory because he still held power in his own country. Encouraged by Bush, the

Shias, in particular the Marsh Arabs, rose against Saddam and his regime fully expecting US military help. None came and the Marsh Arabs were practically wiped out before Saddam built a canal to drain their homeland in a terrible ethnic and environmental rape that alone should condemn him in any court.

Against this backcloth in 2003 the Coalition invaded Iraq, and the legitimacy of that invasion has been endlessly and futilely debated ever since. Did Saddam have weapons of mass destruction or didn't he? Everything I've heard on the intelligence grapevine in Iraq suggests that he did but in the nick of time moved them across the Syrian border before the invasion. There are stories of long convoys of Scud missiles arriving in Syria, an event which may have marked the end of a rift between the Ba'athists of Iraq and those in Syria, where a version of the party also holds power.

Justified or not, the invasion is a fact, and once Saddam was ousted the insurgency was inevitable; nothing could have stopped the resistance movement, which happened very quickly. In the Sunni Triangle and Baghdad the remnants of the old regime activated a plan they'd drawn up long ago and the irreligious Ba'ath Party joined with the zealots of al Qaeda in an unholy alliance. It's highly likely that the man who helped forge this alliance was Izzat Ibrahim al Douri, vice chairman of Saddam's Revolutionary Command Council and the only deeply religious Sunni in the regime. Said to be one of the men who met Saddam in a car at a Baghdad park to trigger the uprising, he was on the run with a $10 million price on his head, but died of cancer in 2005.

The uprising turned from a murderous nuisance into a full insurgency in the summer of 2003 when the Jordanian embassy and the United Nations headquarters were both subjected to devastating explosions courtesy of al Zarqawi. Then in the summer of 2005, after the elections and just before a referendum on the constitution, al Qaeda stopped beating around the bush and openly declared war on the Shiite majority, whom they see as heretics. At the same time the Shiites in the Basra region became increasingly active against British troops in a separate insurgency fomented by Iran and aimed at beefing up the power of the Mahdi Army run by the militant cleric Muqtada al Sadr. Iran is a Shiite state and as soon as its new militant president, Mahmoud Ahmadinejad, was sworn into power in August 2005 he upped the ante. His aim was to destabilise southern Iraq so that when a full civil war breaks out the Iranian government can take control of the strategic Shatt al Arab waterway on the Gulf together with the marshes and the whole of the oil-rich province of Basra. The Iran–Iraq War was a border dispute fought over these very regions.

So, you have a Sunni minority backed by al Qaeda

and supported by Syria fighting to regain control of the whole country and its oil fields, and you have Iranian-backed Shiites squared up against them, with the Coalition as piggy in the middle trying to rebuild a country filled with armed men desperate to tear it to pieces. But I'll bet a barrel full of oil that before this is over al Qaeda and Saddam's Ba'ath insurgents will be at each other's throats. Al Qaeda want to convert the world to Islam and impose what they call a global caliphate on us all; the Ba'athists simply want to regain total power in their own land and don't give a fig about religion. They deserve each other and I'm certain they will fall out.

Only in Kurdistan in the north of the country is there any sort of stability. Here the hard-grafting, business-minded Kurds have set up a decent semi-autonomous state after years living in the jaws of a nutcracker between Turkey and Iraq, where their language and culture has been suppressed and they have been pitilessly slaughtered for generations. At the end of the First Gulf War they fled from Saddam's pursuing avengers into the snow-covered hills but the Royal Marines piled in between them and the Bully of Baghdad, and a no-fly zone has allowed them to flourish for a decade.

The geography of the insurgency is simple, then. The entire country outside Kurdistan and the heavily fortified Green Zone in Baghdad is known as the Red

Zone, and it's here that Coalition troops and foreigners move around at their peril. Some areas are more dangerous than others. Ramadi, Fallujah, Mosul, Tikrit and the notorious town of Tall Afar near the Syrian border are virtual suicide runs, but even beyond these hellholes nowhere in the Red Zone can genuinely be called safe. In Baghdad the road from the Green Zone to the international airport is supposed to be heavily protected but in practice it's a honey pot for suicide bombers and IEDs. The city suburbs of al Dourah, Aadamiya and Gazaliya are hotbeds of the insurgency and the Ba'ath Party housing projects in Amiriyah and al Jihad are also fertile recruiting grounds for anti-Coalition groups.

It goes without saying that bombs are the most deadly weapon in the insurgents' arsenal. Suicide bombs have claimed thousands of lives in Iraq – most of them, it has to be said, innocent Iraqi bystanders but the Coalition and PMC's have suffered from them too.

The weapon that has claimed the most lives of soldiers of fortune though is the IED or Improvised Explosive Device. And that's just what it is, a concoction of explosives with artillery rounds or mortar bombs thrown together to effect the most carnage possible. The bombs can be formed in daisy chains or series parallel, but I'm not going to handbook explosive techniques here.

They're usually placed on the roadside and deto-nated as western convoys drive past. Apparently some of the insurgents have developed a real knack of fusing their bombs at just the right moment when vehicles are hit broadside. No wonder the lads prefer to travel low profile.

IED's are usually put into tightly wrapped parcels and a skilled bomb maker can conform the shape of the package to vent the maximum damage. When shaped the effect is to concentrate and direct the energy towards the target (i.e., the road). The deto-nator is generally a cordless-phone base station. You call the base station and the call completes the circuit. When the circuit's activated all hell breaks loose. The base stations, unlike radio handsets or mobiles, can't be jammed by countermeasures They can also be activated by a washing machine or video timer.

The bombs are usually hidden under piles of rubbish and believe me there's plenty of rubbish on the roadsides in Iraq to camouflage them. Real bomb artists with an eye for their work shove them inside the carcasses of dead dogs, sheep or goats so that spotting one is largely a matter of luck. Doubly so when some bombs are actually buried under the asphalt of the road itself and a lot of them are big enough to topple armoured personnel carriers. The insurgents will place the bomb then lay tarmac over it and shower it with dust. They have been known to etch a channel across a highway with battery acid for the cable from the base station to the bomb and then tarmac over that, too.

The Shia terrorists around Basra have their own take on it and use IED's activated by an infra-red beam and that's an idea that came originally from the IRA, through to the Hezbollah in Lebanon on the terrorist grapevine and then courtesy of Iranian intelligence agents into Iraq. They either have a constant infra-red beam which explodes the bomb when it's broken (for use on lonely roads when you think the target vehicle will be the first to come along) or rig up a beam which can be activated to hit the bomb detonation when they spot the target; once again, skilled timing is required. Basically all you need is the channel-changing kit from a TV and a battery for power.

IED's are a weapon you can't fight, you just have to rely on good fortune to avoid them or to survive them.

The reason no road is safe is that the insurgency was unwittingly accelerated by decisions which the Coalition must now bitterly regret. The first of these was made a decade ago at the end of the First Gulf War when, as I've mentioned, the United States encouraged a Shia uprising then allowed it to be crushed by Saddam's regime. I wonder how you would feel if you were an Iraqi Shia. How would you react when a few years later the same characters fetched up and demanded respect and your total cooperation in something they called a road map to democracy? Remember that your society has no history of democracy but strong traditions of tribal and clan loyalty with a strong religious under-pinning. Remember also that's only the Shia majority I'm talking about. The Sunni minority hate your guts anyway because they were in the pound seats until the Americans and British came along; they ruled the roost and it was their man Saddam who was crowing on the top of the muck heap.

The second mistake came with the waste of intel-ligence effort in the run-up to the war in looking for WMD to justify the invasion. It was pretty obvious the Coalition was going to mallet Saddam and his boys whatever so the intelligence effort should have gone into discovering what his long-term plans for nonsense were. If they'd just taken the time to look under the mattress Western intelligence would have found an insurgency long planned and waiting for activation.

It's difficult to paint a picture of your average, everyday insurgent. It doesn't work like that. They come from all sorts of backgrounds and they come in all shapes, sizes and from different age groups too. The leadership are no doubt men loyal to Saddam, possibly from the same Tikrit background, who were trained and then sent out into society as sleepers to be activated after an invasion or a coup against their master. Many of the foot soldiers come from units of the defeated Iraqi army, which were obliterated or disbanded without pay at the end of the war. The police force was disbanded too in another short-sighted move by the Coalition. Many policemen joined the insurgency to be ordered by their terrorist bosses to rejoin and subvert the new police force.

Ironically, many of the thousands of criminal, as opposed to political, prisoners released from jails like Abu Ghraib by Saddam then joined the policemen who originally nicked them in the ranks of the insurgency. I've no doubt that even as they walked out of the prison gates they were given a number to call if they wanted to earn some dollars fighting against the invaders. The police situation is particularly nasty. Everyone knows the IP is riddled with insurgents and I believe they cynically and in cold blood have used police recruitment as a way of culling out decent Iraqis who want to make a difference to society. I don't believe for a second that the queues of police recruits targeted by suicide bombers contained insurgents wanting to infiltrate the force; they would have been told by their masters exactly which recruiting queues to join and which ones not to join. The rest are blown to hell.

The motives of those joining the insurgency are varied and complex but the X factor is the chests full of US dollars paid to Saddam's regime in the scandalous food-for-oil deal brokered by the corrupt United Nations. Literally billions of dollars meant for the hungry and sick children of Iraq are now fuelling the Sunni insurgency and paying for al Qaeda support. Whatever a man's political or tribal loyalties there's nothing that makes him feel more like fighting than a wad of cash to take home to the wife and kids, and in that respect the insurgents are just as mercenary as the PMCs. The essential difference in the south of the country is that the insurgents are Shia and the paymasters the Iranian government and their agents.

At this point it might be useful if I explain as best I can the difference between Shia and Sunni Muslims. It's something I made it my business to bone up on when I got out there as it's so central to much of the mayhem in Iraq. I'm not an Islamic scholar so I apologise in advance for any offence I might cause through errors of fact or emphasis.

As the story goes, Ali was the honoured cousin and son-in-law of the Prophet Muhammad and was chosen to be the Prophet's successor on his death. However, when Muhammad died the majority of his followers decided to follow Abu Bakr, who became the first great caliph of the Muslim world. Ali eventually became the fourth caliph but was assassinated and his son Husayn subsequently rebelled against a later caliph. Husayn was however defeated and killed in battle, and most of his family massacred. But many stayed loyal to Ali's memory; his martyrdom and that of his son became the focus of a split in the Muslim religion which produced the Shia – followers of Ali – and the Sunni. Ali was buried at Najaf in southern Iraq, the spiritual centre of the Shiite world.

There are two more things about the insurgents that should be clearly understood. The first is that they are courageous and tenacious fighters worthy of respect. The second is that they can't shoot for shit and inevitably lose when sustained and accurate fire is brought to bear on them. The speciality of the British-trained soldier is sustained and accurate fire but sometimes a situation comes along that turns all the conventions on their head and that happens quite often in the upside-down world of Iraq.

May 2005. Another long black snake of tarmac twisting through another anonymous rock-strewn sun-grilled landscape. This time it's just south of Mosul, another suppurating abscess on the arse of the Coalition. A trio of 4 x 4s carrying eight British PMCs is hurrying back to its forward operating base on the edge of the city. They're hurrying but they're doing it slowly because one of the vehicles in the convoy has broken down and is being towed by another with the gun vehicle in the rear.

Ex-Para Chris was in the lead vehicle towing the breakdown and he told me what happened. He was twitchy, they were all twitchy, and who wouldn't have been in a limping wagon train deep in Indian country when the road was about to pass a low hill to their right that looked as though God had created it with an ambush in mind. Chris was about to say something when a huge eruption lifted the side of the road into the air and said it for him.

The blast swatted the car and nearly rolled it but his mate Jim, an Australian I think, gripped the wheel, steadied it and kept it on the road. Whoever had set the IED hadn't packed it properly and had placed it just a bit too far off the road. 'Fuck,' said Chris, knowing what was coming next, and right on cue a burst of machine-gun fire raked the side of the car. Then as they pulled in to take cover and return fire a second IED showered them with earth and rock, but that had been a shit job too.

The team in the third car had reacted instantly, jinking and swerving off the road, manoeuvring to position for a best-effect retaliation. Chris heard them through his earpiece as they spotted the insurgent. They'd pinged his position and now they'd fire fury at him.

'Right at the base of that top feature rock.' The voice was urgent and precise.

'Roger that! Roger that!' Other voices joined in as

they spotted the enemy fire position among the rocks. As they poured considerable and accurate fire on the position a young man, late twenties, standard baggy trousers and leather jacket, broke cover and doubled to a new piece of cover to return fire with his RPK, whipping steel-cased rounds into the gun vehicle.

'Cheeky fucker!' The voice that had first pinged the insurgent was frustrated now.

Eight weapons rained lead on the insurgent's new position, expecting to mallet him, then without warning he was off again. 'He's like a fucking rabbit,' snarled Chris into his mouthpiece.

A few seconds passed before the guy got his wind back to rattle off more machine-gun rounds at them. He wasn't great but the rounds were close enough to keep everyone's head down. So it went on. Bobbing and weaving. Taking cover, breaking cover, demonstrating that the seemingly flat backcloth of the hill had a third dimension in among the rocks. He was up again, leaping like a goat from one rock to another, machine gun balanced on his shoulder. For the briefest moment he turned to look down at them on the road, total defiance implicit in that moment's pause.

Chris looked at him up there on that crag and wondered why he was taking them on alone, then realised that this young man must have sworn an oath to kill an infidel or die in the attempt. Perhaps his brother or father had been killed by the Coalition and he was out for revenge but Chris knew for sure that this was one insurgent who was running from no one. Far from it; he was calling on death to follow him into those rocks if it dared.

It was then that Chris heard the hornet buzz of two Apache helicopter gunships. There'd been no call to them but they'd evidently been passing nearby on patrol and had come to see what all the flash bang was about. It didn't take the helo crews long to work out what was happening and Chris and the lads watched their thermal imaging devices moving like sinister robot eyes, probing the rocks below with their alien technology as they brought *The War of the Worlds* to this barren corner of the desert. Inevitably they found their target, just flesh and blood with the heart of a desert lion. They locked onto him and the big automatic cannon slung under the nose of the nearest Apache streamed out rounds like a sawmill and vaporised the lone insurgent. Later an American army ground force examined the area and found three more IEDs laid alongside the road. All this set by one man whose heart had been filled with hate and revenge.

Chris and the others stepped out of their cover and looked up into the rocks where they'd witnessed that display of raw courage. Their respect for his valour led them to reflect on the waste of a young life and Chris told me, 'I sort of wanted to salute him. I just didn't know how.'

This remarkable one-man army summed up the qualities and the inadequacies of the insurgents. If I were asked to write his epitaph I would suggest: 'He was as brave as fuck but couldn't shoot for shit.'

6

UNUSUAL BUSINESS

It was a steam bath of a day in the Congo jungle and I was bodyguarding an Arab businessman from Qatar. It wasn't just the weather that was steaming either, but the 400 miners at his diamond concession, who hadn't been paid for six months. The mine was owned by my boss, the government of the Congo and another company which appeared to be run by Zimbabwe military commanders. The mine was producing 'blood diamonds', which I believe helped pay for the war in the Congo and the support of the Zim army for the government side in that conflict.

We'd flown up from the boss's luxury home on a big estate in Zimbabwe. There are no unions on the diamond field and the negotiations were being carried on Congo style. That involved taking one of the British site managers hostage and giving him a good kicking. The boss was rattled and he'd brought the cash for the wages owed with him, which I put in the safe at the site office as soon as we arrived. Then we took a deep breath and went off to negotiate with a mob of very fed up miners. Our bargaining stance was that obviously no cash was going to be handed out till our manager was released without further harm.

I'd expected to have to go and meet the miners alone, but to be fair to him the boss had some bottle and he came into the lion's den with me. We drove from the office down to the site of the opencast mine, a huge mud bath of diamond-bearing alluvium with millions of pounds-worth of processing machinery designed to consume great loads of riverbed soil and spit out the precious stones.

The place was buzzing like a wasps' nest that had been poked with a stick. Waiting for us was a crowd of very angry workers armed with spears, machetes, broken bottles and large hammers, in fact anything to inflict a savage wound on those who failed to hand over their beer and whore money. As we pulled up in our Toyota flatbed they were chanting and stamping their feet in time to try and intimidate us. I say try but actually they weren't making a bad job of it. They were a frightening sight.

I had known it would be an explosive situation so I'd arranged the deployment of a platoon of soldiers from the Federal Army of the Congo on the hill behind us. They were garrisoned at the mine to protect it from rebels but at that moment the rebels were inside the wire. The troops were dressed in vests, shorts and flip-flops, and as far as I could make out had never been paid either but for some reason were still up for a bit of pay bargaining on my boss's behalf. Under two ex-Gurkhas I'd hired they were spread out with heavy machine guns in the centre.

So there we were: a crowd of angry men baying for money or blood, a platoon of knickers, handbag and trumpet troops, and standing between them me and a millionaire Arab businessman. And of course I mustn't forget the British mining engineer trussed up like the last chicken on the supermarket shelf. The self-appointed shop stewards stepped forward and some very tense negotiations took place while I stood next to the Qatari, weapon at the ready, tensely scanning the crowd for the one hothead who'd kick it all off. There was a palpable sense of fear and I knew that if something did go down there was a strong possibility that we'd quickly be hacked to death. At that moment it's fair to say I had some perception of how General Gordon must have felt when Khartoum went tits up.

The deal was done and they brought our man to us while I radioed for the money to be got out of the safe and brought down. Perfect. Get the engineer to a medic; watch the miners set off on the seven-mile walk to town where they'd sink a few beers and then everything back to normal in a day or so. Not quite.

A voice crackled down the radio; it was one of my
Brit security staff.

'Sorry. Bit of a problem. Bob's forgotten the
combination to the safe.'

'He's fucking what?' I asked, trying to keep the
hint of alarm out of my voice as the crowd of wound-
up miners watched.

'He can't remember the combination.'

Bob was the other engineer and site manager
renowned for his civil engineering expertise. Bob
looked as though he had stepped straight out of the
pages of a Graham Greene novel. He was a hangover from colonial times, an Englishman with 'Land
of Hope and Glory' stamped all over him. I liked
Bob but wondered how he'd survived in Africa. He
was a small dapper man who lived on site, miles from
anywhere in strife-torn Congo with his wife and their
two pet dogs.

Anyway, in the excitement of it all Bob had forgotten
the combination to the safe and a lot of impatient
men waving meat cleavers were waiting for their money.
What were we going to do? I managed to get the boss's
attention for a moment and quietly told him about
our little problem with the safe. He looked as though
he'd been informed of a bereavement, possibly his own.
Then it came to me.

'I've got an idea,' I said. 'Keep these lads talking
while I phone a friend.'

I took his satellite phone and dialled a number in England, hoping it would be picked up by Jim, an old SAS mate who in his time had been the finest exponent of demolition and safe breaking in the history of special forces. Thank God he answered. You can just imagine the conversation as I explained the predicament I was in.

'Nice one, John,' he said. 'Is the safe fixed to the wall?'

I had my gun on the back of the flatbed now, useless if it all popped off around me, as I used the radio to communicate with the office and the satphone to talk to Jim. I was surrounded by the mob, which was silent and wide-eyed now.

'Yeah, it's bolted onto the wall.'

'Right, rip it off the wall.' I passed the instruction along via the radio, and so it went on as I explained, blow by blow, how they should crack the safe. Jim's instructions worked perfectly – in fact, they worked so well I'd best not upset the police by revealing all the details – and within twenty minutes the cash was with its rightful owners and the battered engineer was untrussed and safe.

So, you might ask, what the hell's all this diamond-mine-in-the-Congo stuff got to do with the war in Iraq? I would have asked the same question myself until November 2004 when I saw Bob the Builder striding towards me across the lobby of the

Sheraton hotel in Baghdad with his hand outstretched.

'John, how marvellous to see you.' He grasped my hand.

'Jesus, what the hell are you doing here, Bob?' I could barely believe my eyes.

'Well, pastures new and all that. I'm going to sell refrigeration and air-conditioning equipment to the Americans. We've heard that they're short of that sort of stuff and the boss has a good supply lined up in Qatar. We can have it here for them in double-quick time. Lot of money to be made.'

'Yeah, well, that's great, mate. When do you start?' I think I was shaking my head in disbelief.

'Tomorrow actually. I've got an appointment with a buyer up at Camp Eagle. I'm pretty confident I'll get a deal.'

'Camp Eagle? You know the road to Camp Eagle is festering with insurgents? Have you got some protection?'

'No. I'll be fine, old boy. Piece of cake. In fact when I get this business going I was thinking of getting an apartment here in Baghdad and moving the memsahib and the dogs over.'

I couldn't believe what I was hearing. The idea was so mad that at first I couldn't think of anything sensible to say.

'Are you mad, Bob? Muslims can't stand dogs. In their culture dogs are vermin.'

'Really,' he answered sniffily. 'Well, I'm sure it'll be fine.'

'No, Bob, it really won't be fine. The whole place is alive with fucking terrorists and they're falling over each other they're so desperate to find Westerners to mallet. They'll have your balls for cufflinks before you know it. Believe me, Bob; you can't do it.'

He gave me one of his I-know-best smiles and said, 'Don't worry, John. It'll all settle down. Believe me.'

Don't worry, John! I wasn't the one who had to worry. 'Bollocks! It's never going to settle down, Bob. Sell your fridges and fuck off home – that's my advice.'

I didn't see Bob in Iraq again and I haven't bumped into him since, but I know he did heed my warning and worked safely out of Qatar. I hope he stays safe.

Bob's not typical of the businessmen who head for Iraq. Most of them are not out there looking for speculative sales. They are mostly men from corporations all over the world with contracts already in the bag. The risks are huge but so are the rewards and in my experience only men with balls of steel visit Iraq to execute the contracts. Most of them are level-headed, quiet and thoughtful. A lot are dedicated family men with children in expensive schools and wives they want to provide for. Some of them run their own specialist engineering or electronic companies and see a lucrative contract in Iraq as

worth the risk to establish the firm's future. Others
are vice-presidents of big multinationals, the centu-
rions of the corporate world, prepared to go to most
places and take big risks for the sake of the business
empire they serve; but they do it for huge rewards.

Diplomats need protection too and the US and
British governments both entrust that job to PMCs
rather than regular troops. Twenty years ago in Beirut
it was a special unit of the Royal Military Police,
trained by the SAS, which was given the job of close
protection of UK ambassadorial staff, but not any
more. The Foreign Office contracted the work out in
Iraq and it looks as though that will be the trend
in future hot spots. Some of the most important
security assignments involve the protection of economists and bankers from the International Monetary
Fund and the World Bank, who are pivotal to the
financial future of the country. Their protection too
is entrusted to PMCs, and some of the people
assigned to them are among the most unusual
contractors working in Iraq. I'll be describing them
in a later chapter.

So, on any given day, there are thousands of businessmen, engineers, bankers and diplomats on the
move around Iraq and it's a real credit to the
mercenary army which protects them that relatively
few of its clients (principals as they're known) have
lost their lives. I reckon the number would be in the

region of thirty or forty and of those only a couple were UK citizens – including, of course, Ken Bigley.

Ken was a sixty-two-year-old engineer from Liverpool and by all accounts a decent bloke. His fate and that of two US colleagues in October 2004 was particularly indecent. He'd been held hostage for three weeks, forced to make several video appeals to Tony Blair and the Coalition, his captors demanding that all women prisoners be released. Only two women, both weapons scientists, were being held by the US, which made the demand a bit of a red herring; they were just playing games. In the end it seems that one of the members of the Tawhid and Jihad group holding Ken had some humanity and helped him escape, but he was picked up again after half an hour's liberty in the back streets of the town of Latifiya, to the south-west of Baghdad. That must have sealed his fate – and probably the fate of the guy who sympathised with him – because they forced Ken to make another video appeal.

I've watched this disgusting film and it seems to me that from his dignified demeanour Ken was a man of more courage than the cowards who held him. This final video shows six armed and hooded men standing behind Ken, who is made to kneel, and after his appeal for help he utters his last words: 'I have a very short time left.' The man behind him then makes a minute-long speech in Arabic before taking a wicked blade out of its sheath and falling on Ken from behind like a dog. Three of the others grab him and hold him as he is beheaded with the knife while the pack scream '*Allahu akhbar!*' time and time again. Good protection is a lifesaver and it is the presence of highly trained PMCs that gives the brave men who want to give Iraq the lifeblood of trade the confidence to keep doing business there.

I always point to the case of two Finnish businessmen, part of a trade delegation, who were murdered on the infamous Baghdad airport highway in March 2004. Seppo Haapanen and Jorma Toronen were hoping to revive old business contacts in Iraq and represented high-tech firms, but their protection certainly wasn't high-tech as they drove to the Ministry of Electricity offices near the airport. A large black car, probably one of the BMWs favoured by the insurgents, drove alongside their vehicle and the gunmen inside opened fire with automatic weapons. The Finns were shot to shit.

The two Finns didn't have any close protection and their Iraqi driver was only carrying a pistol. Great. Even if the driver could have got his pistol out in time – assuming he wanted to have a shoot-out with a couple of machine guns – he wouldn't have been able to drive and fight effectively simultaneously. A couple of trained PMCs, alert and on the lookout for just that sort of attack, on the other hand, would probably have seen the Finns come out of it alive. I don't know who advised their delegation on security but they should never have been in that car without a couple of armed men protecting them. It makes me angry when I hear of wasted lives. Of course Ken's death and the death of other hostages in similar circumstances has had a sobering effect on the men and women who travel to Iraq to help rebuild the country, but it hasn't stopped them coming.

March 2004 and I was in Baghdad doing the usual. I came back to the Sheraton after a day out on the ground with a client and the receptionist handed me a message with my key. Ahmed had called. He'd been a mate for ten years or more. He was a Palestinian I had very good reason to trust. I went to my room, showered then called him.

'How are you, old son?' I asked.

'I'm very good, Johnny, very good, and my family are good too, but I wanted to talk to you about some business,' he said.

'Okay, sounds good. How can I help?'

'Well, you see, I have a friend who does business out of Kuwait. He's got hold of some oil concessions in Iraq, but he wants to organise security. At the moment the oil facilities are not working but they are expensive, as you can imagine, and he wants to make sure they will not be damaged when they are

working again. I mentioned you and he would like
a meeting.'

'Where?'

'In Baghdad, Johnny.'

'Okay. He could come here and meet me at the
hotel.'

'I don't think so, my friend. There are people in
all the hotels who report back to the Ba'ath Party
and the al Qaeda people too. Believe me, Baghdad
is spy city these days and he will not want to be seen
in a hotel full of Westerners. Not a good thing.'

'Well, it's not a good idea for a Westerner to be
wandering around Baghdad either.'

'I know, I know, but if you could see him I would
consider it a great favour,' said Ahmed.

Well, long story short: I owed him a great favour
so I agreed to do it, and anyway I trusted Ahmed
and he'd given me his word the bloke was sound. The
arrangements were made and I met Mr X two days
later. But when I did I broke the one and only rule
in the hitchhiker's guide to Iraq – I accepted a ride
in his car.

It was early evening but darkness was falling as
we drove away from the centre and across the river,
me sitting on the back seat with Mr X. I was getting
more than a little bit uneasy and the fact that we
were heading in the general direction of the insurgency slums of Sadr City wasn't making me feel any

better. Nor was the fact that he wasn't Kuwaiti at all, but Iraqi. What did make me feel slightly easier was the pistol in a concealed holster under my jacket. Slightly – but not a lot.

We turned off before Sadr City but then the car started winding through the backstreets and it wasn't more than five minutes before I had no idea where I was. I felt in my pocket to make sure my personal security card was there. I did that a couple of times. Then the car pulled up and I was invited into a building that appeared from the outside to be some sort of office. Mr X, who was very courteous and spoke good English, took me into a room filled with about five of his associates, as he called them. To me it was a room full of Saddam lookalikes and when I sat down across a desk from him I didn't make any pretence of it: I just put my hand inside my jacket and gripped the pistol. Just in case.

The conversation wandered around a bit, but to be honest I was thinking less about what was being said than about leaving the place and whether I'd get back to the hotel in one piece. He asked a bit about prices of security but he seemed more interested in who else I'd worked for – not a subject I was willing to discuss. In the end I bluntly asked to be returned to the Sheraton and said I'd wait to hear from him. I never did, but I do know that his business was none of mine.

What I'd done was foolish even on the good word of an old friend and I resolved never again to hitch a lift in Iraq.

Perhaps the most eccentric and downright charming of all the businessmen I met in Iraq during eighteen months of protection work were two ex-British army NCOs looking for oil contracts in Basra. If Bob the Builder could easily have stepped off the pages of a Graham Greene novel, then central casting would have replaced Sean Connery and Michael Caine with these two in *The Man Who Would Be King*. I'll call them Doug and Mick. When they first arrived in Iraq they had a South African team bodyguarding them as they went about the Basra area doing recces and building relationships in the oil business for a Qatar-based company, but after a couple of weeks the PMCs told the two old sergeants that the contract was over and dumped them at Basra airport. They were on their own. They managed to get a cab back to Basra and were a striking sight when I first met them as they walked into the Murbad Hotel dressed in 1980s army camo jackets and olive-green trousers. Each of them proudly wore his old beret, one Guards, the other Parachute Regiment, but they had no other rank or insignia on their uniforms.

They told me their story and I was fascinated. Like everyone they came into contact with, I thought they were great blokes. Doug and Mick were old rogues in the best traditions of the British Army. They were brave as lions and had probably known Queen's Regulations back to front – and every way of getting round them. Doug had been living in Texas and working in the oil industry for years, but when the official war in Iraq ended he fancied his chances and thought he'd head for the gold rush. He'd flown to England first and met up with his old mate over a few pints in the British Legion club in a famous cathedral city.

'It was just plain good fortune, John,' Doug told me at that first meeting. 'Mick was at a loose end and he was up for it. You know yourself the value of a partner you can trust and I'd trust Mick with my life.'

'You may have to out here, old son,' I told him. Then I asked, 'Where are you going to go now? You can't stay here without any minders; you'll get chopped.'

'Oh no, we're not leaving yet,' said Mick. 'There's money to be made and we're going to make it.'

'For fuck's sake, Mick, get a grip. I'll make sure you two get safely down to Kuwait, then you can get a flight home. You'll be back on the piss in the Legion in a couple of days' time.'

'Not a chance, John,' said Doug. 'Fortune favours the brave and we're going to strike oil one bloody way or another.'

I didn't see them for a couple of weeks, then they pulled up in the hotel courtyard in a beaten-up old Range Rover they'd obtained somewhere.

'Where are you two staying?' I asked.

'We're camped down at the Mitsubishi oil jetty on the docks,' said Doug. 'It's lovely down there – sea breezes and a view across the docks. Couldn't be better.'

Mick nodded in agreement as I pointed at their old shed of a 4 x 4. 'You been driving around in that thing with your berets on?'

'Yup,' replied Doug.

'And you haven't had any trouble?'

'No, not a bit of it. We wouldn't mind getting hold of a couple of rifles just in case, though.'

I shook my head, unable to credit that anyone could be so bonkers, then I made the only contribution I could to ensuring their survival: I gunned them up.

'I should be able to fix you up with a couple of AKs,' I offered. 'I'll give you a quick rundown on their works. I think we'd better get that done sooner than later.'

'Thanks, John. Much appreciated. Why don't you come down to our place with them? Then we could try them out over the water,' said Doug.

'I'll do that. See you there later.'

I was gobsmacked when I got to the jetty. Their

camp was like an outpost of empire, an old khaki tent pitched on the jetty at Shat al Arab with a Union flag flapping lazily in the bright sunshine on a pole next to it. Hats off to them, they had it all set up military style, shaving mirror on the upright, water cans in the shade and the two old soldiers obviously quite happy with their lot. Again they'd huffed and puffed their way in, and the Mersk oil authorities had allowed them to set up on the jetty, which before the war had been a key oil exporting point. They'd even let them use a hut as a temporary office.

I knew that they'd endeared themselves to one and all with their theatrical parade-ground mannerisms, but the extent to which Doug and Mick were admired and welcomed precisely because of their old-style British army ways was unbelievable. I was to witness their hypnotic powers at first hand that afternoon. About 500 metres away a unit of Royal Engineers was set up and before I'd had a chance to get the AKs out and put them through their paces the second-in-command of the unit came striding down the jetty towards us. He'd only just arrived, was obviously going about like a dervish whipping the place into shape and wanted to investigate this satellite British camp which had been set up under the walls of his castle.

'What the hell's going on here?' he asked.

The boys snapped to attention, chins up and out, big moustaches bristling forward. 'SAH!'

Doug stamped one pace forward then did a bit more stamping and snapping to attention. Mick was doing a bit behind him too.

'Sorry to inconvenience you, sir! We were about to come and make ourselves known!'

They explained their situation. No money. No provisions. Guards. Parachute Regiment. Those were the key words and phrases I heard Doug rattle out and within ten minutes the engineer officer was completely won over.

'We can't have you out here exposed and without rations,' said the officer. He turned to the sergeant who'd been glued hard to his right shoulder and ordered, 'Get these men inside the base. They can have the empty Nissen hut on the east edge of the perimeter. While you're at it put them on the ration roll, and they can have a NAAFI card, and I expect they'll probably need some fuel as well.'

All the while he was talking Doug and Mick were feebly uttering, 'Don't want to put anyone out, sir.' They were trying to make out they didn't want to be any trouble but he wasn't listening. He was determined to make sure his new charges were well looked after and brushed their feigned objections aside: 'Nonsense, nonsense. See to it, Sergeant.'

'He seems to be a good bloke, that young officer,' said Mick, as the engineer strode back to his duties.

'Salt of the earth,' said Doug. 'Salt of the earth.'

I slipped them the guns and left them to get their feet well and truly under the table, which of course they did with well-rehearsed ease.

A couple of days later I bumped into them in the hotel. They looked cheerful and spent five minutes telling me what a wonderful outfit the Royal Engineers were. Then Doug said, 'Actually we've been looking for you, Johnny, old son.'

'Why's that?'

'A bit of an opportunity has presented itself. Thought you might want to cut yourself in.'

They explained that the bloke they'd been working for should have been in country but had been running them by remote control while sitting comfortably at home in Belgium. The company had rumbled him, probably with Doug and Mick's connivance, and put the skids under the Belgian. Doug and Mick were now blokes with a budget and they were off to Dubai to strike some deals.

'Back in a couple of weeks, Johnny, but you're a mate and we want you to do all our company security when we get back. What d'you say?' Doug proposed.

'Yeah, always up for some business. I've got some mates I'll tow in on it and we'll get some teams together.'

There we left it and they went off to Dubai, where, according to intelligence reports that came in later, they lived high off the hog and blew their budget. I forgot about Doug and Mick until I bumped into them again in the hotel. I'd been out of town for a while but as always the sight of them in their signature kit of berets and olive drab fatigues brought a smile to my face.

'You two pull off your big deal?' I asked.

'Nearly there, Johnny boy, nearly there,' said Doug, his face a picture of innocent enthusiasm.

'We've run into a bit of a hitch, though, John,' said Mick.

'Go on.'

'Yeah, usual thing, Johnny. Cash flow. You know how it is,' said Doug.

'Okay, so what happened?'

'To cut a long story short the company wouldn't go all the way down the road with us. We know we can clinch this deal but they've got reservations,' said Mick. 'They're not the ones on the ground, though, Johnny. We're here and we can see the potential. Exclusive jetty rights are a licence to print money and we can get them.'

'We'd like to go independent on this one, Johnny,' Doug said. 'But our contract says we have to pay back the money the company subbed us if we do. Frankly we're in the mire, Johnny.'

I could see what was coming but I asked anyway: 'How much do you need?'

'Hotel bills, travel expenses. What d'you think the lot comes to, Mick?'

'About twenty thousand, Doug, but that's only dollars,' said Mick with a look of perfect accounting on his face.

'And if I sub you I get fifty-fifty on the oil deal?'

'Of course you do. Who else, mate? Who else?'

Well, I was flush, I liked them and there was an outside chance that there might really be some work in it for me, so I subbed them the money. There was some toing and froing for a few days then they vanished.

I haven't heard of them since, but maybe one day I'll roll down to that beautiful cathedral city, take a look in the British Legion and see if they'll buy me a pint or two. It was my only foray into business while I was in Iraq, and afterwards I stuck to the day job.

7

THE CITY OF
THE DEAD

IT was August 2003 and Najaf was hotter than hell. I was in the city, a hundred miles south of Baghdad on the west bank of the Euphrates, with a British TV crew and their regular Iraqi driver. I'll call him Hamdany. I loved Hamdany; he was a really warm, funny guy.

He would often give me a bear hug and say, 'You are my son.' Sometimes his hand of friendship would be followed by the bonding words, 'When you are with me you are Iraqi.' He wasn't bullshitting. Like many Iraqis he was a man of great heart and humanity, and when we drove past some scene of carnage you could almost see him wince. He would shake his head, a deep sadness would fill his voice and he'd say, 'This is my new democracy? This is my new democracy?'

But that day it was too hot even for Hamdany, and the hugs and bonding sessions had been deferred to a cooler season, while his new democracy would have to wait to be mourned even though it had barely been born. The TV crew were doing a piece on the growing influence of the Shiite organisation known as the Supreme Council of the Islamic Revolution in Iraq, centred around the Imam Ali Mosque, which holds the Tomb of Ali. The top Shiite cleric Ayatollah Muhammad Baqir al Hakim was based there with his Badr militia; the town was also home to the Madhi Army. As I said, it was hotter than hell and I don't just mean the weather.

As we drove into the suburbs we passed a vast plantation of tombs and graves, acres of burials, and Hamdany said something in Arabic.

'What's that?' I asked.

'It's named the City of the Dead. Every Shia wishes to rest here within sight of the Tomb of Ali. They want to be near the Martyr when they die. It is said it is the biggest cemetery in the world.'

'The City of the Dead, eh? Nice one.'

Then I saw it, rising from the ground like an explosion of golden light, glittering and glinting as it transmitted a million reflections of the sun over the city. The Imam Ali Mosque. It was awesome and humbling and it was real gold too, thousands of solid tiles of it, but I remember thinking as I saw it that gold usually spells trouble.

We parked a good half-mile from the mosque and

set off on foot through the labyrinth of market streets with their overhanging balconies, the shops closed with their corrugated metal shutters all slammed down. Before we left we'd had some intelligence on the PMC grapevine that there'd been trouble earlier in the day outside the mosque. A bloke had been beaten and carved up outside the gates. Apparently he'd been taken for a Sunni spy – maybe he'd even been one. We'll never know; it's history and so was he.

But you could definitely smell trouble in the air. Everyone knew it was brewing even if they didn't know exactly why and the sense of fear was palpable. I'd taken the decision to go in unarmed. You have to weigh these things up and at that time the Badr and Mahdi forces weren't considered insurgents; they were seen as militia policing their own communities for the general good even if they were a bit on the volatile side. I could have stashed the AK and just taken my Tariq pistol, one of those heavy Iraqi hand-guns a bit like coshes with bullets in them, but that might have been seen as disrespectful. Why? Because we were being sort of hosted by the ayatollah and were being allowed near the mosque after a couple of days negotiating by the producer.

We kept walking. The cameraman had been well briefed and I'd made him wear really bright, gaudy clothes so he looked like the locals' idea of a film-maker. I even got him to wear a brightly coloured hat in line with the old maxim, 'If you can't fight wear a daft hat.' I carried his tripod so as to look like one of the crew. We neared the mosque and hundreds of eyes turned to watch us as we worked our way through the crowd. It was Saturday and the faces glaring at us were entirely male, which was intimidating in itself. Many of them were hostile but a lot of the faces seemed genuinely surprised to see a group of Westerners in that place at that time and their eyes registered grudging respect that we had the balls to be there at all.

We got to the walls of the mosque and represen-tatives of the ayatollah came out and handed us a written safe passage to be in the area of this most sacred place. It allowed us to enter and film the outer courtyard of the mosque in front of the magnificent gates to the inner sanctum and the Tomb of Ali. It was prayer time and the place was thronged with worshippers.

It was a fraught time. We were getting mixed signals from the crowd and a large group followed us around gawping and chattering as we filmed. There was some real hostility in the air but the word had got round that the ayatollah himself had allowed us in so those full of real hatred for Westerners had to curb it. Any questions and we just waved the magic piece of paper.

We finished filming in the courtyard and left but

the cameraman said he had to get some shots from above and wanted to go into a building overlooking the lines of men at prayer. 'We really need that to set the piece off,' he told the correspondent and they dispatched the linkman, who was Hamdany's son, to ask a shopkeeper on the ground floor if we could go up.

I'm thinking, For fuck's sake, let's get out of this place, but I know that cameramen don't see anything except through the lens. They're among the most disassociated and detached people on the planet. Nothing matters but getting the shot. It's different for me. I've got to worry about them and nothing matters but not getting them shot.

The magic paper opened doors again and he went up two storeys for his wonderful fucking shots of the Shia at prayer. Marvellous. I was really chuffed to be walking back to the car swept along by a sea of men who'd just been wound up by their mullahs and whose eyes were lit with the fire of religion and patriotism. Of course we were infidels and, in their eyes, representatives of the forces of oppression. Oh well, only half a mile to walk in their company.

You've seen those pictures of Muslim men beating themselves with chains in an act of mass self-flagellation? Well, that's this lot mourning the death of Husayn on the Day of Ashurah. They're hardcore and soon we were being jostled and cursed. Some of them who spoke English said, 'You shouldn't be here. Go home!' Others asked the question that answered wrongly would have invited a mob lynching. 'Are you American?'

'Not American. English. British,' we kept saying.

'Ah, we like British,' said one of the crowd. Not that much though.

I was getting really worried about the way things were going and I told Hamdany's lad to go ahead and warn his dad to turn the car round and get ready to roll. The last fifty yards were really tense and some anti-Coalition chanting had begun. I have only basic Arabic but I got the message because the names of Bush and Blair featured heavily. I don't like chanting; it numbs the mind and gets people into that state of oneness that allows a thinking mass to become a mob.

I hurried the crew on, cursing the cameraman and his precious prayer footage under my breath. They were all loaded up and I had one foot on the ground about to swing myself in and close the door when four sharp cracks sounded one after another, kicking up dust and chippings of stone from the road around us. Only then did I notice that the crowd following us hadn't come right up to the car. Had they known what was going down? I think so.

I slammed the door and ran the equation through my mind in a split second. Returning fire equals calling down the mob and getting the crew and me torn limb from limb!

I kept my AK dormant and yelled, 'Put your boot down, Hammy!'

'I can't! I can't!'

Shit! I looked at the road ahead and saw it was filled by two looming 4 x 4s heading straight towards us. Bearded men in sweeping black robes bristling with weapons hung off the sides. Fuck! The Mahdi Army! I gripped my AK and began sweating like a paedophile in Mothercare. Too much booze the night before.

'Re—' I hadn't finished ordering Hamdany to reverse the car into the alleyway behind us when the two trucks full of fighters swept past us. It wasn't us they were after; they were looking for the sniper who'd broken the word of the ayatollah. Whoever he was, he'd be split in two and barbecued before the day was over. Hamdany didn't need telling; he was off down the road like a rocket as soon as it cleared.

One of the crew asked, 'Were those shots meant for us?'

'Naah,' I lied. 'Just some stray rounds fired off by a hothead.'

Hamdany and I looked at each other out of the corner of our eyes. We knew. The crowd had known too. Like an agitated hive they'd sensed something was brewing and two days later a massive car bomb exploded outside the gates to the Tomb of Ali. It was parked right below the balcony where our cameraman had been filming and it dispatched the ayatollah and 142 worshippers to the City of the Dead. It was an outrage that pushed the Shias onto the offensive.

But we were safe and Hamdany drove off muttering his usual doleful complaint: 'Ah, so this is my new democracy?'

Three weeks later and I was taking care of a different crew, Irish television this time and in the ancient city of Nasiriyah. We were in the city centre and the crew were filming an interview with an Iraqi making a living taking passport and ID card photos with a home-made pinhole camera made from plywood.

It was going to be a positive, hopeful piece highlighting the resourcefulness of the Iraqi people just for a change. Then all hell broke loose. A huge blast about 150 metres down the street opposite the police station demonstrated the sinister side of the ingenuity and inventiveness of the Iraqi people. An IED had detonated in the crowded shopping street.

It's hard to know which came first, the all-consuming sound of the blast or the piece of corrugated steel sent hurtling by the shock wave into the cat's cradle of power and telephone lines hanging over the street. Showers of sparks fell around us followed by a confetti of shredded rubbish and a rolling cloud of dust. I managed to keep on my feet but the cameraman was bowled over onto the paving and damaged his kit. The rest of the crew were fine. They'd been standing in the shelter of a building just around the corner from the pulsating wave generated by the bomb.

Focus, you've got to focus in those terrible, unreal, dreamtime minutes that come after a bomb blast. On the other side of the street I saw a boy lying on the ground, blood pumping out of a wound in his thigh. Right. I was with him in a second, ripping the cover off a shell dressing, US isssue – the British ones are rubbish with the absorption qualities of a 1950s sanitary towel. The kid looked up at me, his big brown eyes vacant as if some invisible tentacle of the blast had scooped the inside of his brain out. There was nothing to read in those eyes. No pleading, no shock. Nothing. Why subject a boy like this to the hellish lottery of a bomb blast? For a moment I felt a savage anger but I knew the injury wouldn't kill him now and I had the crew to sort out.

Scores of people rushing away from the site of the bomb were ballooning out into the small square we were in and they were in a terrible fury. I think the fact that I'd been seen treating that kid made a difference. They were looking for scapegoats and someone helping wasn't going to attract their anger. Not for a few minutes anyway. A hail of gunfire followed as a battle broke out between insurgents and Coalition troops based in the police barracks but there was no point us being there without a working camera. The box camera too had been knocked over in the stampede.

We were isolated from friendly troops. I took a look at the crowd and then looked at the crew with the broken camera. It was my call. 'Come on, we're off,' I ordered and ushered them towards the car about forty metres away.

I knew what had happened. It was common knowledge that the locals got on really well with the Coalition guys stationed in their town, and they especially liked the captain in charge of the detachment, which I think was Italian. Apparently the captain was a charismatic man with an instinctive political touch, a man they could do business with. Well, that was no good, was it? The insurgents weren't going to let such a cosy relationship take root so they moved in to obliterate it with a bomb.

I stood on the corner looking down bomb alley. Across the way the street photographer was trying to salvage what remained of his equipment. Down the street I saw the body of a man sprawled in the gutter. He was wearing a distinctive red and green striped shirt. I'd seen him only a few minutes earlier as he'd left the photographer clutching a new ID picture in his hand. He'd looked pleased with the results but he wouldn't be needing his photograph now. I wanted a drink.

I'd moved on. It was August 2003 and I was back with a British crew, down south again in Basra, where the summer heat was boiling peoples' brains. A lot of Basrans were so head-cooked that mobs of them were on the rampage, venting their rage over the shortage of petrol. They needed fuel for generators to power the air con units they needed to unboil their heads, so, with the logic of brains transformed into haggis by heat, they attacked the only three petrol stations in town that were open, thereby increasing the scarcity of the very fuel they wanted to get their hands on. To make things worse, tankers were being hijacked and so suddenly there wasn't any fuel at all, causing those clans or tribes not in on the tanker heists to go crazy. There were even gangs trying to hunt down the garage owners and their families to extort fuel out of them.

They'd created their very own catch-22 situation and they'd done it very violently.

In the absence of any effective policing it was the poor bloody British infantry who had to sort it all out and their officers insisted they didn't fire on the mob but instead issued them with riot gear. There they were, I think it was the Princess of Wales' Own, wearing heavy gear, swinging batons and charging the crowds with plastic shields in a ninety-degree breeze blowing off the gigantic kiln of the Arabian desert. It must have been like wrestling in a sauna. It's a testament to their training that they didn't flinch even when soldiers were collapsing from heat exhaustion and being dragged out of the line to be rehydrated.

At one incident we saw a thin line of infantry bashing people's heads to get them to back off from the petrol station when suddenly a youth – he was no more than seventeen – appeared from nowhere clutching an AK that he looked far too comfortable with. A corporal on the flank of the infantry line pinged him immediately, broke ranks, ran over to him and grabbed the AK, twisting it out of the kid's grip. Then he butt-swiped him with it, dragged him twenty metres by the neck to a Land Rover, hurled the gun into the back and plasti-cuffed the would-be gunman before you could blink.

It was a superb example of the brilliant work the British army puts in; that corporal was a hero who certainly averted a catastrophe on the streets of Basra. We saw the same sort of raw courage and complete discipline in Basra in September 2005 when a Warrior armoured personnel carrier was set alight during the rescue of two SAS men from the so-called police. Our lads stand their ground and do not overreact.

In both of those situations in Basra their US counter-parts would have brought extreme force to bear on the mob and shot the shit out of them.

My crew were busy filming but I noticed that we were getting cut off by the mob so I said to the correspondent, 'I think we should go; we're getting isolated here. Have you got enough?'

He looked around, had a chat to the cameraman and said, 'Yeah, we've got enough.'

That's the way it usually went – a balance between safety and their need to get good footage. It was my job to draw their attention to the security implications of any situation they were in. I wasn't making judgements about what I would do if I were only responsible for my own skin; I had to think of the group and make sure they all survived.

As we were driving back to the hotel a great bang on the roof heralded a stoning, and soon an erratic thumping and clattering filled the cab of the vehicle as we were pelted with rocks and bottles. On the road ahead of us a UN 4 x 4 was being systematic-ally smashed to pieces and we were lucky to get out of it and find a new route to the hotel without me having to fire a shot. Then the streets fell quiet as the thermometer rose to a point where rioting became a physical impossibility.

We were staying in the Hotel Murbad in town. It's a family-owned business and all the boss is interested in is offering a safe haven to travellers, whoever they are, in exchange for their money. He had a simple view of the insurgency – he thought it was bad for business – and was always ready with a robust response to any incursion into the peace and prosperity of his hotel compound.

It stayed quiet and the crew went to their rooms and got their heads down for an afternoon kip, but I just couldn't sleep. I may have been on the lash for a couple of months but my instincts hadn't been completely shot away by booze and fatigue. I just knew something was going to happen. Usually I can sleep through gun battles when the shit's going down a couple of streets away, then when my position is threatened I'm up and standing as though my brain is sounding its own bugle call. That night, however, even though it was really quiet, I lay awake on my bed restless. I got up. I thought I'll just have a little look around.

Five minutes later I was on the roof of the hotel among the usual scrap heap of air con units and ducts. On the far side of the roof there was a movement. I froze for a moment then I saw him. It was Bill, an old mate from the Regiment, a real top-slice operator with a proven record, and he was doing exactly the same thing as me. I thought his call sign – there were four of them – was out on the ground with another media crew but Bill had come back a day early for some admin reason or other. I knew Bill well; I'd worked with him in Northern Ireland and a couple of other strange places too.

'You get a bad feeling too?' I asked.

'Yeah, John, I did.'

'It's too quiet, isn't it?'

'Yes, mate, it's too fucking quiet out there by half.'

'Have you found anything?'

'Yeah, I have. Take a look over here. There's a fire escape bridge between this place and next door. It's about ten foot long, made of steel.'

'Nice one. If they come at our place I can get my people out across it,' I said.

'There's a couple of call signs with clients over there. They might want to come the other way if their place is hit,' said Bill.

'Let's take a stroll across and find 'em.'

There were two big gunned-up teams in the other hotel with a couple of ex-Blades and a load of Paras, and we quickly found them. A ten-minute chat had the deal worked out. We'd butt out to their position if anything hit the Murbad and vice versa. Bill and I were happy. We'd have eight seasoned ex-army lads and two bang-on Blades in our gang if the night erupted.

I got back in time for the routine six o'clock RV with the crew in the editing room, when they'd usually have a debrief on the day's work, discuss plans for the next day and take on any orders from London. Quite often the cameraman would then go up to the roof and get some sunset footage looking out over the city. I'd be asked if I had any contribution before the meeting broke up.

'John?' Everyone looked across at me as the producer asked for my call on the day.

'Okay. It's like this. I don't want to worry any of you but it's too quiet and it's been too quiet since this afternoon. It's time to talk about our escape route if the hotel is attacked. I've had a recce and talked to some security call signs staying here and at the hotel directly behind this building.

'If anything or anyone hostile comes through the front gate of the hotel do not go to the vehicles. I want you to go upstairs to the roof and I'll be with you. That guy Bill who's been around will be with us. Is that clear? Get up to the hotel roof, keep your heads down and wait for instructions.'

They all nodded. They'd had lots of briefings and every one of them is serious in a place like Iraq, but I knew I'd got across my conviction that something nasty was imminent.

We went down to the dining room for our evening meal but we didn't even finish the soup before it started. I jumped up and turned the corner into the hotel lobby and there was an armed mob pouring through the gates. I watched the old guy who seemed to be the gateman scuttle across the courtyard to the building as fast as he could. Not just any night-watchman, he was swinging his AK behind him every ten steps to fire a burst at the gunmen pouring into the courtyard.

All hell broke loose as the waiters abandoned the soup bowls, AKs appeared in their hands like rabbits conjured out of magicians' hats and they began laying down fire on the gatecrashers. At first a lot of the incoming was pistol fire and the UN cars in the court-yard were riddled with small holes in seconds. Metal shutters appeared from nowhere and were placed over the front windows under fire. Can you believe men risking their lives to protect a fucking window?

Cooks and bottle washers in their whites charged out of the kitchen. Ladles and whisks had been aban-doned for AKs but wicked kitchen knives were held in reserve in the bands of their aprons. They deployed at various key points and started banging out an unvaried menu of lead. I know top chefs call their cooking team the kitchen brigade but Gordon Ramsay has never had anything like that lot. And they were all harder nuts than Gordon too.

Our cameraman was gagging to get to work. 'I've got to get some shots of this, John.'

'Where's your gear?'

'In the room.'

'Oh for fuck's sake, get it on the way to the roof.'

I had the crew waiting at the restaurant door. To the right was the lobby and the firing line. Left were the stairs. Rounds were tearing into the facade of the building and the odd one or two whined into reception like lead wasps trying to register. I was waiting for the kitchen brigade to get their eyes in and lay down enough fire on the perimeter wall to suppress the incoming rounds.

I judged it was time. 'Okay, let's go! Up the fucking stairs! Sharpish! Don't stop till you see the stars.'

I hustled the crew along and the cameraman diverted to grab his gear before joining us on the roof. The air up there was like warm milk and thick with cordite. Bill, who had no one to look after, was already there of course, laid up in the far corner behind a parapet picking his targets as he used his AK to effect. A couple of waiters still wearing their aprons were alongside Bill, firing wildly down at the walls and corners below that hid the unwanted guests. Bill grinned at me like it was a big game then turned back to his work. I wished I could do the same but I had a crew to nanny.

'We'll try for some shots now, John,' said the correspondent.

'It's not safe. Just keep your fucking heads down!'

'It won't take a minute.'

I looked at him then at the cameraman. They wanted their shots. 'For fuck's sake! All right. Keep low.'

I guided the cameraman away from Bill and the two waiters – who would be attracting return fire – and behind the hotel sign, which was about three feet higher than the parapet around the rooftop, then into a position where he could just get his camera and eye over the parapet to take his shots. In the dark unlit streets around the hotel I could see shadows flitting from cover to cover like huge low-flying bats, flashes of gunfire giving their positions away. I could also see that Bill's pinpoint aim was making it very dangerous for them. I spotted someone being dragged away wounded and experience told me that the attackers were losing the initiative and being forced back from the hotel perimeter.

I never saw the footage the cameraman took so I don't know how it looked although I imagine it was just a load of flashes, bangs and cracks. When he'd finished I steered him back to the others then pushed them to the far side of the roof away from where Bill and the waiters were at work. 'Just keep your heads down. Don't be heroes.' I didn't want them catching ricochets and I reckoned they'd be unlucky to be hit by any where they were, as long as they kept down.

One of the waiters was a big burly bastard with a moustache. He looked a hard case, a chubby Saddam type with a cruel eye, and he was well into it. I could see his blood was up. His face was glowing and his eyes, lit up now and then by gun flashes, were wild. He was firing away quite happily when suddenly he had a stoppage in his rifle. You should have seen him. He went into a complete strop. He bashed the AK on the floor, whacking it here and there, desperately trying to get it to fire again. Then he moved away from the edge, sat on his arse on the flat roof and took it out on his weapon even more, cursing as he flailed it around.

Bill looked at me and I could see he was laughing like a drain at the absurdity of it all. He told me later that he thought it hilarious that the waiter couldn't serve up a dish of hard metal jackets. 'Go on, Johnny, give the fucker a hand,' he shouted across to me.

'All right, all right.' I ran low and fast across the roof to the waiter and took the gun off him before he crippled it. I unloaded all the rounds then looked in the breech and saw he had a hard extraction – the casing of a cartridge had split inside the mechanism and wouldn't eject, blocking the works completely. The thing was filthy and I remember hoping that he kept the cutlery cleaner than his gun. Rounds thumped into the masonry just above my head as I leaned back against the parapet, got my foot on the cocking handle and jumped on it hard. The split case tinkled like a bell as it fell out onto the roof and the waiter reached for his gun. I pushed his hand away and sprinted across to the air con unit, which had one of those old-fashioned oil cans with a long spout sitting on top of it. I grabbed the can and poured oil into the workings of the AK then ran back across the roof to hand it to the waiter.

He was beaming with delight to have his weapon unseized and serviced mid-battle and was soon back at it with gusto, firing like fuck into the darkness.

Our producer had called the army quick reaction force at the start of the shoot-out but they didn't arrive until forty minutes later, when they did a drive-past and reported there was nothing to be seen. It was all over and the gunmen had melted back into the night.

That was the first and last time I've acted as gun bearer for a waiter during a battle on a hotel roof.

'What's going on in reception, John?'

'No idea. I'll have a look.'

I was in the bar of the Baghdad Sheraton and the usual drone from the huddles of media types, businessmen and hard-nosed security guys had been temporarily drowned by bedlam coming from the lobby. As I turned the corner from the bar into reception I was confronted by a jabbering, animated party of forty or so Japanese of all ages and sizes. Chubby little women mingled with inscrutable teenagers, all kitted out in designer gear. It took me a second to work it out. Unbelievably, they were tourists, and for a moment I could have fooled myself that I was in the entrance hall to the British Museum. Something was wrong though. For one thing there wasn't a single camera in sight and for another they were milling excitedly around a growing pile of labelled suitcases and bags being brought in by the porters. The luggage looked as though it had been ripped open and everything tipped out.

Two well-dressed but dishevelled-looking young European men with the Japanese party broke away from the chattering group and headed into the bar, obviously in search of a cold beer. They seemed dismayed and looked around anxiously. That's because there was no bar. Instead you got your drink from two or three booze vendors who'd set up their stalls at the hotel entrance. They did a roaring trade. When you'd bought your booze, maybe a bottle of whisky or a slab of beer cans, you just went into this big room full of tables and chairs with a running buffet laid out on trestles at the far end – the same buffet every night. You'd have your meal then settle down for a drink.

I collared them.

'Fancy a drink, you two?' I asked.

When they had their beers we made our introductions and they turned out to be two Danish students from a town somewhere near Copenhagen. They were tourists too. They'd been travelling around the ancient sites of Babylon in a car they'd hired in Jordan and had met up with the Japanese group at the Hanging Gardens of Babylon. Hard to believe, isn't it? Sightseeing in the middle of an insurgency.

They'd decided it would be a good idea to tag on behind the group's convoy, figuring they'd be less likely to get lost following someone who knew the roads. At one stage they'd lagged behind a bit and when they caught up again the convoy had pulled over and the Japanese were being held at gunpoint on the roadside by a group of what I used to describe as BSIs – bandits stroke insurgents. The BSIs were relieving them of enough camera gear and top-of-the-range mobile phones to open a branch of Dixons in Baghdad. The Danes wisely kept on driving. However, the Japanese made such a racket that the BSIs, struggling badly with the language barrier, just loaded them all back on their vehicles and sent them on their way. They were so desperate to get rid of the babbling tourists they even spared their drivers; normally they would have slotted them and dumped them in a ditch. On the other hand, two English-speaking Danes would have been a much better proposition as hostages so it was just as well they hadn't stopped and eventually they'd all got back to the hotel.

The Danes, whose names escape me, joined me and Tony for a couple of drinks and we got chatting.

When they learnt what I did for a living and that I was taking a cameraman and sound technician back to Amman in the morning for a crew change, they pleaded to be allowed to join us. They were nice young blokes and obviously scared shitless. It had dawned on them that coming to Iraq had been a big mistake. Why not take them? I thought.

'Okay, we leave at six on the dot. If you stop for any reason you're on your own, and I don't run a breakdown service.'

'No, no. We won't be stopping for anything.'

I believed them. That night they looked like they wanted to hang out with us and get really pissed but they went to bed early. I don't think they wanted to miss the convoy.

Tony was a utilities engineer, water or electricity, I'm not sure which, and he'd been around for a while. He knew the correspondent I was working for but I'd only met him that night. Tony was a really nice bloke – quiet and self-assured but obviously with plenty of bottle. He'd done the job, some sort of assessment for a tender, and was relieved to be going home. In the morning he'd be picked up by a security team that his company had hired; meanwhile there was nothing else to do but drink and enjoy each other's company in the more or less relaxing surroundings of the Sheraton bar.

The Baghdad Sheraton was expensive but grubby.

Not surprising really considering the hotel's situation, and to be fair the staff tried hard and were always charming. The carpets were shabby, the furniture worn and threadbare and the whole place needed a lick of paint but I could live with all of that. It was the chained and padlocked emergency exits that worried me. I suppose the management thought they'd keep out any insurgents but common sense should have told them terrorists would bomb the place rather than try to storm it. That's just what happened in October 2005 when a huge bomb was detonated nearby, killing several Iraqis.

Anyway the chained doors were a bit of a headache because I had a TV crew to look after. The solution was a big pair of bolt cutters placed close to the door of the room we used as an office and editing suite. I insisted we practised escape drills in case of attack often so when the signal was given we'd all head for the designated emergency exit with me in the lead. Normally in such a situation I'd have my Kalashnikov stuck in front of me but during the drills I had to sling it and make for the exit with my big, bugger-off bolt cutters as an alternative. We'd all run down the stairs; I'd simulate a bit of chain destruction then I'd unsling my AK ready for action when we burst through the emergency exit into the open.

We never did any bursting through the doors, which was a real pain in the arse because I had to check the alleyway outside every day to make sure we had a clear run in case of a real emergency. It was just another madness in the catalogue of insanity I had to deal with. Still, the Sheraton had been home on and off for months and it was better than kipping in a pioneer camp. That night in October 2003 we'd done a day's filming around Baghdad and the crew had finished their feed. That doesn't mean they'd had their supper; it's TV jargon for sending an edited piece back to the studio.

I'd developed a routine for when my day's work ended: I usually took a shower and got into the bar by six o clock, ate, then went on the lash with the crew. I'd start on gin and tonics and move on to Jack Daniel's by about eleven. I'd keep drinking as long as there was someone to drink with. I'd been on the piss like that for about seven or eight weeks, but every morning I'd be up again and back on the road, bleary but unbowed.

Tony poured me another whisky and we settled in for a long night, then around midnight two blokes arrived in the bar obviously looking for someone. It turned out to be me. They had a quick word with the waiter, who nodded in my direction and they came up and introduced themselves. Even I was surprised at who they were. The tourists in Iraq were mad enough but these two were right out on the edge of sanity. They were Israeli Jews, who'd been wheeling and dealing trying to pin down some oil contracts. Being a Jew was dodgy enough in Iraq but they were carrying their Israeli passports as well. They may as well have brought their own orange boiler suits with them. And they looked Jewish too. I'm not racist and I don't mean to be offensive but they just looked Jewish.

'Nice to meet you, guys,' I said, trying to avoid giving them a 'dead men walking' look.

'You too,' said the bigger of the two with a beam. 'We've been told you're a bodyguard. They say you're the best.'

'That's absolutely right,' I said. 'How can I help you?'

No time for false modesty and there's nothing like a compliment when you're half cut but I can see now that he was playing me with a line straight from a cowboy movie.

'Well, we've been here for two weeks and we've done about all we can business-wise so we've decided to leave in the morning. The security situation is getting worse.'

'Great. Good luck with the journey.'

'Yeah, thanks, but we think we should get some security for the trip out.'

'You mean you've been driving around for two weeks without any?'

'Sure. Protection is very expensive. We thought we'd be fine if we just kept a low profile.'

'Well, you've been lucky. It seems to have worked for you. So far.'

'So far yes, but we thought we should get some protection for the journey out; they say the road's very dangerous.' I nodded agreement. 'How much will it cost to hire you for the day.'

'Well, how's six hundred pounds a day sound to you?'

'Six hundred pounds, you say, not dollars? It's too much.'

'Really. So tell me, friend, how much is your insurance policy worth?'

'What do you mean? You're joking.' He smiled.

'No joke. I'm deadly serious. I bet your wife will collect a packet if you're killed out here.'

'Maybe she will.'

'So maybe it's worth paying six hundred pounds to make sure some other bloke doesn't share it with her.'

He wasn't smiling now and I was already regretting my words. There'd been no need for that. I relented, ashamed of my dig at his marriage. 'Listen, guys, I'm leaving at six in the morning. Be there on the dot and you can follow us. If you stop on the way, tough. We don't stop until we get to the border.'

'We don't have to pay?'

'No, you don't have to fucking pay but remember, if you stop you're on your own.'

'We won't stop.'

I believed him. They drank some of my beers then headed for bed.

That left me, Tony and a few other diehards, including my correspondent and his two crew, who were shipping out with me in the morning. The lights dimmed. Not for the cabaret but because the power had failed again. From somewhere in the basement came the drone of the generator as it kicked in. Pissed, we watched a couple of nocturnal flies as they weaved in and out of the blades of a fan which barely turned.

Tony broke the silence. 'John, what are the chances of me coming back to Amman with you guys in the morning?'

'Why'd you want to do that, mate? You've got a complete team to nurse you back down the Highway.'

'I know, I know, but I don't really get on with those guys. I suppose they know what they're doing but I just haven't gelled with them over the past three weeks.'

'I know them; they're a good team, mate, believe me.'

'I'm sure you're right but I'd feel happier with you. I just have more confidence in your ability.'

I knew he wasn't feeding me a line like the Israeli and I appreciated that he was willing to put his life in my hands, but I tried to put him off.

'Remember what I said to that Israeli guy?'

'About what?'

'About the insurance.'

He raised an eyebrow and I quickly explained: 'Nothing to do with your wife, old son. No, what I mean is if you travel with me and it all goes pear-shaped you probably won't have any insurance because you should be with the team assigned to you.'

'Fuck it. I don't care. Will you take me? I'll pay you, of course.'

'Ask the boss over there. If he okays it, I'll be fine with it. Forget the money.'

A couple of minutes later the correspondent gave me the thumbs up across the room and Tony rejoined me. We had another drink. So there I was. Big-time hero. Everybody's safety net. I was pissed and in about four hours I was intending to ride the most dangerous road in the world. Like some wagon train master I was taking the fate of a completely random group of people into my hands.

I'd ridden lone shotgun on scores of protection runs and was making huge amounts of money because there were no middlemen taking a cut. I was getting the premium rate and it was virtually all profit. But that profit came at a price: I was paying it in stress and paying in spades. I'd started drinking with the media crews. I suppose I was trying to drown the stress but it had got completely out of hand until

I found myself in a cycle of fatigue, stress and drinking.

There'd been some close shaves since I'd returned to Iraq after that first six weeks with Bungo immediately after the war ended, and it had got to the point where I had become the most dangerous man to be with on the most dangerous road in the world because I should have been sober and together. I should have been doing the job SAS-style not media-style and I knew in my bones that it had to stop before it all went terribly wrong. Sure, it was during this period that I'd sorted out the guys in the black BMW and I knew I hadn't lost my skills, but I also knew that I was blurring my hard edge with the life I was living. The drinking was part of it but it was the stress of riding shotgun alone with media crews and the responsibility of keeping them alive that was really wearing me down, and the worst thing was that I was beginning to dwell on the past. I was thinking a lot about the mates I'd lost in battle.

And yet there I was in the bar of the Sheraton pissed, agreeing to bodyguard people on that terrifying roller coaster ride back to Jordan. I was like some John Wayne figure walking tall into the saloon. Perhaps I was fooling myself that I really was the Duke; I was certainly acting like a cowboy. In the morning it would be wagons roll but I'd be lucky if heads didn't roll. I was going to be taking the wackiest convoy you could dream of down the road past Fallujah and Ramadi: a correspondent plus two-man camera crew, a brace of Danish archaeology students, a couple of Israeli Del Boys and a British engineer who on the strength of a night on the piss preferred to be with an ex-SAS man rather than four perfectly capable ex-soldiers. Five of them weren't paying me a bean and I thought they were the ones who were mad. I knew it had to stop but I thought, Fuck it. One last time and let's hope it isn't the last time.

How the fuck had I managed to end up in a state like that?

8

AL AMARAH

I suppose I could turn to the old cliché and say I blame the press. After all it was the media I had been working with and it was their drinking habits that I'd fallen into step with. I have always enjoyed a drink but those people go for total immersion on a regular basis. Hand on heart though I don't blame my dealings with the media for my fall off the more or less straight and narrow.

There are a couple of things I should get straight. First my boozing all took place over a relatively short period of time, a three-month period at the most, out of the eighteen I worked in Iraq in total. Also a lot of people would think the amount I was putting away was nothing compared to what a really hard drinker will consume, and I never drank at all during the hours of daylight. But set against all that, and what made it a potentially acute problem, was the fact that I was operating with a hangover nearly every day in the most lethal and hostile military environment on the planet. That was extremely foolhardy and dangerous. I'm not proud of it.

While all this was going on I began to dwell on the past, particularly on the friends I'd lost in combat operations. Steve Prior was on my mind and I kept hearing the words he had spoken to that frightened eighteen-year-old paratrooper in his section as we sailed to the Falklands: 'Don't worry. If it comes to it I'll die so you can live.' I remembered how he had died saving life instead of taking it, as time and time again he had dragged wounded soldiers into cover during A Company's bloody struggle on Darwin Hill. I replayed those moments at Goose Green over and over in my mind. There were friends who'd died in SAS operations too and they kept coming back to haunt me. They call it survival guilt and that's what it is. I felt as guilty as fuck.

There was another fallen comrade whose face kept coming to mind in those days, one of the most ballsy guys I've ever known, an old SAS mate called Nish Bruce. He was one of the finest and most courageous free-fall parachutists in the world and pivotal in the development of the high altitude, low opening tactic used to insert special forces. Nish had parachuted into the South Atlantic with an SAS patrol and had swum ashore as one of the first British troops back on the Falkland Islands a couple of weeks ahead of the fleet carrying the main task force to retake the islands in 1982. Nish was tall and hawkish-looking with a vicious sense of humour. He was very popular and I'm proud to say we were best mates.

But years of stress had left him scarred by depression. Nish himself believed his psychological problems stemmed from the effects of the decompression chamber training he did for his planned attempt on the world's highest free-fall jump in 1993. I'm not sure about that but I know that like many other Regiment guys he was stretched to the limits by non-stop operational cycles.

I visited Nish many times when he was a patient at the Stonebow psychiatric unit in Hereford. I'd sit for hours with him just talking shit then I'd return the next day and talk the same shit again because the lithium drugs gave him a memory like a gold-fish.

In 1998 Nish wrote a painfully honest book about his military career and his descent into depression and, with no little irony, called it *Freefall*. Then in January 2002, while flying over Oxfordshire with his girlfriend Gail, who was the pilot, his mental problems got the better of Nish. He simply opened the door of the light aircraft and made his last free fall, this time without a parachute. True to Nish's huge personality he'd even ensured his death was as spectacular as it was tragic and it inevitably attracted a huge amount of publicity.

The warmth of his friendship stays with me to this day but then, in what were relatively tough days for me in Iraq, it was his illness that I focused on. I began to wonder if I was beginning to experience the same demons that had tormented Nish. These were not comfortable thoughts. Strangely though it's been while I've been writing this book that I've thought most deeply about those events — what propelled me on a dark carousel of Jack Daniel's and stress — and I've come to realise when it began and what triggered my months of recklessness. It was events at a dust-choked hole called Al Majarr al Kabir.

It was a place of treachery and death where six lightly armed British military policemen were summarily butchered by a mob after the Iraqi police officers they were supposed to be working with abandoned them to their fate. God knows how terrifying their last minutes were. My heart truly goes out to their families. You see, for three days I thought my son Kurt, who was serving in the Parachute Regiment, had died in that shithole thirty kilometres south of Al Amarah. At the time I was just getting started as a freelance operator in Iraq but I was still hanging out with Bungo.

The Paras had been assigned to the Al Amarah area, which is about 130 kilometres south-east of

Baghdad. It's a strategic place, quite close to the Iranian border and on the highest navigable reach of the River Tigris for small commercial boats. The area is on the northern edge of the Shia region but just close enough to Baghdad to have had a large Ba'ath Party spy network. It was also the place where Ali Hassan al Majid, the infamous henchman of Saddam known as Chemical Ali, was raised; he was the man who gassed the Kurds. Being so close to Iran it was alive with Iranian agents. In other words the place was full of stroppy insurgents who hated everything and everyone including their own shadows.

I should tell you a bit about Kurt. He's a cheeky hard bastard who was born with 'army' stamped on his forehead. From his earliest days he was a tearaway. I can tell you I was really proud when he joined the Parachute Regiment after passing the tough P Company selection process. When I saw him wearing his red beret I had a touch of moisture in my eyes but of course with the rivalry of an old stag I told him it was harder in my day.

When he got to Iraq Kurt and his unit were not crows. Far from it; they were the heroes of an entire country – and I'm not talking about the UK, where too many people don't realise just how much they owe our armed forces. No, they were and are the true heroes of the people of Sierra Leone, whom they rescued from a horrifying civil war and years of hand-chopping anarchy at the whim of gangs like the infamous West Side Boys. Things came to a head when the Boys seized eleven British soldiers from the Royal Irish Regiment and held them hostage with some locals in the hamlet of Magbeni against demands for guns, ammo and drugs and the release of their leader, a psycho called General Papa, from jail.

A negotiator did a bit of seriously dangerous toing and froing into their camp in the hamlet and came out with accounts of cannibalism and serious communal instability brought about by fierce drug taking and drinking. Five of the hostages were released but the man doing the talking, a sadistic clown who went by the nom de guerre of Colonel Cambodia, was getting more and more crazy. SAS guys had been moving through the swamps of the creek where the hamlet was located and they'd been observing the goings on in the village and seen mock executions of the Irish lads. So it was decided to go in and get the hostages out.

At first light on 10 September 2000 a hundred or so guys from 1 Para went in hard under the cover of Chinook helicopters using the downdraught from their rotors to knock the flimsy roofs off the huts and cause maximum confusion among the enemy. The SAS were there too of course and the only casualty on our side in Operation Barras, as it was called, was a tremendous character from the Regiment called Brad Tinnion, who tragically failed to beat the clock. Showing incredible courage, he died from gunshot wounds received during the difficult operation of loading the hostages onto a helicopter to get them out.

About fifty or so West Siders were wasted including Colonel Cambodia. The rest were taken prisoner, including their leader Foday Kallay, as the whole of the country first breathed a sigh of relief then burst into spontaneous celebration at their final release from the daily and indiscriminate terror that had stalked the land. The Paras still have the status of demigods among the people of Sierra Leone.

I heard that Kurt had acquitted himself well in that textbook special forces attack and it goes without saying then that he could already handle himself when he arrived in Al Amarah, the armpit of Iraq.

Anyway, it was Sunday evening about 2100 when I heard that six Paras had been killed in an attack near the city and that several others had been wounded. I can't remember for sure how I heard but I think it was a phone call from another PMC. I don't think I've ever experienced anything like the feelings I had over those next two or three days as a mixture of anxiety and anger consumed me. I made frantic calls to anyone I thought could shed more light on the situation but it was no good. There was a news blackout. It was then that I began to realise how my family and loved ones must have been feeling over the years as I went off to trouble spots with the Regiment and since my SAS days wandering all over the globe as a PMC. I'd just cheerfully said my goodbyes and not really and truly considered the worry they would be going through. Never once had I seriously considered what it's like to be sat at home fretting about the safety of a loved one and being totally unable to communicate with them or even get a briefing on where and how they are from their superiors.

So it came back to me in spades when I was unable to find out whether my lad was hurt or not. Now it was me fretting and feeling impotent over the fate of my son. Kurt was incommunicado and it was me who was left behind to worry. I learnt then that the words 'No man is an island' are among the truest ever written. No SAS man is an island either. I knew something else too. I knew that those first figures of dead and injured that we'd heard meant that there was a high probability that Kurt was a casualty. I had to find out.

We were in Baghdad and Bungo suggested that we should wing over to the British embassy compound within the Green Zone. He'd remembered he had a mate there, an officer who'd done some time in Northern Ireland with a surveillance unit. He was now in command of the Para detachment guarding the embassy and there was a chance he'd know something.

We slipped into his command hootch and Bungo made the introductions. 'John's got a bit of a problem. His lad's down the road in Al Amarah with 1 Para and John's obviously worried about him since the shit hit the fan. He's called Kurt Geddes.'

The officer was sympathetic. 'I honestly don't know any names but I can tell you that there are no dead Paras. The six dead soldiers are all redcaps. They were bottled up in the local police station and killed. The Paras were in a firefight about the same time, maybe a couple of hours later, with insurgents about five klicks away, and they had seven wounded, but they slotted about eighty of the other side. That's why there's been some confusion about just who got whacked because the MPs were being done over at around the same time. None of that came from me.'

An almost overwhelming sense of relief overtook me as I learnt that at least Kurt was alive – even if there was still a possibility he'd been wounded in the firefight. I looked at the officer and thanked him with a couple of words that could never have conveyed just how grateful I was for his intelligence on the incident.

Bungo summed it up, the relief evident in his voice: 'Thank fuck for that, John. Someone would have died tonight if that kid had been killed.' I just looked at him.

Bungo was right. If Kurt had been killed I would have tooled up and gone looking for serious trouble. In the end there was no need to do it. My lad was alive and my rage had gone.

It was another two days before I learnt that Kurt hadn't been wounded either and about a week before I saw him. He was in a canteen in Saddam's palace, where he and his mates were stagging on at the embassy compound. I saw him across the room shovelling food into his ugly mug and I just strode over and gave him a big hug in front of all his mates. If he was embarrassed at this demonstration of his father's relief in front of his mates he didn't show it. None of them seemed to want to take the piss either, which would have been the normal thing among Paras. Anyway, I didn't give a fuck; I was just pleased to see my lad alive.

Dave didn't talk about the fighting and I didn't press him about it. I know how he felt. It wasn't the time to glory in combat; we both were just thankful he'd come out of the other end in one piece.

Later through official sources I was to find out about the Paras' action at Al Majarr on 24 July 2003. Two call-signs of 1 Para were ambushed by a strong contingent of insurgents and called in the QRF, who arrived in a Chinook. Just as it was putting down the helo came under fire too and seven guys were wounded including an RAF medic shot in the foot, and they were taken to 202 Field Hospital. Scimitar light tanks then escorted a second QRF force by road into the town and Kurt was in that detachment. They quickly deployed and dealt out a lot of punishment with their accurate fire.

I heard that once again Kurt had acquitted himself in the finest tradition of the airborne, fighting an effective battle and slotting a few of the enemy. Much later he told me just one thing about that battle. 'It was the strangest thing, Dad,' he said. 'We were heavily engaged with the enemy but all the dogs in the town were going mad. They were running around between us snarling and snapping. We had to shoot them all.'

My son was alive but that still left six military policemen dead, murdered by treachery in a scruffy room in a sun-baked flat-roofed police barracks. They'd been there by appointment on a training mission and I firmly believe they were set up by an insurgent in police uniform. Later it was said the locals were furious about searches of their homes. A mob had taken the law into its own hands and killed the MPs in a spontaneous action not connected to the attack on the Paras. Crap. It was a carefully coordinated double whammy with the stench of Iranian agents all over it.

The redcaps who died were Sergeant Simon Hamilton-Jewell, Corporal Russell Aston, Corporal Paul Long, Corporal Simon Miller, Lance Corporal Benjamin Hyde and Lance Corporal Thomas Keys. They served with 156 Provost Company, Royal Military Police. I never met them. I wish I had.

The road to Amman stretched ahead as we left Baghdad and the rising sun behind us: a two-man camera crew, a brace of Danish archaeology students, a couple of Israeli Del Boys and a British engineer who, on the strength of a night on the piss, preferred to be with me rather than a complete gunned-up team. We had watched the Jap tourist group load up into a coach and leave with a military escort and now we were hurtling along, the two hire cars containing the Danes and the Israelis so close to our tail they looked as though they were attached to us by a tow bar.

The road is basically a motorway and for much of its length in the city is higher than the housing that flanks it. As you leave Baghdad it arrows through an industrial area with many oil processing plants belching steam and smoke and the occasional flame where venting waste gases are burnt off. It's a busy arterial route that all too often sees real arteries opened.

I preferred to travel early because I figured that most insurgents would be tucked up in their pits or busy with their morning prayers, and by the time they'd got their shit together and decided to wander out onto the shooting gallery I hoped to have left Fallujah and Ramadi well behind me. Generally this worked but when you'd been on the piss into the twilight hours the strategy had some obvious disadvantages. For one thing your tongue felt like the bottom of Saddam's flip-flop and for another you had to perform monumental feats of concentration just to keep your eyes open.

Tony, the engineer, was sat in the back, stuffed between the two crew members, and was the first to speak after the tension of the Ramadi bypass.

'John?' he asked quietly.

'Yeah.'

'How the fuck do you do it?'

I paused, conscious of the burning fatigue behind my eyes, and said, 'Don't know, mate. Suppose it must be practice.'

'Anyway, thanks for the ride,' he said as he closed his eyes and did what I was desperate to do and went to sleep.

There was a really dangerous choke point at Ramadi where a Yankee 'JDAM' smart bomb had hit an elevated section of the highway so that traffic had to come down off the dual carriageway and crawl around a dusty contraflow before being guided back onto the motorway. It was a favourite hang-out of insurgent sharks, who used to bask there while they eyeballed the passing traffic looking for likely targets to prey on. I always kept a sharp eye out for them but that day it was fine and we were back on the fast road with no problem.

I wound my window down after Ramadi, adjusted my AK-47 on my lap, put my shades on and let the warm desert air pour over my face as I scanned the road and my rear-view mirror for unwanted interruptions. It wasn't long before I noticed that our last car, the one with the Israelis in it, was starting to lag behind. Their fucking problem, I thought. I'd warned them I wouldn't be stopping and that was that. Now and then they'd put a spurt on and catch up but they kept fading away again. I tried not to take any notice. Their problem, their fucking problem, I kept telling myself.

We'd just passed one of the local versions of a greasy spoon dotted along the highway when I saw the BSIs in my rear-view mirror. They were in a scruffy white BMW 7 series just pulling out of the dusty car park at the back of the cafe throwing spurts of gravel into the air as they accelerated towards us.

Here we fucking go, I thought. I've read this script before.

I knew for sure that whoever was in that BM was up to no good. The way they'd rushed out onto the road, the intent way the motor was being driven told me they were scumbags on a mission, and I knew in my guts that they were out to hunt down the Israelis, who were now well behind us, three hundred to four hundred metres or so. Sure enough they latched onto them and pulled alongside. A gun barrel poked out of the window of the Beemer and I watched as the Israelis pulled into the side of the road, the 7 series close behind them.

No! No! No! I said to myself. I'm not getting involved. I told them: no pay, no play.

But I knew in my heart I couldn't leave it at that. I wouldn't leave it at that. They'd be headline news on CNN in the morning and it would have been my fault. But then I told myself, No, if they got slotted, it's their own fucking fault for being in Iraq in the first place. The arguments for and against stopping, for and against breaking my self-imposed rules tussled inside my head. Then tails – they won.

'Oh fuck it!' I said out loud.

The driver had seen too and so had the rest of the traffic but the herd didn't bat a collective eyelid as it kept moving along the highway. The people of Ramadi were used to this sort of stuff and most of them approved of the actions of their young warriors anyway. The driver was looking at me questioningly and I nodded at him to pull off the road. The Danes, still attached to our Range Rover by the invisible tow bar, came straight off after us. I was going to break all my own SOPs and take back my own dire warning to the hangers-on who'd been following me. I unsealed the car and trotted back to the Danes.

'Out of the car and into the ditch.' I didn't have to ask twice. They'd seen what was happening back down the road and were crapping themselves.

I could see the Israelis standing at the side of the road with three BSIs shaking them down but the really rough stuff hadn't begun. I knew that would begin the moment the BSIs found their passports and saw they were Jews. The two of them would be on the road to Al Zarqawi and it wouldn't be a pleasant ride; they'd be tortured every step of the way.

They were about 400 metres away, I reckoned, and the heat was causing the air to shimmer and swirl above the tarmac. Not the best of conditions for a clear accurate shot even for a trained sniper – which I am. Still, clear air and a telescopic sight would have been nice for starters. And have a look at 400 metres some time. Pace it out in a park. It doesn't sound very far but is quite literally a long shot with a rifle. Especially when you've got a hangover.

This is no way to be fucking doing this, I thought as I clipped down the bipod on the front of my RPK light machine gun, dropped to the ground and took up a fire position by the rear wheel on the ditch side of the Range Rover. I glanced at the two Danes cowering down waiting for the worst to happen. I looked across the slight curve in the carriageway at the unfolding drama down the road. The only good thing was that we'd been just far enough ahead for the BSIs not to have noticed us and they still hadn't pinged us. They were too intent on their prize to be looking about and one of them was actually lifting his AK into the air and whooping in triumph.

'Oh well, fuck it. It's now or never.'

Crack!

'Shit!' I couldn't believe it. The shot was short and I had only managed to hit the wanker doing the war cry in the ankle. At first he hopped around doing a strange dance that wouldn't have been out of place with the rifle waving and the ululating. Then he fell to the ground screaming. One of his mates who'd been searching the Israelis spun round as he heard the *crack* and *thump* then started firing in all directions. He had no idea where the shot had come from. Good. This gave me a precious fraction of a second.

I put fifty metres on my sight to lift the shot and gently squeezed the trigger again.

Crack!

It whacked the gunman in the shoulder, maybe the chest; I couldn't be certain. He crumpled to the floor like a sack of fertiliser still pulling on the trigger. Rounds burst all over the place, kicking up around the two cars and narrowly missing the Israelis. The third of the tough guys proved to be a real hero: he jumped into the white Beemer and sped off, leaving one wounded and one dying comrade on the side of the road like dogs that had been run over.

The two Jewish guys were in their car before you could blink and screaming up the road towards us as we surged back onto the road without waiting to see what we had left behind us. The Israelis didn't drop back again and were tailgating at 160 klicks all the way to the border. I never learnt why they'd dropped back in the first place. I reckon they just got complacent and had been chatting away like Israelis do.

I don't particularly like Israel. I know the score on the West Bank and I don't like seeing unarmed children shot in cold blood just because they've hurled a few rocks. I have mixed feelings about Israeli policies and think a lot of the trouble in the Middle East, including Iraq, can be laid at their door. Why, I ask myself, does a nation born out of the ghettos of Europe then put the Palestinians in ghettos too? My mate Bob was on a media protection job in that neck of the woods one time and he was thrown against an Israeli tank by a soldier who said, 'I know you're not crew. If I see you on the streets again you're dead.' Nice people.

Nothing was said about the incident back on the road; I wasn't in the mood for chat. When we got across the border and then into the suburbs of Amman the two hire cars kept following. They tailed us all the way to the Grand Hyatt Hotel and pulled up right behind us. I dismounted and walked back to talk to the four of them as they climbed out of their cars. The Jews started pouring out effusive thanks but I just put my hand up to stop them.

'Just shut it. I don't want to fucking know.' I didn't either but I wondered why they were all still with us so I asked, 'Are you lot staying here?'

They looked nonplussed then sheepishly shook their heads. Of course they weren't. They were like little chicks following mother hen; they'd been so terrified on the highway they couldn't let go. They hadn't realised their dependency on me was over.

'Well, I suggest you get those fucking cars back to the hire offices before you scratch the paintwork,' I said.

One of the Danes looked close to tears from the stress of the drive and I've no doubt he'd spent the

entire journey wondering what would have happened
if they'd had a flat tyre. The Jewish guys were apparently going to head off to the border to see if they
could wangle their way across the Allenby Bridge
back into Israel. Not recommended but nothing much
they'd done so far on this trip had been. Me, I just
wanted a coffee, a shower and some sleep, but what
I didn't know was that someone had spotted me
through the big plate-glass window of the hotel.

A huge back confronted me as I walked up to reception in the Sheraton. I'd have known that back
anywhere and I moved up and put my arm round
the man's waist.

'Johnny! How are you, boy? I saw you coming in
earlier,' a big Welsh voice boomed as Mike Curtis
turned to look at me. As he did, his voice dropped
a couple of decibels and he said, 'Fuck me, you look
rough, boy. What have you been doin' to yourself?
You look as though you've seen a ghost.'

I told him I'd nearly seen my own then sat down
and related the whole story of my hungover, terror-
laden dashes across Iraq over a glass of mineral
water and a jug of strong coffee. It took some telling,
and he sat there, his eyes full of concern, occasionally laughing at the more ludicrous turns to my tale.

'So, Johnny,' he said at last, 'to sum up: you've
been rocking up and down the highway and around

the arse end of Iraq minding media crews, and you've been doing it all on your fucking ownsome?'

I nodded. 'Yup. That's about it.'

It was his turn now. Mike waded into me and gave me one of the biggest bollockings I've ever had in my entire life. 'Who the fuck do you think you are, John? Zorro? No, that's not it, is it? You're the Scarlet fucking Pimpernel, aren't you? Come on, mun, tell me; I'm fucking fascinated.' He squeezed his forefinger and thumb together as he went on, 'You're a living legend, mate, but you're that close to becoming a dead fucking laughing stock. It's got to fucking stop, John. This Lone Ranger act has got to fucking stop or you'll be dead within a month.'

I was too knackered to argue. Anyway I had no case to make. He was absolutely right and I knew it. But it needed someone like Mike to tell me. It needed a Blade who had worked with me. It needed a man who'd fought side by side with me and had my absolute respect and loyalty. Only someone like that could tell me exactly how it was. Anyone else would have got a slap.

'When you going back in?' he asked.

'Tomorrow, six o'clock. It's a crew exchange.'

'On your own?'

'Yeah.'

'No, you're fucking not. You're going at eight

o'clock because I've got five gunned-up wagons going then and you can join them. All right?'

'Great. I think I'll get my head down now.'

'Good idea. And, John . . .'

'What, Mike?'

'Remember. Bread always lands on the buttered side.'

'What the hell does that mean?'

'Fucked if I know, boy.' He roared with laughter and I knew I was among friends again.

The trip back into Iraq was a total relief. No hangover, sharp as a knife and twelve mates to fight with if the shit hit the fan. I still had eyes in the back of my head; I was still keyed up and ready to rock, but what a difference a day makes, I thought as we bowled along the Fallujah bypass. I kept my eyes peeled for the spot where I'd shot up the two BSIs but there was no sign that anything at all had happened except for a dark brown patch of sundried blood on the side of the road. No white BMW in the parking lot at the greasy spoon though.

That twenty-four hours marked a sea change for me during my time in Iraq. From then on I only worked in teams. I sometimes worked with Bungo, sometimes with Mike's guys but never alone. I was still a gun for hire but I wasn't up for solo jobs any more.

I slotted back into a proper routine as well. Instead

of showering and going on the lash with clients you'd find me running up flights of stairs in the Palestine or whichever hotel I happened to be staying in. If my memory's correct there were eighteen flights of stairs in the Palestine and I'd grind up and down with a pack on my back, passing other guys also in training. Any locals I happened to pass on my high-rise concrete treadmill looked at me as though I'd lost my marbles. What they didn't know was that I'd really just found them again.

I also had a long stint, lasting months, back in Basra. The city was relatively quiet again after the fuel riots and the Shia majority were content to police themselves and more or less lay off the British Army on their patch. That was to change a year or so after I left with Iranian agitation and a series of attacks on our lads culminating in the taking of two SAS men by local police in August 2005.

Basra was good for me because there was no drinking down there. The reason? Well there'd been three or four attempts at off-licences in the town but the ayatollahs had them dealt with summarily by whacking them with RPGs and the booze supply was obliterated. Licence refused. Happy fucking days.

So it was that I re-established some normality in a life that by its very nature was pretty abnormal. I had a couple of runs home too, which were a real blessing, and I no longer took my family for granted.

But there was one more thing that needed to happen to completely restore my self-esteem and predictably it happened on the Highway. That road had become my own, personal hell on earth. But first there was other business to take care of.

9

BAGHDAD BABES

A group of four people was enjoying a quick lunch in the bustling canteen of a Coalition base north of Baghdad. Two of them were dressed quite formally in safari-style tropical kit they'd picked up in a smart New York department store especially for the trip. They were bankers on a mission to gauge investment needs and audit the schemes that money had already been spent on – big cheeses in the business world and a precious cargo for the team guarding them. You don't want to lose any of the customers but especially not clients like these. The other two at the table were dressed in the usual PMC garb – kit vest, body armour, cargo pants with pockets everywhere – MP5 assault carbines on the table close to hand even in this relatively safe haven. They were all picking away at their food. It was a hot day and even in the air-conditioned environment of the canteen they had little appetite.

Whoomph!!

Without warning a mortar round exploded just outside the canteen, cutting out the lights. Soldiers dived for cover under tables as two more rounds thumped into the ground outside, the blast smashing crockery as the kitchen wallahs screamed with terror.

But the bankers were already on the move as their close protection dragged them in the opposite direction to the incoming rounds and out through the flap of an exit on the other side of the big temporary building. 'In the car! Quickly!' one of them said.

The bankers obeyed immediately and without question even though the PMC giving the orders was a tall, stunning blonde who looked like she could have been a fashion model in another life. The other guard was a babe too. Within seconds they'd ferried their VIP charges across the base and out of the firing line. Cool as ice, tough as whipcord and crack shots, the two were from the elite handful of close protection women working on the Highway. They're known as Baghdad Babes, and not needing to be politically correct because they are unique, they use the title with pride.

There are hundreds of women involved in security work in Iraq and many of them are British. A lot of them come back after a stint in the most frightening country in the world and boast of working on the front line. They're right to be proud of the fact that they have worked in Iraq at all but 99.9 per cent of them are not the real thing. Their jobs are mostly confined to bag searching inside Baghdad International Airport. Most of them fly into BIAP, stay in the on-site accommodation with its bars, clubs and cinema, do their shifts then fly home again without ever driving through the gates. They never progress into the combat zone.

But a very few women are the real deal. There are six from Britain, I don't know of any from the US and a handful from Eastern Europe. I met one from Italy and one from France. You could probably number them on the fingers of three hands.

These days women claim the right to equality in the armed forces and this is viewed as some bold new departure in the history of warfare, but women have been at the sharp end of conflict for thousands of years. In Britain we have one of the great women of war in our history, the tempestuous Boudicca who came so close to kicking the Romans out of Britain, and in fact Celtic women traditionally fought alongside their menfolk. In classical mythology the Amazons were characterised as the enemy men should fear most, women who could fight as well or even better than them, and there is some archaeological evidence to suggest that the legend of the Amazons may derive from Georgia in the Caucasus. Many of the warrior graves there contain the skeletons of women and their weapons.

Alfred the Great had a daughter who went by the wonderful Saxon moniker of Aethelflaed. When Dad wasn't around the flaxen-haired princess tied up her braids, unsheathed her sword and led the Saxon thegns against the Viking invaders. From Orléans in France there was Joan of Arc of course, who routed the English and paid for the trouble she caused by being burnt at the stake for wearing men's clothing and witchcraft. In the First World War the French used Moroccan women mercenaries in the trenches and in World War II some of the most skilled and feared snipers fighting in the rubble of Stalingrad and Leningrad were formidable females. And in many of the African civil wars of the past thirty years or so women have been partnered with the ever present AK-47 to fight alongside men; in 2005 Liberian women fought as mercenaries in the Ivory Coast. The countess of Pembroke, Dame Nicolaa de la Haye, Black Agnes the countess of Dunbar – all were women warriors.

Of all of these women the one who really sets my imagination alight is another princess with a wonderful name. She was Sichelgaita, a ninth-century princess of Lombardy who married a Norman mercenary against her father's will then joined the business. Described as long-limbed, strong and striking in her looks, she fought alongside her husband, riding to battle with him and vowing to live or die as he did. Sichelgaita took no shit and personally executed deserters. Some woman.

I'm dodging the issue a bit because my personal view of women in the front line is that all the rights in the world can't make them a match for men – with of course notable exceptions now and then. Women will certainly never be able to perform to the standards required by the SAS and other special forces units, although a levelling factor is the development of modern weapons. A woman who can shoot straight with an AK or some of the lightweight composite plastic rifles on the market is on the face of it as good as a man.

One great example of sex equality at the end of a barrel is the Danish woman gunner in a Leopard tank in the Balkans who took out two Serbian Bofors guns which had been playing havoc in the Goradze valley. She was the best shot in her unit and did it with just two rounds, one for each gun. Hats off to her; she did a fantastic job. But there's more to war than sitting hundreds of metres away from your enemy and taking pot shots at him.

Personally I just take them as they come. I'm not some unreconstructed male in the business of dissing women because of some chauvinistic attitudes; I'm just rationally looking at the military facts. Some women are brilliant in certain very dangerous roles and they have my absolute respect, but they have to earn it just as a bloke does. You meet men who look the part and talk the part but I run my gimlet eye over them and wait to see how they pan out. One thing's for sure: I don't rely on anyone, man or woman, until I've seen how they perform.

But back to Iraq, and one of the two women in that Coalition canteen really stands out as a bit of a Sichelgaita figure. Also tall, long-limbed and striking in her looks, her name is Penny and she was the first female PMC in Iraq. The original Baghdad Babe, she's a woman I respect and admire in the male-dominated world of close protection work. Penny's been a mate for years. I used to do close protection work with her on the Middle Eastern royal families that Mike Curtis and I looked after in London. She's had a fascinating and dangerous career in covert units of the Met Police and became a very good pistol shot. When she left the force she went into security work and then in 2003 found herself in Iraq.

It was her first time in a war zone and true to type she performed brilliantly. I'll let her tell you the story of the Baghdad Babes as she told it to me. It's a fascinating insight into a very exclusive world.

I'll never forget the day I got a call from a guy from another company. I can't name the company for various reasons but he was a bloke I'd worked for before. I didn't expect the question he asked, I didn't expect it at all.

'Penny,' he said, 'I'd like you to go to Iraq and get involved in some close protection work out there. We need a woman to get involved with client protection. What do you think? You up for it?'

'Let me think about it,' I said, and I came off the phone feeling quite stunned at the request.

This would be my first foray into a war zone so I spent the next couple of hours working out all the options in my mind – the options being the number of ways I could get killed – and as I worked them back from being blown to bits by a car bomber in Baghdad to getting run over by a cab outside Terminal 4 at Heathrow I realised I was going to do it. Ever since I was a little girl I've had this funny idea fixed in my head that I was going to live until I was eighty-seven so I just thought, Yeah, I'm not going to die for a long time yet so I'll take the job.

I rang the guy back and said I'd do it but I persuaded him to let another girl come with me – I'll call her June. She was someone with a great deal of experience too. We flew out to Baghdad a couple of days later and you'd have paid for tickets to see the faces of the guys from the team waiting for us at the airport. The boss back in London had just put our initials on the manifest and hadn't told them we were women. We weren't just any women either because, without boasting, I can truthfully say me and June both turn heads. We're both real lookers. The guys were stood there mouths gaping when we checked through passport control. One or two of them had real sneers on their faces and I could see they were thinking, 'Why have we been lumbered with these two silly tarts?'

It didn't phase me or June; we're both used to being looked upon as silly tarts in a man's world. I've found though that the higher up the PMC food chain you go the more tolerant and accepting the men are. The SAS guys are at the top of the chain and people like you and Mike Curtis and Bungo just watch and wait to make their judgement on an individual. You can't ask for more than that.

Anyway we began with some range work with our new weapons. We were both familiar and competent with pistols but we'd not fired rifles before so we had a crash course with MP5s and once again we attracted a lot of looks as we stood up and did our stuff. After that we spent a lot of time on the ranges and a lot of time practising escape driving routines – U-turns, J-turns, all that sort of stuff – on the big parade ground in front of Saddam's giant crossed swords of victory. I can remember looking at the famous crossed swords and thinking, God, a couple of weeks ago I was playing Scrabble on a boat cruising down a river in Norfolk. What the hell am I doing here? I used to get cheesed off with the driver training because in the police you're always involved in chases on the streets so you don't need to practise. The army guys are right though; they say practice keeps your blade sharp and they're bang on.

After the rifle training we started work almost immediately. We'd be in a team of four and we'd work long hours on close protection of very high-level officials. You're guessing they were bankers and economists. You could be right but I'm not going to comment. Our chosen method of movement was low profile. We'd have good fast vehicles but they were soft-skinned and we'd bash the bodywork round a bit just to make the car blend with the Baghdad background.

You can imagine there aren't many six-foot blonde women in Baghdad so I would often wear a burka when I travelled and keep my face reasonably well covered but not so much that I couldn't see what was going on. I'd be sat there in the car, a big blonde bird smothered in a burka with an MP5 across my lap. I suppose it's a hell of a strange sight but it worked because it gave the impression that this was a local group travelling through Baghdad.

First impressions are everything in Iraq. That instant impression that we were locals gave us the split second we needed while any potential enemy was doing a double take. By the time they'd decided *we weren't all that we seemed at first glance we'd have vanished. It was a good scheme for operating and it largely kept us out of trouble; as I said, our clients were very important people. They really loved the female close security operators. They weren't phased by us; in fact they were impressed that we were in the country at all and I can honestly say that to a man they behaved like perfect gentlemen. There was no bottom pinching or anything like that but then you might not want to chance groping a girl with an assault rifle in her hands.*

June and I were so popular that in the end the company had six girls working rotations out in Iraq. There were two ex-police and four ex-army. All the girls were British and I don't know of any female teams except ours. There were no American women to my knowledge and I only know of one Italian girl who worked out in Iraq as a full personal bodyguard.

We were a small and elite number of women who put ourselves at risk and the risks were considerable. I had no illusions about what would happen if we were taken by the insurgents. There's no doubt that we would have been subjected to gross physical and sexual torture if we'd been taken alive and I would be lying if I didn't admit that this was one of the most terrifying thoughts on our minds.

We all knew what would happen because two

Scandinavian aid workers had been kidnapped and killed by the insurgents. The two women had had enough of Iraq and wanted to go home so they went to a cafe around the corner from their base to get a cab to the airport. The cabbie turned out to be an insurgent and they were driven off and horrifically tortured to death. I didn't want that to happen to me so I knew that I would do anything rather than be captured. I vowed to keep one bullet in the magazine and use it on myself. I know that sounds melodramatic but was it really so melodramatic to consider that sort of extreme case in modern Iraq? I don't think so.

We all talked about it and the other girls felt the same. I have doubts whether I would have done it in the end if I had been captured because my survival instinct is so strong but I wanted to feel that I had the option.

Eventually we became known among the men as the Baghdad Babes – not to be confused with a porn movie of the same name, which needless to say wouldn't be our line of work. We didn't find the name offensive; in fact the reverse is true. None of us are feminists in that mouthing-off sense. We all felt quite confident enough in ourselves and what we can do not to have to shout it from the rooftops. So we took the name in the spirit it was meant and now it has become a badge of pride for those of us who

*were involved. We even posed for a website publicity
picture but our faces were never revealed.*

*Scary times? There were a lot of scary things
happening in Iraq while I was out there. It was
nothing to have bullets flying all around you, and
you honestly never knew whether some of them
were meant for you or not. I lived through a few
mortar attacks and a couple of near misses from
RPGs but none of us ever had a contact in the sense
of a full-on shoot-out. It was our job to avoid those
situations so I think from that point of view our
low-profile tactics and our burkas worked.*

*One of the most sinister things that happened was
on a bridge over the River Tigris. There was an armed
group out on the street and one of them was taking
photographs. He took a picture of me through the
car window and I really didn't like that. The thought
that I was on some insurgent's file made me feel very
uncomfortable. I felt almost violated and I remember
wanting to get out of the car and do something about
it. We had a client with us though and he had to
come first. That's the way it was.*

*We used to cause a real stir round the place with
the locals and you could tell the sight of a blonde-
haired Western woman carrying a machine gun used
to get the Iraqi guys going. Knowing that, we used
it to our advantage because we knew for sure that
some of the local police, militia and private security*

guards were working as dickers — that's jargon for a spy or spotter — for the insurgents. Sometimes we'd just wander out to a checkpoint or hotel entrance and chat up the guards until one of our call signs had whipped through the gates and got off on their way. That way the dicker didn't have time to make his call to the bad guys and a chance for them to make a hit was lost.

Unashamed use of sexuality? Yeah, maybe, but women members of the Resistance would act out almost exactly the same role to distract Nazi guards in occupied France during the Second World War. If it works, it works.

Sometimes we'd go into the banking district in Baghdad with our clients. It was a strange area, busy but extremely tense as of course it would be a great hit for the insurgents. It was surrounded with concrete barriers to keep the car bombs out and there was a generally high level of security. But just looking around made you aware that the place was heaving with insurgency dickers.

We'd go in low profile as usual and park in the basement garage of the building. Then we'd head for the boardroom of the particular bank or institution; these were generally on the upper floors of high-rise buildings. It used to give me a really strange feeling to be so high up, and you'd feel really exposed and wonder how you were going to get your client out

*in the event of a bomb. Those visits were always a
bit surreal because from the moment I got through
the door and whipped my burka off I'd be followed
by a crowd of women who were no less fascinated
by the sight of a tall blonde woman with a machine
gun than the Iraqi menfolk were. They'd literally be
pulling at your clothes and chattering around you,
and it made it difficult to keep an eye on the client.*

*Once I took an American principal to the banking
district. He was a really nice bloke – tall, distinguished-
looking, iron-grey hair, perfectly turned out and a lean
fit-looking figure. 'I think it would be nice to take the
stairs, don't you?' he said.*

*No, I bloody didn't, but he was the boss and he
set off with a long stride, eating up the stairs two at
a time with me trotting after him. Unbelievable. It
only took me a couple of minutes to work out there
was no air conditioning in the stairwell. I was
wheezing as I tried to keep up with the sly old goat.
I had all my kit and my weapons and by the time
we'd got to the twenty-seventh floor I was dribbling
and nearly fainting from the effort.*

*I quickly recovered and gave him a sick smile when
he said, 'That was invigorating, wasn't it?'*

*There was a lot of comradeship in Iraq and I found
that most of the men were prepared to give you a
chance. Of course, you got more than your fair share*

of the little woman stuff but I really don't think it mattered. I'd been a female in a man's world for a long time and I'd learnt to cope with the crap. I'd usually just ignore it and as I said earlier the people that really counted didn't come at the situation in a negative way.

I think the worst individual was a South African guy who actually I thought was a good bloke at first but then he really had a go – a lot of stuff about shooting blacks in the townships and how women were shit and should stay in their kitchens. He went on and on, blah, blah, blah. I know what it was all about. Some guys sort of put out to you and when they realise that sex is not on the agenda and you're just there as a professional they round on you and attack you for being unprofessional because of all things you're a woman.

I just told him, 'Look, mate, you think you're tough but when I was a nineteen-year-old I was patrolling the streets of Brixton with a truncheon. You'd have been afraid to go out on those streets without your big gun so don't give me any more crap.'

Really I should have done what I usually do and just let it roll over me but I just got fed up with him. Some of those South Africans just make it their business to get on your wrong side. They're a really cussed lot.

There are definitely a lot more women involved in security work these days but in Iraq they're mostly employed as searchers and airport processors. A lot of girls get into the business through martial arts skills which take them on to nightclub door work, that sort of thing. Then they want to get into the real world of close protection, which they fail to do and end up in Baghdad airport searching bags.

Close protection, now that's another world, and the best people come with an army or police background. You get women who've served with specialist army units like 14 Int (14 Intelligence Company) who are absolutely expert at surveillance work, and that goes for women with a background in specialist police work too.

I came up through the Met Police mill and was on the streets when I was quite young. I saw all the worst riots in London when I was in my twenties. You learn certain things in those situations. It's that awareness of what's happening all around you. It's being one step ahead. Even if it's just the ability to read the signs that tell you there's a choke point in the traffic ahead and that you'd better take a turn and go a different way. It's the ability to look a man in the eye as you sit in your car and know with your every fibre that he's weighing up his chances of taking a shot through the car window, but your look tells him he'd better try another day.

Like I said, none of the girls had a full-on shoot-out with insurgents but some heroic stuff was done. There are things I simply can't talk about because they would give away operating procedures still being used to convey people in safety. But the girls did some great work and displayed courage on a daily basis. We thwarted suicide bombers and we kept our clients out of harm's way. And there was an X-factor too because the clients really took courage from the fact that they had women minding them. That day in the canteen, for instance. All hell broke loose and there was chaos all around us as the rounds kept coming. Later on though the clients told us that they'd got a huge boost from the fact that they were with two women who remained cool, calm and collected through those terrifying few minutes. I think that was a great testament.

Was there any romance under the desert skies? People always ask. Afraid there wasn't for me. I'm single but out of the thousands of alpha males on the loose in Iraq I never saw one I fancied. It hardly seems fair does it, but I was out there to do a job for good money. I wasn't looking for love. As for the other girls. Well, none of them had a fling, at least not while I was there.

I think the serious thing is that there's this huge army of mercenaries in Iraq and among them are a handful of women prepared to match the men for courage and devotion to the job. I'm proud of that and I hope with all my heart that in some small way I've helped the Iraqi people on their journey to reconstruction and shown two fingers to the insurgents who'd like to take them back to the Bronze Age.

There you have it – the story in Penny's words. I'd really like to underscore one thing: the fact that the Baghdad Babes have not been involved in any fire-fights really stands as a testimony to the skilled way they move around the warscape in Iraq without attracting attention to themselves. I hope they never have to fire a shot in anger and their low-profile style of operating keeps them out of trouble for the duration.

I did hear a story that an Eastern European woman was involved in a shoot-out north-west of Baghdad. Supposedly her vehicle was hit by an IED and she staggered away from the wreckage and fell to the floor a few yards away. She kept screaming but she was only pretending to be badly wounded and when a couple of insurgents ran in to make the capture she malleted them with her rifle. That's the story but I simply don't know if it's true or not. I do know that having seen the Baghdad Babes I am convinced that they are more than capable of providing that hallmark British military skill, sustained accurate fire.

One thing is certain: there is a place for women in the PMC line-up.

It was 4 November 2005. Four Iraqis, one of them a woman, were tearing down the Highway on their way to Jordan. They were determined to create their own miniature hell on earth. The four rented an apartment in west Amman and a few days later took taxis to three separate hotels. Three of the Iraqis then blew themselves up; the woman's device failed to detonate. The explosions ripped through the hotels, causing devastation and massive loss of life. They had carried out the attacks in the belief that the Kingdom of Jordan had defiled the purity of Islam. Whose Islam had been defiled? You might ask, and that's a bloody good question. It's one the Jordanian security services came closer to answering when the failed suicide bomber was captured and detained.

Her name is Sajida Mubarak Atrous al Rishawi and as she was being grilled the streets of Amman were filled with crowds baying for her blood and the blood of her close friend Abu Musab al Zarqawi, the head of al Qaeda in Iraq. It was not the effect those psychos had intended. The thirty-five-year-old came from the nest of al Qaeda vipers at the heart of the insurgency so the Jordanians kept her arrest secret at first hoping to get a location for al Zarqawi and with it the possibility of capturing the Sheikh of the

Beheaders. Just how close Sajida was to the leadership is demonstrated by the fact that she is the sister of Mubarak Atrous al Rishawi, the former right-hand man of al Zarqawi, who had been killed by Coalition special forces in Fallujah.

The other three suicide bombers who attacked the Grand Hyatt, Radisson SAS and Days Inn hotels killing fifty-seven innocent people included al Rishawi's husband, Ali Hussein Ali al Shamari, an al Qaeda lieutenant in the Anbar province of Iraq.

The Jordanian security services were not giving out too many details but I heard on the grapevine that al Rishawi had deliberately chosen to target the Radisson, where 300 people were attending a Jordanian–Palestinian wedding feast in one of the hotel's ballrooms. It appears this excuse for a human being wanted to turn another woman's happiest day into a nightmare – her belt of powerful RDX explosive was packed with ball bearings, like those of her comrades, to cause the maximum amount of injury. Al Rishawi walked into the wedding reception with her husband but when he noticed she was having trouble detonating her bomb – she was tugging at the primer cord with no result – he pushed her out of the ballroom then blew himself up.

I have no doubt she was given a real going-over by her Jordanian interrogators and I have no sympathy for her whatsoever. I am certain she gave them a lot of information that meant al Zarqawi will have lost safe houses and operators. This will have limited his options and means he is one step nearer to death or capture. As for al Rishawi, she looked a pathetic figure when she stood in the caged dock of a court in Amman, Jordan in September 2006 wearing a blue prison headscarf and long gown.

After her arrest she admitted her part in the dreadful bombing plot in a televised confession then recanted her guilt and said she'd had no intention of killing herself or anyone else but had been tortured by the security service.

But experts showed how the mechanism of the explosives belt she was wearing had indeed jammed, providing the lie to her story. This evil woman was sentenced to hang.

There was however a strange twist to the story that emerged in court because although she has been characterised as the first of the so-called Black Widows of the Iraq conflict it seems that in reality she was a Black Maiden. The judges of the military tribunal were told that she had married her husband Ali Hussein al Shimeri just before their arrival in Iraq in November 2005, but it had never been consummated. It sounds as though she came from acceptable terrorist stock so al Shimeri was ordered to marry her to tie her into the bombing plot; they effectively created a sham marriage to catastrophically ruin a decent, loving union.

Sajida al Rishawi was the first of the Black Widows and was followed by a perhaps even more sinister figure, a Belgian woman called Muriel Degauque, a thirty-eight-year-old from Charleroi who converted to Islam after marrying a Moroccan immigrant who also happened to be a radical Muslim. Muriel Degauque's mother Liliane reckoned that after her conversion and marriage in 2000 the former Roman Catholic became more 'Muslim than Muslim'. She'd tried without success to contact her daughter for three weeks before Muriel carried out her suicide attack in Baghdad on 9 November, when she tried but failed to take out a patrol of US troops with her.

The radicalisation of the quiet Belgian woman took place quickly as she moved from wearing a simple veil to donning the full head-to-toe chador. After thorough indoctrination she passed through Syria into Iraq, where she became the first female European bomber there. The Syrian government of course denied any knowledge of her travelling through their country but they bear a heavy responsibility for a lot of al Qaeda's activities in Iraq. The chilling thing is that she could have come from any country in Europe including Britain, where anti-terrorism legislation introduced in 2005 seems to have had little impact on radical imams; they were still preaching violence and hatred and praising suicide bomb 'martyrs' even as Muriel Degauque was killing herself.

In December 2005 there was a blood-curdling double act in Baghdad when two Black Widows blew themselves up in the police academy, killing twenty-seven students and wounding thirty-two more. One detonated her explosives in a classroom full of students during roll call, the other in the busy mess room where young officers were eating a meal. The two were believed to be students at the academy and had not been subjected to a search. They took five other female police officers, Muslim sisters, with them. It was a dreadful act and the type of terrorism that is the hardest to combat.

10

THE POWER OF LOVE

You'd think that Cupid's arrows wouldn't stand a chance against the assault rounds and car bombs in Iraq. Even if it wasn't a war zone you'd also imagine that being surrounded by the prohibitions of an Islamic culture would dampen the ardour of the thousands of Westerners in the country all on their own.

Don't believe it for a moment. Love finds a way even in Iraq, and there are countless affairs and romances and even scores of marriages between Coalition troops, PMCs and locals. In practice that means male US soldiers marrying Iraqi women, female US soldiers marrying PMCs they've met in theatre, and PMCs marrying Iraqi women. What I've personally never heard of is an Iraqi man being involved in this complex triangle of love. Why? Because these romances depend on one thing to survive: a marital home and a life outside Iraq. These are things Iraqi men aren't generally able to supply.

And of course when I talk about the marriage surviving I don't mean there's a shortage of marriage guidance counsellors in Iraq. No, what I mean is that the happy couple would be slotted and dumped in the Tigris before the groom could carry the bride across the threshold.

The centre of this marriage bazaar is the relatively safe Green Zone where the Provisional Coalition Authority operates and literally hundreds of local women work in secretarial, clerical and catering jobs. Naturally the locals meet the men from the Coalition and the mercenary armies as they go about their daily work and relationships begin to flower. There's a lively social scene inside the zone with discos and bars and it's easy enough for them to chat each other up in the day then make an RV to meet again in the evening.

It's like the fifty-first state of the Union inside the zone and when I was there I always felt like I was inside an alien craft with some sort of force field surrounding it. Outside is bedlam and anarchy where nothing and no one is safe. Inside the alien invaders and the Iraqis are able to interface and evolve their own unique culture.

All sorts of relationships flourish inside the zone, from the purely platonic, through total lust and on to true love. But I reckon a lot of the Iraqi girls, and there are some real lookers among them, set out to get a Yank by hook or by crook so that they can get out of the hell of Baghdad and across the world to relative safety and a good life in the greatest consumer society on the planet. And that's exactly what they do, because as soon as they get married there is no going back home. They are on a marriage conveyor belt that plucks them from one culture then takes them halfway around the world to drop them in another.

The women keep their arrangements totally secret, sometimes not even telling their own parents. Then on the big day they bring their luggage into the zone with them and have it ready to go when the civil ceremony has been performed. All the vetting and visa arrangements have to be done by the US Immigration people, who have their own bureau in the zone too. The couples make their marriage vows in the presidential palace, which is at the heart of the Green Zone tucked into a great bend in the river. The marriage ceremonies are held in one of the garishly painted state rooms with high stuccoed ceilings inside Saddam's very own version of Versailles. When they've finally tied the knot there is only one way to go and that is down the road to the airport in a protected convoy and straight onto a flight out of Iraq.

While I was around Baghdad there were so many marriages taking place they had special wedding days up at the palace. I knew three or four Yank PMCs who took the plunge and married Baghdad brides. There's apparently been a big fall-off in the number of mixed-religion marriages taking place between Shias and Sunnis but perhaps the weddings between Westerners and Iraqis in the Green Zone are making up some of the shortfall.

It was a quiet evening in the bar of a Baghdad hotel in July 2003 and I was relaxing over a drink with the British correspondent I was bodyguarding. He'd invited a couple of members of one of the international news stations to join us and we were chatting about the usual stuff. Where was the latest hot spot in the insurgency? Who'd had a contact? How many people were killed in the latest bombing?

One of the journalists was a woman I'll call Jasmine. She was in her late thirties, dark and quite attractive. I was to discover that she was on the lookout and hungry for love. We'd only been introduced about twenty minutes before she cornered me and deftly turned the subject away from the 'situation' and onto my personal life.

'Yeah, I've got a steady girlfriend. We've been together for years. We're really happy,' I said.

'I'm happy too,' she said. 'My husband and I are close but we don't keep each other on a lead. You know what I mean. I think the expression is we have an open marriage.'

'Really?' I said.

'Yes, we're very understanding of each other's needs. He knows I have certain needs and of course when I'm in a place like this he knows that there's a certain de-stressing factor involved and he knows that sex is great relaxation.' By now her foot was going up my trouser leg and I'd got the message loud and clear. 'Obviously, it has to be no strings attached, but that's fine, isn't it?'

Now if I had agreed it would have seemed like I was accepting her advances, but on the other hand, if I said it wasn't fine then I might have sounded a bit rude. I settled for the diplomatic course.

'Suppose so,' I offered.

She smiled seductively and gave me a look at her room key fob. 'There's my room number. Shall I see you later?'

I know that refusal can cause offence but some of the man-hungry media women were more scary than the insurgents. Most of them were fantastic at their jobs and kept everything on a professional level but some were real prick mangles. And with all the alpha males of the PMC community around them with testosterone levels that must have been near the top end of the safety guidelines they were like kids in a sweet shop.

Still she had to be told. 'Don't think so. I've got an early start tomorrow and I love my girlfriend.'

It sounded rather limp but that's how I felt. A few of my mates, especially the ones that weren't too seriously attached, got well into the female correspondents. They're formidable women. You can imagine that the networks don't choose them for their bad looks and they're not exactly shy. Those girls know what they want and they go out to get it.

They're not the only women out there either. There are a lot of businesswomen in Iraq as well, high-powered executives representing top corporations. They mostly stay inside the relative safety of the Green Zone to conduct their business with executives of oil companies or the Iraqi utilities who come in to meet them. Once again they're mixing with the whole range of people involved in the Iraq project so where there's attraction there's opportunity. You get liaisons between women execs and senior officers, interpreters and inevitably with the PMCs who are assigned to protect them.

Put yourself in the woman's situation. You're in a strange and dangerous country. Along comes the hunk assigned to protect you on your occasional forays outside the Green Zone. He's got his own wants and desires too. That feeling of vulnerability and not a little fear then throws you into his arms. It happens a lot. One of my mates, a bloke called Mac, had a passionate affair with a corporate executive from the States. He was divorced; she was single and wanted to ship him back home to New York, shower him with cash and presents and love him for the rest of his life. Perfect. Apparently not.

'She's a cracking looker, mate,' I told him. 'You could do a lot worse for yourself.'

'I know, Johnny, but I just can't do it.'

'It's not because she's American, is it?' I asked. 'They're great when you get into their way of thinking.'

'No, it's not that.'

'What is it then?' I was really curious now.

'The trouble is, she just wants me to hang around while she's working. She's told me I can have all the toys I like – fast cars, a superbike. She's even said she'll get me flying lessons. It's all there for me, Johnny. Skiing in Aspen every season. California. Flights home to see the kids whenever.'

'Fucking hell, Mac. Move over, son, I'll have her,' I joked.

'You wouldn't, mate.'

'So what's wrong with her?' I was exasperated now.

'She's told me I can have it all but I'll have to give up the Highway. No more jobs.'

'You're kidding?'

'No.'

'Tell her to fuck off, Mac. You've got to keep your balls.'

'That's what I've been trying to tell you,' he replied.

One of the most unusual relationships I saw spring up in Baghdad was between three of the lads and three Iraqi sisters. They were beautiful girls, members of the small Christian community, and they had been working for some company the boys had been ferrying clients around for.

One thing led to another and they would sneak into the hotel for nights of passion with the lads but it had to be kept very secret, not because the hotel might not like it but because they'd get malleted if the word got out. If I had to go and see one of the boys there'd always be a pause until they were certain it was me, then the door would open and I'd be allowed in just as the girl was coming out of the wardrobe. They were absolutely paranoid about being spotted by one of the cleaners or by room service in case they were recognised. I'm sure it was all a big exotic game for them and the lads seemed to enjoy it too, but there is danger out there in Iraq for illicit lovers. It's a very real and present danger that can end in terrible tragedy and for one famous soldier it did.

Brian Tilley was relaxing after supper in the lounge of a comfortable villa-style house in the smart suburb of al Dourah in Baghdad on a warm evening. His bags were packed and he was ready for an early night; he was catching a flight back to the UK the following morning. He'd already missed a flight two days earlier and didn't want to lose the next one out.

Brian was a forty-seven-year-old veteran of the Royal Marines elite Special Boat Squadron and a man with a fantastic military record. As a special forces soldier he attracted immense respect and was extremely popular with his 'boatie' comrades in the SBS.

Life was sweet for Brian at the time. He was making a good living as a PMC and had sorted out his routine to make life work for him. Not for him the anonymous walls of a hotel room and the same old couscous buffet in a tatty restaurant every meal-time. No, Brian had done better – with all the resourcefulness that had made him a hard-core SBS operator, he had set himself up in the villa with all the comforts. He had good home cooking, comfortable informal surroundings and an excellent social life which included the passionate attentions of a beautiful Iraqi woman.

But a knock at the door that evening in May 2005 heralded a tragedy that was still unfolding eight months later with all the twists of a crime thriller. There were five other people in the house with Brian that evening. There was his lover, her sister together with a woman friend and an Iraqi man who worked with Brian. The last was a pretty teenage girl, the daughter of Brian's mistress. The Iraqi guy opened the door to be confronted by four police officers who calmly asked to be let in on official business. Brian must have heard the conversation at the door but there was no commotion and he remained relaxed. The police uniforms must have allayed any fears the occupants of the house may have had. Mistake.

The IP officers came into the lounge and what happened afterwards is largely a matter of conjecture. They probably jumped Brian Tilley before he could arm himself and put up a fight; I cannot imagine he didn't have a weapon somewhere near to hand. One of the cops shot him in the foot, presumably to disable him, then they dragged him into another room as the screaming women watched. We can only imagine what was being shouted and screamed. Maybe Brian was told that he was infidel filth and he should keep his hands off Iraqi women. Maybe he was told to beg for mercy and refused. We simply don't know because Brian Tilley was then executed with a shot in the back that smashed his vital organs and killed him instantly.

The cops then went on to execute in cold blood the three women and the man in the house. The fifteen-year-old girl, who'd come out of her bedroom rubbing the sleep out of her eyes disturbed by the noise, was shot in the neck and left for dead. But she survived to give investigators the vital evidence they needed: the perpetrators were police officers and not only that she was able to identify them.

Iraqi forces arrested the cops with the PMC community awash with rumours – he'd been jumped leaving the house and they'd tortured and mutilated his body before shooting him; the cops were part of an insurgent hit squad out to get any PMCs who strayed into the community; and so on. However, it doesn't appear that he was tortured or mutilated and it doesn't seem to me he was the victim of insurgents. The best theory I heard was that the cops were paid by the woman's family to warn Brian off but when they got into the cage with the tiger they found themselves completely out of their depth and had to shoot him before he tore their throats out. That done, the rest of them had to die too.

Brian's home in the UK was in Dorset, not far from the SBS base at Poole where he'd served with such distinction, and the local coroner ordered a police investigation, which was headed by Detective Superintendent Phil James. In the winter of 2005 the superintendent was no nearer to closing the file to his or the coroner's satisfaction. What DS James had come up against was the Iraqi factor – an absolute unwillingness on the part of the authorities in

Baghdad to move things along. This could be for a variety of reasons. Perhaps it's because the Iraqis have a lot on their plates. More likely they have a certain sympathy for the men who killed an outsider, a non-Muslim who'd brought shame and dishonour on an Iraqi family. Or it could be that tribal loyalties – which are complex and intertwined in Iraq – together with a few well placed bribes are keeping the officers immune from justice. Because believe it or not in December 2005 the bastards were back on the beat.

The girl, the only witness in the case, provides another twist to the story. Apparently it was only through a chance encounter in the Baghdad hospital where she was being treated that the girl spotted the killers. How much of a chance that actually was I don't know. Maybe they were planning to finish the job but she spotted them first and bubbled them to the authorities. Anyway, it was immediately recognised that she was in mortal danger and it was even suggested that she could be given asylum in Britain in return for giving evidence at the inquest in Dorset. But Dorset inquests don't hand down Baghdad jail sentences and then the girl vanished from protective custody. Without her there could be no trial, but on the other hand turning up to give evidence might have amounted to a death sentence. So there's a dilemma: what's more important, justice for those who were murdered or life for the teenager?

Personally I don't think there's an argument. That girl's life is paramount; after all you can't bring the rest back from the grave. DS James thought it was pretty certain she'd been spirited away by friends of Brian. That suggests one thing to me. Those Baghdad cops with blood on their hands had better be watching their backs. If anything goes for cops in Iraq then I think anything might go for friends of Brian Tilley with the skills to move in and out of the shadows at will.

There are lessons to be learnt from this tragedy and unfortunately that means I'm going to have to speak frankly about the actions of a man who was held in high esteem when he lived. But first I think we should look at Brian Tilley's record a little more closely because he was some man.

Born in Derby he served for twenty-two years in the Royal Marines and fought in the Falklands, Northern Ireland and the First Gulf War. In 1997 he was awarded the Queen's Gallantry Medal for outstanding courage. But it wasn't just his military career that marked Brian out as a special bloke, even by special forces standards. He was also a qualified paramedic, a diver and a talented mountaineer who'd been on expeditions to three of the world's four highest mountains. On two expeditions he used his medical skills to save people's lives. When he left the marines he set up his own security company called

Peak, and in 2002 when a plot to kidnap David and Victoria Beckham was exposed it was Brian Tilley who was called in to beef up security. He became friendly with the Beckhams who were apparently delighted with the way he improved their close protection by retraining their civilian security staff. Quite a CV, isn't it?

But it's plain that Brian Tilley succumbed to special forces invulnerability syndrome. If we're honest, all of us in the world of special forces will put up our hands and admit there have been times and situations when we chose to believe that we were supermen. I've done it myself. For 99.9 per cent of us the outcome is fine – we either realise in time that we're wearing our underpants outside our trousers or luck carries us safely through whatever the situation may be. But some don't realise or their luck doesn't hold and they pay the price.

I don't know what verdict the coroner will record on Brian's death but in my judgement he all but killed himself when he broke every rule in the book by going native. He became complacent in his cosy berth at his girlfriend's villa. He didn't believe anyone could get the drop on him and he exposed himself as surely as if he'd gone onto a mountain glacier without an ice axe.

I don't want to upset his family or any of his old mates in the SBS but I'm sure that, hand on heart, they know he should never have stayed in that villa on a regular basis in the first place; he should have taken steps to carry on the romance in a more secure environment. Even Jordan would have been infinitely safer than the suburbs of Baghdad. But Brian had a lovely girlfriend back home in Poole and he surely never meant his Iraqi liaison to last anyway. It's a crying shame. A man like that had a lot left to offer.

Thirty days hath September and so forth . . . and February has twenty-eight and twenty-nine in a leap year. Well it was leap year day in 2004 and I was back on my old stamping ground, staying at the Hotel Murbad in Basra.

The night of that attack on the hotel when we'd taken cover on the roof seemed a lifetime away and the old chap who owned the place was in great spirits. He was pleased to see me and patted me on the back as he kept repeating, 'Welcome, Mr Johnny, welcome!' And the Saddam lookalike waiter gave me a conspiratorial wink as if he'd been initiated into the brotherhood of men who know how to free up an AK-47 jammed by a split case. It was nice to be back on familiar ground and it had the feel of a bit of a homecoming. Even the insurgents put out the welcome mat at dusk by starting a firefight under cover of the fading light.

I was with a team of guys who immediately started

deploying together with other call signs. The odd shot in the dark was cracking into the outer wall of the Murbad but I noticed the old nightwatchman – installed in his hut at the gate again – didn't seem inclined to move. So rather than rush around like a headless chicken I asked the owner what was going down.

'Oh, not to be worrying, Mr Johnny,' he said gravely. 'Tonight they are killing each other.' I knew he was right so I just settled down in a corner of the car park to watch the phosphorescent muzzle flashes on buildings a hundred metres or so away. There was some tribal or clan dispute to be settled and they were too busy sorting out matters of honour to be bothered with us.

As the battle reached fever pitch my satphone began jumping around in my vest pocket; the sound of the rifle fire joined by the steady rattle of a machine gun made it impossible to hear it ringing. I pulled it out of my vest pocket and pressed the receive button.

'John.' It was my long-term girlfriend Emma.

'Hi, darling,' I bellowed down the phone.

'What's all that noise? It's a terrible line,' she said. Terrible line? The only lines were the occasional luminous streaks of tracer rounds.

'Hang on, doll,' I shouted as I ran further away from the shooting and crouched down on my knee behind a vehicle. 'That any better?'

'Yeah, much. What's going on?'

'Nothing much, babe, just a bit of a firefight across the road.'

'Oh God, are you okay?'

'Yeah, I'm fine. Safe as houses.'

Emma had been with me for eight years and had learnt to accept that when I said I was all right then I was all right, so the conversation moved on.

'You know it's a leap year, don't you, John?'

Well I did, but I hadn't spent my waking hours thinking about it. 'Yeah, what about it?'

'Well it's leap year day today, isn't it?'

Once again I supposed it was but still I hadn't twigged and I might even have been getting a little bit impatient at being quizzed about my knowledge of the calendar in the middle of a gun battle. 'Really? I suppose it is,' I replied.

'Well you know that a girl can take the initiative on leap year day—' *Boomph!* An RPG round hit the side of an apartment block about 150 metres away and drowned Emma out.

'What was that, babe?'

She was shouting now. 'John, will you marry me?'

For a second I was stunned as I realised where the whole conversation had been leading, but I wasn't stunned for long. Emma is a beautiful, caring woman who just tunes into the way I am. There was only one answer. 'Course I will, darling.'

A crescendo of firing drowned out the conversation again but she'd heard me accept and next trip home, we were married. Mike Curtis was my best man. Who else? So I know from personal experience that the power of love works even in war-shredded Iraq and I'll never forget the day I went down on one knee to take cover for a proposal.

II

OUT-TAKES

It was July 2003 and the people of Baghdad navigated their way around the pools of sewage leaking from cracked pipes in the streets. Down one of those streets a slightly built young man with a thousand-yard stare in his eyes clutched the steering wheel of a truck as he drove it straight towards the concrete 'jersey' blocks barring the way to the Baghdad Hotel.

A first glance would not have revealed that this was a suicide bomber on his route to paradise but a second would have disclosed something very strange about the young man's face. He had a bulldog clip from the end of a set of jump leads, with wires dangling from it, held open between his teeth. The armed Iraqi guard at the hotel checkpoint probably didn't have time to see the bulldog clip but he must have known what was about to happen as the car ignored his signals to stop and kept coming. Later on, eyewitnesses told how the guard pumped several rounds through the windscreen of the truck. The bullets thumped one by one into the driver, and as he died the bulldog clip fell from his mouth. The metal jaws of the clip snapped together in a vicious bite, completing the electrical circuit to the bomb in the truck which would kill six people and savage scores of others.

We felt the earthquake of the downblast under our feet only a second after we heard the massive blast reverberate around the Palestine Hotel. No time to fuck about; we were out of the door, into the car and heading for the Baghdad Hotel. I was with an Irish TV crew and we were first on the scene. The carnage caused by a suicide bomb is difficult to describe. I'm sure you've seen pictures on the news channels – smoke, debris, dust. But seeing it on TV is one thing, being there right in the thick of it is something else.

People were rushing everywhere; victims were staggering about with gaping holes in their clothing and their bodies. The horrible epicentre of it all was a smoking hole which used to be a building full of living, breathing people. It had become a place of screams as those trapped in the rubble wailed in their agony. Some of them were wailing their lives away.

As we got closer we saw bits of the suicide bomber mingled with pieces of his victims. Scraps of flesh were everywhere, fragments of anatomy thrown here and there in a haphazard rearrangement of bodies – a leg here, someone else's foot there. And the smell.

It's not the mouth-filling stench of decomposition. Too soon for that. No, this was different. The air was like that in a slaughterhouse on a busy day. There was the hot steam of eviscerated guts but everywhere too was the metallic scent of blood. It's not just the smell either; you could taste the iron tang of it on the air all around, where the blast had sprayed it like an aerosol.

A small crowd was gathering now but the military and the police hadn't yet arrived. I guessed they were standing back and counting to twenty while they waited to see if there was a second bomb meant for them. The cameraman was struggling to get a clear shot of what was happening over people's shoulders and was being bumped around and jostled. For him it was a nightmare in the midst of a nightmare.

'John! John! I need some height.'

I looked around and homed in on a construction site about seventy metres away, opposite the hotel. There were some workmen standing in front of it obviously in shock and I went over with the camera-man asked if any of them spoke English. One of them nodded and I said, 'Irish television. Can we go up?' He nodded again and we legged it up the open staircase to the second floor. There was a big open square waiting for a window to be fitted on the corner of the building. The cameraman decided it was the spot but he wanted to be back away from the edge for the best shot. I think he wanted the concrete hole to frame the pictures.

I didn't like it. Back in the shadows with a piece of kit over his shoulder he'd look as if he was aiming a rifle or mounting an RPG. 'Come on; move forward to the window,' I told him.

He didn't like that. Let's be fair, he didn't like me and resented taking instructions from me. Why? Well, he was from Ireland, he was a staunch Nationalist and he knew I was ex-SAS; he'd put two and two together and decided I had been involved in anti-IRA operations. Maybe I had, but that was none of his business. I was out there to protect him, end of story. I didn't give a fuck what he thought. He wasn't going to get shot up on my watch if I could help it whether he disliked British soldiers or not. 'Get across to the fucking window,' I snarled. He knew I meant it and moved forward grumbling.

He was standing about five feet back from the window opening facing the hotel. I was at an opening just behind him on the opposite corner to the hotel looking back up the street. Just as he moved a convoy of US Army Humvees came down the road. They had 50 cals mounted on the backs which were being swivelled around in threatening arcs.

I leant out and showed myself, both hands in the air, waving as I shouted, 'Irish film crew!'

Those guys with the big fuck-off 50 cals don't look

at you with their eyes, they look at you with their guns. Where their eyes go the barrels follow, and a couple were trained on me as they sized me up. And their eyes, army-issue Coyote shades, are large, dark and reflective like sinister dragonflies' eyes. Then one of them shouted, 'Okay, man, we got you. You're fine.'

I knew that if the cameraman had stayed back and then been spotted as a shadowy figure those guys on the Humvees would not have hesitated. They would have ripped him apart with lead and he knew it too.

'Enough?' I asked.

'Enough,' he said grudgingly and we went back down to the street outside the blitzed hotel where the correspondent and the interpreter were waiting for us. By now our driver had joined us. It was my old friend Hamdany. You have to understand that these guys are not hired drivers; they come complete with a set of vehicles and are proud businessmen who are well paid for a high-risk job. I admire them and their families and I had great affection for Hamdany in particular.

The correspondent filmed his piece to camera and we decided it was time to go. Almost invariably three phases take place after such atrocities among the survivors and those who come to witness events. The first is trauma brought on by the shock of what has been perpetrated. The second I'll call the post-operative phase, to use the military term, when the need to aid and save the injured and trapped is paramount. The third is anger. This is a real wave of fury that thrashes around looking for somewhere to vent itself and the media is often the target for that frustration. It's quite understandable even if it's not very fair; it's just a variation on the old shooting-the-messenger routine but in this case there's a real danger the messenger will be shot before he's even delivered the message. No surprise then that I always aimed to get my crews out of those situations before phase three kicked off, and usually I did.

But the phases can overlap and that day in Baghdad anger began to spill over while the rescue operations were still underway. A huge crowd of locals was pressing up against the line the military had thrown around the site. Most were people who feared relatives were among the dead or injured in the awful tangle of concrete and metal, and many were hysterical with grief or fear and were becoming hostile.

The cameraman spotted a concrete bus shelter. I knew what was coming. 'John, I need that shot.' Oh shit, I thought, this is borderline phase three and he wants to set up on top of a bus shelter for one last shot. Five minutes felt like five hours, then he was finished and we were moving. He had taken one hell of a risk but I had to admire him.

I had the tripod over my shoulder and a pistol in my belt but no body armour on; we'd left in such a

A routine client pick-up in a low-profile saloon.

A British call sign after an accident on the road. One of the many RTA's that private military contractors are involved in. Even without the insurgents, driving through the desert is a risky business.

The real Desert Storm. More than a decade after the Gulf War and a sandstorm is about to engulf a coalition outpost during an occupation that's been vastly more costly than the 1991 operation.

US armour storming into Fallujah, just forty-eight hours after four American PMC's were killed and mutilated in the city.

American soldiers examine a defused IED. The years of the insurgency have seen the US Army become the most skilled bomb disposal experts in the world.

Another IED, another smoking hole. This one is on the Coalition's designated Main Supply Route near Talil. IED's have claimed more PMC lives than any other insurgents' weapon.

Tak's 4x4 after his battle with insurgents on the road from Kuwait. The bullet holes in the windscreen were made by outgoing rounds as Tak took the fight to the enemy.

The blood of a hero. The running board of Tak's vehicle is covered in blood leaking from his thigh wound. There's a bullet hole there, too, but it's low, proving most insurgents can't shoot for shit.

The 'spot the rock competition'. The guys walked away from the burnt-out wreck of their gun wagon after an IED attack but this dickhead's not convinced.

A typical PMC call sign. There are guys here from around the globe, and from elite units, including the SAS.

One of the three Horsemen of the Apocalypse. Andy is very handy with that Minimi he's holding.

This call sign didn't make it. The guy on the left is covering them, watching their backs as they pick up the pieces.

Four American PMC's died in this burning wreckage in Fallujah. The question is, did the deaths of this call sign signal the infamous first US invasion of the city?

What a lucky man. Call sign medic Mick has three tears in his combat vest – and he's not ripped it on barbed wire.

Peel off a layer and closer examination shows that his body armour has been torn too, by some closely-grouped shots from an AK fired by an insurgent, one who could actually shoot.

LEVEL III

Pull the ceramic plate out of the armour and you can see it stopped the rounds from smashing into his body and almost certainly killing Mick. The lads say he's got the plate framed in pride of place above his mantelpiece.

hurry I'd forgotten it. We pushed the correspondent and the cameraman against a wall and Hamdany put his big arm round me as we formed a scrum to walk back to the vehicle against the human tide still arriving at the scene. The interpreter kept telling people we were Irish TV and that deflected most of them. A few cursed us, some spat. Eventually we got to the car and shoved the crew inside. Someone aimed a blow at me from the crowd. Hamdany deflected it. My hand was on my pistol.

'What a time to forget my body armour,' I said as Hamdany pushed the attacker to one side.

'You are my friend. Today I am your body armour.'

I'll never forget those words and now and then I wonder how he and his family are getting on.

That story of the Baghdad Hotel and the Irish cameraman I was minding contrasts starkly with the tragedy of Mazen Dana, a Reuters news agency cameraman killed by machine-gun fire from a US Bradley fighting vehicle in August 2003. Dana was belly-shot while filming near the notorious Abu Ghraib prison the day after a mortar attack there had malleted six Iraqi civilians. His death led me into a heated debate with a famous British staff correspondent over what he called the 'trigger-happy' military and the 'shit rules of engagement' of the US Army.

Accounts of Dana's death differ in detail and emphasis depending on who you hear it from. Journos tend to play up the fact that twenty minutes or so before he was shot he'd been allowed to film at the prison gates by the military. However, Dana and his soundman then moved a third of a mile away to film the prison from a river bridge. He might have been a world away from his original filming position. Everyone who was there is agreed that Dana and his colleague had called it a day and had packed their kit into the car and driven off towards the Reuters office. Dana then spotted an armoured column coming directly towards him and stopped to film it with the prison in the background. He got out of the vehicle and set up his camera with a built-in microphone as his soundman lit up a fag. Within ten seconds he was clutching his belly and bleeding to death.

What he'd done was jump out of his car, which by the way had no press markings on it, drop to one knee and mount his camera, which was swathed in a dark-blue padded canvas cover, onto his shoulder. This precisely mimics the way an insurgent would mount an anti-tank weapon or RPG onto his shoulder before firing. Add another element, the fact that Mazen Dana, as you have probably guessed from his name, was of Middle Eastern origin – I think he was Palestinian – and you can easily see why he was mistaken for an insurgent.

International journalist groups claim that from fifty metres the camera would have been clearly recognisable. I don't agree. When I took up media protection work in Iraq the possibility of a camera being mistaken for a weapon was one of the most contentious issues. Could a highly trained US soldier really believe a camera was a weapon? I decided to find out for myself by conducting a little experiment. I got a cameraman to kneel behind a low wall with his kit on his shoulder while I paced out fifty metres, a hundred, two hundred. At each distance I spun round as if in a combat situation and I am convinced that I could not have differentiated quickly enough between a camera and say a 66 mm rocket launcher, a Stinger or even a Milan, if my life had depended on it.

Instead of pointing fingers I would ask media people to put themselves in the skin of the nineteen- or twenty-year-old marine on a coaxial machine gun that day at Abu Ghraib. He saw what he took to be a local man hurriedly dismounting from an unmarked car and raising a potential weapon onto his shoulder. At that point his training would have been screaming at him, 'Tank action!' He only has seconds. His vehicle and his pals depend on him for their lives. He fires. An innocent man dies. War is shit.

Every media person I met poured real venom on the US forces for Dana's death and blamed their rules

of engagement for his shooting. It's bollocks. They
seem to believe the media can go to these places with
some force shield around them. Are they so foolish
as to believe a soldier would hesitate and put his own
and his pals' lives at risk? Do they seriously believe
a young soldier will look down his barrel and say to
himself, 'Ah, there's a media cameraman. I'll shoot
him and pretend I thought he had an RPG.'

As I said, it's bollocks. It was Mazen Dana's own
rules of engagement that were at fault and I am
convinced that if he'd had a PMC with him he would
never have been allowed to behave the way he did.

I briefed all the camera crews under my protection to look like what they were and not dress in
paramilitary style – which some dickheads did with
cargo pants tucked into their boots, that sort of thing.
One of my guys used to wear a big floppy hat to
mark himself out as a civilian. I taught them to infiltrate slowly into their filming positions and to be
deliberate in the way they set up the tripod and
camera. They learnt to be aware of what was going
on around them and not just what they saw through
the lens; they learnt to look at troops and make eye
contact and wave at any soldiers they thought hadn't
spotted them – in short anything and everything to
make them stand out as film crew.

During my career I've taken countless risks that
other people might think crazy, but as a soldier you

know that at some point you are going to have to put your life on the line to tip the balance in a battle. Taking a risk for a bit of footage of a Bradley fighting vehicle trundling past a prison was foolish but I'm sorry he had to pay for it with his life. His colleagues should learn from it, not whinge and blame.

I'd worked with the media a couple of times in the 1990s, long before my experiences with them in Iraq, when Mike Curtis and I were out of the Regiment and up for adventures. The first time was when a mate from the *Daily Express* called us. Could we give them a hand?

This was a celebrated case of two British nurses held in a Saudi jail for eighteen months for allegedly killing their flatmate, another UK nurse called Yvonne Gilford. Deborah Parry had been sentenced to public execution and Lucille McLauchlan to 500 lashes and imprisonment The two had been pardoned by the Saudi king and released, and were jetting into Gatwick the following day. There was bound to be a bunfight at the airport, he said, and they needed some professional help. He introduced us to John Coles, the *Express* reporter in charge of the job, and off we went.

Well, there was a bunfight and the nurse in our charge, Debbie Parry, was photographed immediately we left the terminal and fought our way to a waiting

Range Rover. We were tailed to London but we slipped into a private car park, got a mate's wife to dress up in Debbie's clothing and leave in the Range Rover with the press pack pursuing her. Meanwhile we wanted to put Debbie into the boot of a Golf GTI to smuggle her out of the underground garage but she was too nervous to get in.

'Don't worry, lovely, I'll get in there with you,' said Mike.

The sight of the two of them curled up there in the boot, the burly ex-SAS man and the tiny nurse, was unforgettable. First the princess, now the nurse; Mike just seemed to be cuddling up in the line of duty all the time. Anyway, we gave the rest of the pack the slip, got our nurse to a nice country hotel in Wiltshire and the *Daily Express* was able to interview and photograph her at its leisure. The *Daily Mirror* had the other nurse but they were under siege by the rest of Fleet Street for days. For what it's worth, I thought Debbie had been well and truly set up by the Saudis just so they could write off the murder as solved and not have to bring a Saudi citizen to trial.

The other media job was for the *News of the World* but it's one I look back on with a mixture of sadness and fond memories of an old mate. We were asked to look after George Best in the days immediately before and after his liver transplant. I'd got to know George well through his long-time agent Phil Hughes and it was Phil who suggested our names to the *News of the World*. George was pleased to have us on his team because of our friendship. I'd often have a drink with him and Phil in a private gentlemen's club in the West End of London. Mike particularly loved Bestie's company because he has two passions in his life. The first, which generally eclipses everything else, is the Welsh rugby team; the second is Manchester United and George was one of Mike's heroes.

Bestie was ferociously competitive and a phenomenally good snooker player as well as a soccer genius. He was always up for a challenge and I'm not ashamed to say that I once lost a bottle of champagne to him in a bet over the snooker table. I'm not ashamed to have lost the game but on reflection I'm perhaps less proud of the fact that I used to drink with him. I was probably doing him no favours but then, what the hell, he was a grown man.

He looked like shit when he went in for that life-saving operation but when Mike and I went to get him afterwards he was full of hope and resolution. It's a shame he couldn't keep up his resolve to bin the booze. George Best would certainly have lived longer if he'd laid off it but no one can say he didn't live his life to the full.

Those jobs were an introduction to the madness of the press and the frantic lives they lead. I love some of the characters I've met through the media but in a war zone they can drive you nuts. The problem is that many of them, particularly photographers and cameramen, think they are bomb- and bulletproof. They look at the world through a lens. As far as I can make out they believe they are detached from the events going on around them and so take bloody stupid risks that a professional soldier would never expose himself to. They are voyeurs who believe in their own immortality and that makes them hard to look after.

Businessmen just want to get to the job or project they're involved in quickly and safely. Journalists are the same except with them the job is the war and they want to see it. They want to get to the action, so looking after them is a very tricky balancing act. It's particularly difficult when their bosses have a strict no-guns policy.

Most big US media corporations have a very businesslike attitude to guns and travel in well coordinated columns with enough firepower to fight off any large insurgent ambush. Sometimes, when it suited my purposes and usually when I was in a hurry, I would tag onto the end of a big media convoy bound for a bombing or a shooting. At the other end of the spectrum, the BBC now has its own hostile environment security team. It comprises some top operators led by an ex-special forces officer. They have a no-weapons policy because the Beeb sticks to the notion that a journalist must remain neutral if he or she is to report a situation fairly. I don't know if those Beeb protection guys could suddenly conjure a gun out of a hat like a magician's rabbit if they needed to but I do know that I would not like to be responsible for a media team in the Iraqi situation without a gun in my hand.

I remember as a kid looking at replays of those old newsreel films taken during the Second World War with correspondents like Wynford Vaughan Thomas and Richard Dimbleby, who hit the D-Day beaches with the troops. Everyone seems to think embedded correspondents are something new on the scene, but those blokes weren't just embedded they were trusted to bring news from the front without subjecting the troops to a politically correct analysis of every action they took. War is not some sanitised bloodless exercise; it's fierce bloodletting where kill or be killed is the norm.

Moreover, the nature of war has changed with the emergence of Islamic fighters who not only don't heed the rules of the Geneva Convention but despise those conventions and the world order that created them. It is their often stated aim to topple that order and create a new Islamic world which they call the Global Caliphate. Article 79 of Protocol I of the Geneva Convention states: 'Journalists engaged in dangerous professional missions in areas of armed conflict shall be considered as civilians and they shall be protected as such.' These words have a nice ring to them but don't mean jack shit in downtown Fallujah; the only protection a journalist has in modern Iraq is his wit and a man like me watching his back with a gun.

In 2005 one American print journalist based in Baghdad, a *New York Times* staffer called Dexter Filkins, brought the whole debate out into the open when he openly carried a pistol on his assignments. There was a lot of soul-searching and hand-wringing in media circles along 'Should we, shouldn't we?' lines. Many journalists argued that membership of the profession was their best defence. An armed press is a vulnerable press which has joined rather than is observing hostilities, they said. How could an armed reporter argue that he's not a spy or a combatant? But that's what radical Islamists are going to call any captured reporter whatever his views and the fate of American reporter Daniel Pearl is a case in point. He was kidnapped by a fundamentalist gang in Pakistan and beheaded in 2002. His killers claimed Pearl was a spy. Well made arguments about his journalistic impartiality didn't count for a thing among his captors. Theirs is a different world with different values and they recognise nothing of our world as being of any value or honour.

I've never met Dexter Filkins but he must be a realist who worked out the odds for himself. He made a rational appraisal of the men out there in Iraq just waiting for people like him to fall into their hands. He weighed up the risks and thought that shooting it out would be a better option than beheading after a period of terrifying and humiliating capture. In my opinion he's absolutely correct. I take my hat off to him with one proviso: I hope he knows how to shoot straight and handle his weapon safely while in the company of his friends and allies.

There was also another tragedy that opens up all the arguments about being armed and the way the media operates in a war zone and it involved one of the most respected British TV correspondents to die on the front line in recent years.

Terry Lloyd was ITN's longest-serving correspondent when he died during the official war in March 2003. He was a veteran of several conflicts and a man of proven courage loved for his cheerful outlook on life and admired for his unyielding professionalism.

The circumstances of his death and those of his crew cameraman Fred Nerac and translator Hussein Othman are complicated. They were in a two-car convoy of 4 x 4s with Nerac and Othman in one vehicle while Lloyd and French cameraman Daniel

Demoustier were in the other with Demoustier, the only survivor, at the wheel. Both cars were clearly marked as TV vehicles. They were near Az Zubayr and being pursued by Iraqi troops. Demoustier thought the Iraqis may have been trying to give themselves up to the journalists. Subsequent events show the reverse was probably true. In any event they took incoming rounds, possibly from US troops ahead of them as well as the Iraqis behind. They were quite clearly caught in crossfire and an ITN investigation later concluded that the Iraqis had been trying to capture the media team to use as a shield when they ran into the Americans.

Lloyd and Demoustier's car went into a ditch and burst into flames. When he looked across the cabin of the 4 x 4 Demoustier saw the passenger seat empty and the door wide open. The Frenchman was hurt but managed to escape and was picked up by another media crew who sped off with him. At this point he saw Nerac and Othman being taken out of their vehicle alive and well by Iraqi soldiers. He never saw Lloyd again. Later, US troops said they had fired on vehicles marked 'TV' which were among Iraqi troops as they feared suicide bombers may have been using the vehicles.

Six months later, a local civilian emerged to say that he had been driving some Iraqi soldiers to hospital in a civilian minibus and he had picked up

Terry Lloyd, who was wounded in the shoulder and pretending to be a Russian journalist possibly to protect himself. Lloyd, he said, was actually killed when a US helicopter gunship strafed his bus. The Iraqi had taken his body on to hospital in Basra. Eventually a post-mortem in the UK showed Terry Lloyd had two wounds either of which could have been fatal. One was from an Iraqi round, the other from a US bullet. It seems Nerac and Othman may have been handed over to the fedayeen and shot out of hand. The fedayeen went on to become the core of the Ba'athist insurgency in the months and years after the war ended.

I found myself in a ruck with an ITN correspondent just a few months after Terry's death that went along roughly the same lines as my argument over the death of Mazen Dana. The scars of loss and mourning for their hero Terry were still fresh for ITN staffers and one of them, another well-known face on British television, was trying to give me a beasting over his death.

'You military,' he said, 'you're all the fucking same. Trigger-happy fuckers. Terry should never have died. He should never have been shot. His car was clearly marked with "TV" all over it. Then he was finished off in a civilian bus. It's obscene.'

He was right, war is obscene. I wasn't particularly looking for an argument but I couldn't let what he had said go unchallenged. I told him then and I say it again now: Terry Lloyd and his crew should never have been in that position during a full-on battle. Not only that, they should never have been in the field without a PMC team to advise and protect them. The truth is that they made themselves hostages to fortune by making up their own rules of engagement on the hoof. I never met him but if he could speak I believe Terry Lloyd would probably acknowledge that he pushed his luck and it ran out.

I don't care how experienced a correspondent is in front-line coverage, he is not a soldier and he cannot fully understand why events take the turns they do or what propels the course of battle. It's tough enough for a battle-hardened soldier to work out and only the best can really see much at all through the fog of war. I'm not saying that if I had been there they'd have all lived but I am saying that I doubt whether they'd have got caught in that lethal crossfire in the first place.

The fury of ITN staff and executives is futile. Do they think that an Apache helicopter pilot can't spot men in military uniform clambering into a civilian vehicle? Do they think it's impossible for a helo pilot, looking through enhanced sights, to see military uniforms through the side windows of a bus? I've not had the benefit of speaking to the Iraqi who picked up Terry Lloyd but he's a very lucky man because in my experience when an attack helicopter turns its attention to a target it's almost inevitably curtains. Just a single burst from their least powerful machine gun will rip a vehicle into a blazing wreck and shred everything inside it.

Terry Lloyd was moving independently across the battlefield – they call it 'busking it' in the media – and in such a situation you cannot expect dreadful things not to happen. What you can do is pay him proper respect, mourn him and learn from his death.

It seems that in the confusion of battle both sides fired at a civilian vehicle, but bleating about which of two bullets killed him and who was more responsible is a fruitless exercise. I believe his superiors would do better to reflect upon whether they should have allowed him to go where he did in the first place without military experts at his side. It's impossible to say what might have happened if they'd had some top PMCs guarding them but I have a strong feeling that the pursuing Iraqis would not have been chasing a 4 x 4 capable of returning accurate fire.

I'm sure that privately his company has learnt the lesson of Terry Lloyd's death. ITN has now decreed that crews should never travel without experienced military operators watching their backs. If that alone is his legacy it is worthwhile. I know for a fact that

some of the colleagues who followed Terry had their
lives preserved by the actions of their PMC call signs.

A note of advice to wannabe war reporters

The most basic advice I'd offer to any journalist going
to a place like Iraq for the first time is to think very
hard about whether it is the right thing for them to
do at all. We've all got different personalities and
some people will never settle into any sort of comfortable existence within a war zone. If you're not
absolutely certain then my advice is don't go. There
is no shame whatsoever in saying you don't want to
put your life on the line and turning down a war zone
assignment. However it is a shame if when you get
there you are in such a state of fear that you become
a burden and a danger to your colleagues. Chris Ayres,
the *Times* journalist, wrote a hilarious account of his
unwilling days as a war paralysed with fear in Iraq
in 2003. *War Reporting for Cowards* describes the
experience perfectly and it's worth a read.

If you do decide to accept a war zone assignment
there are a number of things you should then address.
The first is to go on a good course which will at least
give you an introduction to military jargon and the
world of the PMC. More importantly you will also
be subjected to simulated attacks and this will introduce you to the shocking flash-bang world of the

terrorist ambush in a controlled environment. It's never like the real thing but it could save your life as the instructor runs you through the options.

You'll be taught how to survive if you're separated from your team during an encounter and given some basic advice on keeping your wits about you if you're captured. You will also learn how to use a GPS navigation system and basic radio communications and signals protocols. Situation awareness is very important in a hostile environment like Iraq. You'll be taught how to recognise the particular threats of different situations such as the approaching flashpoint of an angry crowd or the hostile driving that marks out the insurgent pursuing you. Then there's how to recognise an IED (improvised explosive device), very important knowledge if you want to avoid having your arse blown over your head. Off-road driving and a few escape driving techniques are also useful skills to have in your locker and it's well worth learning some of the tricks.

A vital part of any good course is trauma medicine. If you are attacked when you get to Iraq you may not have the skills to fight back but you can learn how to staunch and dress a bleeding wound. That way you may save a life and you won't feel like you've been a burden during combat. This training ensures you will be a useful member of the team above and beyond your media skills.

I now run training courses for PMCs and also put on courses tailored to businessmen and journalists through my company. We do a lot of work in the UK but also travel to Eastern Europe where we're allowed to do live fire training with AKs and machine guns. Naturally I think my course is the best available, but there are others out there offering similar comprehensive war zone training and a couple of them are run by excellent men with a similar background to my own. Such courses are vital if you're serious about surviving a war zone assignment. Look for a proper course run by professionals and certified by the official watchdog, the Security Industry Authority.

The next thing you should do is to check your insurance situation and make sure your company has you adequately covered for combat situations. This is particularly important for freelance journalists, who may be sent out somewhere to cover for a large company, but aren't insured by that company's own scheme.

Check your blood group and have it dog-tagged with any other relevant medical information and keep the tag around your neck. If you're going to a country where HIV is prevalent you can get an AIDS pack with needles, lines, etc. to use if you are wounded so that you can avoid local, possibly contaminated hospital gear.

Most media people do their background briefing in detail and will have boned up on a country's politics, geography and culture before they get to the airport but remember to think about surrounding countries. Get entry visas for as many of the neighbouring states as you can. They could prove lifesavers if you have to pull off a hurried exit and you never know when a situation is going to spill over and you find the story has moved across a border.

The best journalists I know have their entire kit, including clothing and laptop, in one bag which they can take on board a plane as hand luggage. Cameramen sometimes book an extra seat so their kit doesn't go in the hold. When these men and women arrive at an assignment they're not watching luggage go round a carousel for an hour; they hit the ground running. So an important rule is to always travel light.

These days a satellite telephone is a must, and in Iraq it can be used to help you get good intelligence from US troops. No subterfuge here; you just work on the fact that they are likely to be homesick and a free call home to their family in the States is going to make you a helpful friend. A more primitive intelligence-gathering tool is a six-pack of beer. Remember, the US Army runs dry; in other words they don't let their boys drink until they're officially on leave. I've found a few cans of beer or a phone call home can be traded for vital information and the supplies and ammo I need. It worked a treat every time.

August 19, 2003. A terrible scene of carnage and a turning point in the escalating insurgency in Iraq. The UN building in Baghdad lay obliterated in front of me when I arrived at the scene with a UK television crew.

When I look back at that moment I realise it wasn't just a turning point in the war but a moment of revelation for those who had not understood that the al Qaeda psychopaths responsible for this outrage were operating in the dark forests beyond the walls of civilisation. If they could hit the personnel of the organisation of world governance and peace they could hit anyone.

And hit them they did, a suicide bomber detonating a cement truck filled with explosives parked right opposite the window of the UN special representative Sergio Vieira de Melo. The special representative died along with twenty-one other UN workers and scores were injured as their headquarters building, the old Hotel Canal, was obliterated. The place was chaos with UN officials staggering around injured or blast-shocked. A lot of local people had found work with the organisation as interpreters, secretaries, cleaners, you name it, and crowds of relatives rushed to be there when word got out.

Such situations are difficult to gauge because there's always the danger of a second device. My inclination would always be to sit in a cosy spot half a mile away sipping on a brew of tea waiting to see if there was going to be a second explosion. But life's not like that and the crew need to film what's in front of them for a piece, so you just get on with it. More and more people were arriving at the scene and I can remember there was a great deal of emotion in the crowd, more so than usual. I think the ordinary Iraqis looking on felt a great chunk of hope slipping away with the destruction of the UN headquarters. They'd always seen the UN as an acceptable middle way between the US and the madmen.

Strange atmospheres develop in other ways at these scenes of annihilation and as the emergency services settled into the long slog of digging casualties out of the wreckage the media crews sat back to wait for developments. They were hoping for shots of survivors coming out of the rubble, back from the brink of death. Meanwhile life goes on, and food and drink vendors began to turn up at the scene offering their wares to the media waiting behind a tape cordon. People began chatting just to pass the time away and I made contact with PMCs guarding other call signs.

Bizarre as it may seem, a sort of barbecue atmosphere developed. It was surreal. There in front of us was unfolding a human and international catastrophe and we were shooting the breeze about old times, other jobs and people we knew in common. The press and media guys tell me it's something that happens all the time. They end up at bombings and sieges and there's nothing to do but kill time. So what do they do? Do they stand there in silence out of respect for those who have died or who are suffering or do they chat? They chat.

Like I said, food vendors set up little stalls and there were soon chicken dishes and hot coffee. There was chatting and food and the only way I can describe it is to liken it to a barbecue.

It wasn't long before the street kids started turning up. There are hundreds of them in Baghdad. Some were orphaned by Saddam or one of his wars, others by Coalition bombing. Still others have families but have been kicked out because they simply can't be looked after. We saw a lot of them because they'd hang around the hotels too, scrounging food and generally grifting and working the street to survive. They would move from one opportunity to another and were always on the lookout for a dollar or a can of Coke. When they rocked up at the UN bombing we knew their faces and just fed them. They didn't beg. They were there, we had food and we shared it with them. It was as simple as that.

Most of those I saw around were solvent addicts.

You would see their noses streaming and their eyes ringed red against their brown faces turned a puce green from the glue. There was a real Dickens feel to the plight of these children. I always thought of them as local versions of Oliver Twist. One of them had a strange name that we sort of translated into David. I liked him. There was something about him and every trip to Baghdad I'd slip him twenty bucks, but I'd made him agree to give up the glue.

'I will do it, Mr John,' he told me. 'I do not like it anyway.'

'Okay,' I said. 'It's good you don't like it because it will kill you.'

'Aah,' he said gravely, 'but what will kill you, Mr John?'

A good question, I thought, but one I couldn't answer. He'd go off with his money and the next time I saw David he would show me some clothes or maybe a pair of trainers he'd bought with the money.

'I have a family but they do not like me,' David told me once. 'If I go home they send me away. They have no money to feed me.'

I didn't know what to tell him about his family. What could I say about the fact they'd pushed their son out onto the street? I simply didn't know what they had to cope with. David saw I was uncomfortable with the subject and beamed as he told me, 'Don't worry, Mr John. One day I will have four or five big four by four trucks from the General Motor Company and I will hire them to the film crews. I will be very rich and I will have my own family.'

He was there that day at the UN building with the rest of the feral kids and I wondered then what would become of him and his mates. I hoped David would make something of himself. Maybe, just maybe, he would get his fleet of 4 x 4s. But where would the media crews be then? Still in Iraq or maybe they'd have moved on to Pakistan or Indonesia. Who knows where this madness in the world will take them?

Those Baghdad kids were the news the press never wrote about, the tragedy the TV crews never filmed. The story was right under their noses but they never saw it. In many ways it is one of the most important stories in Iraq, where children have suffered so much.

12

RESPECT

REMEMBER, remember the fifth of November. It was a blazing hot desert afternoon on the road from Kuwait to Basra, a far cry from the cold mists and the early fall of darkness in Britain on Bonfire Night, and the acrid smell of explosives didn't come from sparklers and rockets. Two ex-Blades were driving a pair of brand-new GMC four-wheel drives back to their FOB (forward operating base) after dropping two clients off in Kuwait City. An hour later there would be four Iraqi insurgents lying dead on the roadside with no memory of the fireworks they should never have started on that day in 2003.

The four BSIs in a beat-up old Mercedes decided it was their lucky day when they spotted the two smart 4 x 4s in convoy through the unrelenting landscape of shattered rocks. They decided to split the pair up and mallet the man in the second vehicle. Bad decision.

The Blade in the first 4 x 4 was a Welsh bloke

called Darren who's a great guy and a really hard
case; on his own he would have been more than a
match for those four and another lot like them. But
the guy in the car the BSIs were targeting was something else. It was being driven by a living legend of
the SAS, a man whose exploits are feted throughout the world community of special forces. He's a
Fijian known as Tak and he was about to become
their nemesis. Picture a muscular broad-shouldered
Polynesian warrior who's polite, softly spoken and
invariably gentle with his family and friends. But
when his fighting blood is roused Tak is the most
terrible of enemies.

Tak told me about the contact himself. It was one
of the most spectacular pieces of close-quarter
combat I've heard of involving a PMC in Iraq and I
really can't do better than let him narrate it in his
own words . . .

*You know what it's like, John. I was a bit uncom-
fortable with the company's operating procedures and
I was thinking of quitting and looking for someone
else to work for. I didn't like the business of driving
alone in Iraq. You need someone with you because
you can't shoot if you need to with your hands on
the wheel. I thought it was a bad risk. I didn't like
the soft-skin four by fours either and we had crap
weapons and no body armour had been supplied.*

Anyway, we'd dropped the clients off in Kuwait and we were going back into Iraq for another assignment. At the time we were spending a couple of days resting in Kuwait then we'd go back in and hold the ground for five or six days. We went up the Mutla Pass where the old border post is situated and then we drove off down Highway Tampa into Iraq. I thought we'd vary the journey so I called Darren on the radio and suggested we take the old route that runs parallel to Tampa. Basically we were leaving the motorway to drive on a trunk road. Darren took the lead. It was about three thirty in the afternoon. There's a lot of nothing out there but we'd got well on the way and we had about half an hour of the trip left to do. We were near the oil fields that stretch out towards Kuwait from Basra and I could see the installations on the horizon.

Then we came to a part of the road that does a big S-bend around a burnt-out Gulf War T42 battle tank. The road doubles round the tank then over a bridge above the highway. At that point there's a steep dirt track that serves as an unofficial slip road between the trunk route and the highway. A car came up the bank on the track and joined the road ahead of us. Darren went past them and they pulled in and stopped to watch me go past. I tried to look into the car to see if there were any weapons in evidence but I couldn't see anything. Then they started off again and went past me before slowing right down. I came up behind them and as I went to overtake they suddenly veered out in front of me and forced me to throttle back and fall in behind them again. I thought I'd just give them the benefit of the doubt and tried to overtake them again.

This time there wasn't any doubt about it; they didn't bother with the swerving nonsense, they just fired a burst from an AK in front of me and I realised I was on the menu. I dropped back behind them again and I could see AKs popping up everywhere inside their vehicle. Not good.

One option would have been to ram them. As you know, John, we're taught certain ramming techniques in the Regiment that would have spun them. That would have been great if Darren had been sitting next to me ready to shoot them up as soon as I'd done it. Basically that would have been game over, but he wasn't with me so I decided that ramming wasn't an option. Instead I just whipped the wheel over and off into the desert and drove across the rocks and sand about fifteen metres parallel with them. That didn't last long though because there were lots of rocks and though it looked a bit clearer further over I reckon my wheels would have gone down into the sand.

I was really concentrating on the driving and cursing the company for their crap one-per-vehicle

policy when suddenly I saw a ridge of rocks ahead
of me that I couldn't drive over. I wasn't going
anywhere. I stopped and when I looked up I thought,
Shit! There standing in front of me were three of the
bastards from the car. They'd obviously shot ahead
at speed on the tarmac road while I was concen-
trating on not smashing the vehicle up on the desert.
Then they must have just run across when they saw
where I was going to have no choice but to stop.

I forgot to say that they weren't just standing
there nonchalantly; they were firing their weapons
from the hip too. There were AK rounds going every-
where but none of them were actually hitting me.
I'd pulled up on an angle so most of the rounds
were going in on the passenger side. I had an MP5,
a pistol and a AK on the floor behind my seat. The
MP5 is fine for close-quarter work – it's shorter than
an AK – so I just fired a burst through the wind-
screen at them. I don't think they realised I'd fired
at them they were so busy doing their own thing,
and they were making so much noise they probably
never heard my burst. Maybe they thought it was
their rounds that were hitting my screen. They just
kept coming towards me firing from the hip.

I don't know why but then it just came to me. I
dropped the gun onto my lap and put my hands up
as if I was surrendering. They stopped shooting. They
were right in front of my bonnet by then. They must

*have thought I'd given up and for an instant they
stopped firing. It was all I needed. Just that fraction
of a second. A hesitation. It was just a blink of time
and they probably did blink too, but by the time they
had the MP5 was back in my hands again. I fired
through the screen and this time two of them
dropped. I can remember how they looked. Really
surprised. Like, what the hell's happening – this is
all going wrong.*

*They were wearing long gowns, local style. I think
one of them had a shemag wrapped around his head.
They just fell down when they were hit. But the third
one was standing to one side of my car at an awkward
angle and he was still firing. He looked desperate
because he'd seen his mates slotted and he knew what
had to happen.*

*I was out of the car as quick as I could and
straight at him. I could see the fear in his eyes
because he'd seen his mates slotted and he wasn't
feeling such a tough guy any more. But I knew there
was no fear in mine. His eyes told the story. He was
desperate and he knew it was him or me. We both
knew that.*

*As I came round the front of the car I hit him
with a shot from the MP5 but he was still standing
with his AK and he was firing but I think he was so
scared he was shooting wildly and not hitting me. I
was on him before he knew it and then I smashed*

*him with my weapon. I don't know why. I think I'd
run out of ammo and I didn't have time to put
another magazine in. I knew I had to get that AK
off him and I think it was while I was clubbing him
that a round went off from his weapon and hit me
in the thigh. At that stage he'd been so badly clubbed
that I don't think he even knew he was shooting. He
was in bad shape by that time so I wrestled the gun
off him and finished him with his own AK. Then I
walked back to meet Darren, who'd just slotted the
driver of the car and was coming to help me.*

*He drove me to the military hospital in Basra and
I was eventually flown back to the UK. Luckily it
was just a flesh wound or I'd have been in big trouble.
Those assault rounds from an AK will track right
through your body if they hit bone. It's fine now. I've
been wounded a couple of times before and I've been
quite lucky really.*

When he'd given me his account Tak smiled and said,
'They got me in the head as well, John.'

'What do you mean?' I asked.

'Well, quite a few rounds smacked into my bag,
which was on the passenger seat beside me, and one
of them hit me right in my passport photograph. I
had to go down to the passport office in Newport
to get a new one and when I told the girl at the
counter what had happened she asked me, "Is that

what saved you then?" I just told her, "I don't think so. I really don't think so.'"

That's Tak's story but there's more. He's the sort of bloke who should have his history in a laser show above his head. That way the local scumbags would give him a wide berth and live to fight another day. He was one of the team that stormed the Iranian embassy when those images of the SAS at work went round the world and made the Regiment internationally famous. The operation was courageous, cool, super-efficient and very public. But the embassy was not his finest hour because Tak was also one of the heroes of the battle of Mirbat. That's the battle of Mirbat in Oman, not to be confused with the skirmish at the Hotel Murbad in Basra.

It happened in 1972 and was one of the most gallant stands ever made by the British Army. It was at dawn on 19 July that a nine-strong SAS detachment, under the command of Captain Mike Kealy, fought off 400 Adoo rebels who'd come down from the hills to attack the port of Mirbat in Dhofar province.

The SAS patrol bunkered up in a house near the strategic Wali Fort on a hill above the town and fought off wave after wave of Adoo. Tak's fellow Fijian Sergeant Talaiasi Labalaba ran 500 metres to a gun pit at the fort, where he manned an old Second World War twenty-five pounder artillery piece. Scores of rebel fighters threw themselves at the fort as both SAS machine guns fired until their barrels were literally white hot, while in the gun pit Labalaba kept firing shells at zero trajectory straight into the oncoming rebels until he was wounded. At this point Tak went to his aid, running a gauntlet of tracer bullets and mortar shells to dive and roll into the gun pit.

He found Labalaba still firing the big gun and Tak helped him man the weapon. Tak was also hit but kept firing as the rebels reached the edge of the gun pit, when Labalaba was hit in the neck and killed. A few more of the boys arrived to help in the gun pit and they were about to be overrun when twenty-two members of G Squadron stormed in by helo. The rebels were then driven back with the help of air support. The battle had lasted six hours and around eighty-seven Adoo rebels were dead.

When it ended, Tak, severely wounded in the back, walked calmly to the helicopter to be lifted out when most men would have collapsed. His friend lay dead in the gun pit behind him and no one in the Regiment doubts that both Fijians should have been awarded the VC. Forget the Alamo. Davy Crockett got malleted there but when Mirbat ended Tak and most of the boys were still standing and they'd been fighting against the same sort of odds. About forty to one.

One more thing you should know about Tak: when

he killed those three BSIs on Bonfire Night 2003 he was fifty-eight years old. In December 2005, at the age of sixty, he enrolled on my course because new regulations meant he had to have a diploma to be employed as a PMC. Imagine trying to teach a man like him about tactical awareness and close quarter combat!

After that contact on the Route Jackson some of the guys joked that Tak had been on his way to Basra to collect an Iraqi bus pass when he was ambushed. What a phenomenal man.

There are some other people whose work in Iraq I respect. Among them are three young guys whose exploits have earned them the scary title the Horsemen of the Apocalypse. They got the name because of the sheer number of contacts they've survived and the large number of insurgents they've killed in these encounters. I'll call them Andy, Mel and Cules. I feel particularly smug about the Horsemen because I actually trained them on my first course in August 2004 then waved them off to Iraq. Mel and Cules were both I Para and served in Sierra Leone with my son Kurt. Andy was SAS Signals and when he left the army he did a variety of barmy jobs including a spell as a professional bare-knuckle cage fighter in the West Country. He's a hard case.

They'd only been out there a couple of weeks before they were in a scrape, and that set the tone for the lads, who were involved in shoot-outs and bombings with a regularity that was anything but monotonous. They tot up contacts with insurgents like other people tot up speeding points on their driving licences and to date I think they've been blown up four times (or should I say there have been four attempts to blow them up) and have been in over a dozen firefights. They've had four or five vehicles totalled and still emerged from the scrap alive, well and triumphant. Some people think they're indestructible and I really hope they are.

It was the Horsemen who got into that sad shoot-out with the lone insurgent against the Apache I mentioned at the end of chapter five, but they've had some really wild flash-bang fights too, and one of them was a police matter. It was October 2004 and they were on a routine trip north of Baghdad – if there is such a thing as routine in that corner of the planet – in three armoured 4 x 4s with a gun vehicle in the rear. They were on their way to collect a couple of clients. An unusually hot wind was blowing off the desert that day which had left everyone tetchy and short-tempered. That's how they felt when they arrived at a police road check on the outskirts of a one-mule town but they were going to get a lot more tetchy in the hour that followed.

They pulled up and went into the usual routine of showing their passes to the cops. There's always a lot of eyeballing in these situations. To be honest you find yourself looking into the eyes of everyone you meet in Iraq. You look for the slightest sign of hatred or unease that might tell you something is going down. It becomes a way of life. The Horsemen said later that they'd smelt a rat at that roadblock but they'd driven on anyway because that's what you do – keep going forward. When they went into the town, which I can't name for a couple of reasons, they thought it looked a bit deserted to say the least and they got that Clint Eastwood tumbleweed feeling. This became acute when they saw a group of police officers scuttle into their barracks on the high street as soon as their convoy came into view.

'See those fuckers,' Andy called over the radio.

'Yup,' came the reply from Cules.

'Heads up,' said Andy and they all knew what was coming.

Whak! Whak! Whak!

Heavy machine-gun rounds started thumping into the ground to their right soon joined by the chipping, flinty kicks of lighter rounds. A few smacked into the vehicles and the lads immediately pinged the source of the shooting and returned fire. Mel and Cules unsealed their vehicle and sprinted into a building as the Minimi in the gun vehicle roared a chainsaw reply to the ambush. They were looking for a vantage point to pour shit into their attackers but ran into fire from the back of the building itself.

Back onto the street. Pandemonium. A full-scale battle ensued with the guys smacking rounds into any bastard with a gun who dared give away his position. Six or seven of the insurgents were dead or wounded but there were others still firing away and the lads hadn't been able to take out the enemy machine gun although they had it well suppressed. Time to fuck off and leave the Minimi to say their final farewells.

'Oh fuck my old boots!' Cules was watching the literally depressing sight of the back wheel of the gun vehicle deflating while rounds kept chipping and cracking all around them. It was in rags.

'Bollocks!' Mel had spotted it too.

'Cover me!' shouted Cules. 'I'll sort the fucking thing out!'

'What you gonna do?'

'Change the fucking thing of course.'

Mel shrugged and kept up his fusillade of well-placed shots as he joined the others keeping the enemy fire suppressed. That's the name of the game. Win the firefight; outshoot the fuckers. Don't give them the time to aim. You don't need the time to aim; they do.

Cules had the jack and the spare wheel deployed from the back of the vehicle and was winding the wheel nuts off in record time. Forget those guys in Formula 1 pits. Sure, they're really quick but I won't rate them until I know how fast they can do it under fire. The Horsemen estimate their record stands at about six minutes under continuous fire – and that was just two men remember. Perhaps there's a challenge there somewhere but somehow I can't see the Ferrari team taking it up.

Cules slammed the fresh wheel on, screwed on the nuts in a way that suggested his life actually did depend on it then dropped the jack under the vehicle and chucked it into the back of the gun wagon before hurling the flat tyre in alongside it.

'Get that fucking thing out,' yelled Gus, the man on the Minimi, as the tyre slammed into his weapon and threw it off target, sending rounds tearing down the high street just past Cules's shoulder. Cules grabbed the wheel back and this time tossed it up onto the big metal rack on top of the vehicle where it slid around as they roared out of town and carried on towards the FMB (Forward Mounting Base).

By now the incoming was thinning out under the sheer weight of fire from the call sign but to drive on through the town would have been a bad move.

Tikrit is Saddam's hometown. It's where his clan live; it's the heart of his old power base and it's full of Ba'ath Party pigs who fed at the trough of his regime while the rest of the people suffered. It's not a place where you'd want to buy a timeshare.

The Horsemen were driving through one day and found themselves bowling along the long straight piece of dual carriageway on the eastern side of the city. They'd been shuttling clients around the area for most of the day in armoured 4 x 4s and as you can imagine they were on a high state of alert. As they rattled down the carriageway at speed Cules noticed an old white Japanese saloon stationary at a strange angle, about the width of a car out from the pavement. Its position gave it a view straight down the road for at least half a mile and the lads immediately pinged it as suspicious. Not only that but one of them, sharp as fuck, had noticed it earlier in the day.

'Same car as this morning,' he sang out on the radio.

No doubt then that this was a dicker's car and the way it was lined up suggested there was more to come. A lot more. 'Dicker' is the old British Army slang term for an IRA spotter in Northern Ireland. Then they saw another, dark saloon parked by the side of the road on a long empty stretch with nothing next to it but a length of two-metre-high concrete wall. Why would someone park there? What were they doing? Visiting a section of wall? Don't think so.

The thoughts went through Mel's mind in a rapid-fire calculation and then a couple of voices came to the same inevitable conclusion voiced over the radio at the same time: 'Kamikaze!'

Simultaneously the rear gunner spotted a gunman on high ground to the right and began firing burst after burst. A split second later their front windscreen was crazed by the massive orange flash of an explosion as the car bomb to their right was detonated and the dark saloon erupted.

Cules was at the wheel and won the battle to keep the car on the road then drove it right out of the killing ground of the ambush. Incoming fire poured in but even though they'd just driven straight through a bomb the guys had the presence of mind to ping the firing positions of the enemy.

'Right! Right! Right!' Andy screamed, and concentrated bursts of fire poured from the vehicle that the insurgents had hoped would be a mangled wreck full of shattered bodies. Wrong. The Horsemen rode on and they reckon four insurgents were killed or wounded in their return of fire. This contact was all the more remarkable because the whole thing was filmed by one of those dashboard cameras that UK traffic cops use.

Two of the Horsemen are still riding the Highway but Cules decided to call it a day and I asked him why when I next saw him. 'It's not that I'm scared or anything, John,' he said. 'I really can't put my finger on it but I think it's just that I've had enough of being blown up all the time.' Fair point. The Horsemen have my respect and admiration but there are others who didn't make it and I salute them too.

May 2005 and a convoy in western Iraq is hit by the al Qaeda group Ansar al Sunna. It is an effective ambush and one of the guys is cut off from the rest. Outnumbered and surrounded he is held at gunpoint as the convoy limps away leaving him to his fate as the clients' lives are given priority. The Ansar al Sunna men must have thought they were in for some hostage fun, but this was no ordinary man. This was Akihiko Saito, a modern Samurai who had served in the Japanese paras before enlisting in the French Foreign Legion.

The bristling AK-47s of the mujahidin didn't subdue Saito and he chose death rather than the indignity of prolonged torture followed by a beheading. Although he was badly wounded he pulled a concealed automatic weapon from his vest and wounded two of his captors. He only had so much gas in his tank with his wounds and they nailed him with a burst of fire. He then took many more rounds but still he didn't die. The terrorists dragged him off, beating him without mercy as they fled the scene before the approaching US QRF arrived. Akihiko died later of his wounds.

Subsequently Ansar al Sunna released a video of his broken body accompanied by a commentary of Islamic propaganda – babbling words from empty vessels compared with the indefatigable courage of Akihiko Saito. I'd met him briefly some time before his death. He was a polite, reserved man in line with his culture but even then I thought he had the haunted look of a Ronin – a Samurai without a lord, the original Japanese mercenary. Respect.

13

CHANGING TIMES

THE year is 2015 and the mighty USA is still the world's dominant power thanks to the development of new hydrogen cell power sources and massive advances in gene technology. The war against terror continues unabated and the president feels compelled to act against a fundamentalist state harbouring terrorists somewhere in the Middle East. More shock and awe as the US Air Force strikes with pinpoint accuracy at several terrorist bases. Ground troops are inserted under the umbrella of airstrikes to hit at specific targets and to hold a key town on the country's border. It's not a special forces raid but a much larger endeavour, a medium-sized invasion.

The general appearance of the troops is similar to that of the Iraq War, although the helmet design has been changed to incorporate micro night vision and target designation kit as standard. Much of the soldiers' bodies are also now encased in lightweight moulded-ceramic body armour so that they look like twenty-first-century plastic knights. But there's another much more fundamental difference because this US force is not comprised of good old boys from the States; it's a unit of highly paid PMCs whose allegiance is not to the president or to the star-spangled banner but to a binding contract with the Pentagon.

Some specialists have negotiated lucrative individual contracts but most of the soldiers are hired out by companies. They're free companies, to use the medieval term, from around the globe: Brits, Germans, French, Italians, Aussies and Kiwis, probably quite a few South Africans, Ghurkas and Fijians. A global rental army. They will have plenty in common: complete fighting skills, great experience in war zones and excellent English so that they can fit in seamlessly to the command structure of the client state.

Loyalty? Of course. Loyalty to their comrades and to their ideals of soldierly behaviour. Loyalty to the contract. People might prefer patriotism as a motive for military service and some of history's greatest heroes have been patriots, but for every one of them there have been hundreds of conscripts who, with the best will in the world, were always better clerks than commandos. They call them cannon fodder. No room for fodder in the mercenary army though. Just fighters. You can imagine too how they might be organised – in the American style, along the lines of major-league football teams. The British contingent would probably be called the Bulldogs with a suitably Churchillian emblem; you might have the Everest Gurkhas and the Wallabies too. These legions might even secure ad deals, industry sponsorship and product placement contracts. They'd probably get winning bonuses too.

Far-fetched? Well not entirely, and even on this side of the Atlantic no less a person than Foreign Secretary Jack Straw sees PMCs playing a key role in the future of warfare. He's on record as saying, 'In developed countries, the private sector is becoming increasingly involved in military and security activity. States and international organisations are turning to the private sector as a cost-effective way of procuring services which would once have been the exclusive preserve of the military.'

Top American officers envisage that the US Army of the future will be like the Spanish army of the fourteenth and fifteenth centuries. This was a mercenary force composed of the best fighters recruited from all over Europe and paid for by Aztec gold and silver brought back to Spain in treasure galleons from South America. From my conversations with US officers and PMC bosses this is an option firmly fixed in Pentagon thinking. Who knows? Maybe advances in DNA science will see recruits with the right profile given gene therapy to build muscle and courage too so that SAS or Delta Force selections become a doddle.

I doubt that somehow, but I do believe the battle-field will be dominated by drones in the air and the increasing presence of robots and remotely controlled fighting machines. Like the fighting men alongside the machines in the US new model army it's likely these will also be on hire from a PMC. But to completely understand what may come in the future we should first look at the past.

Some historians believe that the profession of mercenary soldier is the second oldest in the world. Certainly there have been accounts of soldiers fighting for pay since Egyptian times, and right through the Greek and Roman eras. They were even employed in ancient Mesopotamia, the country now called Iraq. Britain has had its fair share of merce-naries too and during medieval times knights with a weapon for hire were literally free lances.

The Byzantine emperors whose capital was Constantinople used mercenaries as their personal bodyguard and one, a Viking chief called Harald Hardrada, took part in eighteen battles and became head of the guard. He next appeared up in Yorkshire where our own King Harold defeated Hardrada's army at the battle of Stamford Bridge in 1066. Five days later

Harold of England was shot in the eye after marching his army from Yorkshire down to Hastings. No wonder the English lost to William the Conqueror and his Norman knights; they must have been knackered. Many of the legendary longbowmen who wrought such havoc on the French at Agincourt were actually paid-to-fight Welshmen. Those blokes were more likely to have cried 'For enough silver to buy a flock of sheep' than 'God for Harry! England and Saint George.' At around the same time the city states of Italy were employing mercenaries called condottieri to fight their battles for them and it was their particular excesses that began to give the trade a bad name.

Look at modern Switzerland, home of neutrality, the cuckoo clock, Toblerone and secret bank accounts. Hard to imagine, but in the sixteenth century it was a ragged-arsed, landlocked, rural society which barely managed to survive from one Alpine winter to the next. The hard life made the men into hard bastards who became more than handy with eighteen-foot pikes, which proved deadly against cavalry charges. Naturally these pikemen were in demand, and the solution to Switzerland's dire economic straits was to hire out their soldiers to surrounding countries as mercenaries. To this day Swiss citizens formally hire out to the Vatican as mercenaries and swear an oath to protect the pope. The Swiss Guard is a familiar sight on TV reports of papal events.

So it went on down the ages. In the fourteenth century hardbitten mercenaries formed free companies to fight in the Hundred Years War between France and England, sometimes on both sides. The most famous of these was the White Company commanded by Sir John Hawkwood, whose exploits became a byword for courageous fighting. Another was formed by a Welshman called Owain Red Hand, who presumably got his name because his hands were steeped in blood. Red Hand fought for the French against the English before he was assassinated by a Jock called Jon Lamb. A Scotsman hired to kill a Welshman by the English – it sounds a bit like one of those jokes about the Englishman, Scotsman and the Irishman – but mercenary warfare was a dirty game in those days and no mistake.

In the sixteenth century bands of colourfully dressed and highly skilled mercenaries called landsknechts dominated fighting forces throughout Europe. The Spanish employed them during the eighty-year war they fought to keep possession of the Low Countries, the nations we now call Holland and Belgium. They were the best of the soldiers from various European countries – British, German, French, Scandinavian, Tyrolean and Italian – the only qualifications required, skill with arms and undaunted courage. But it was during this period that the concept of nationhood was emerging as power shifted from the sovereign and his God-given rights towards the people in general and the rich in particular.

There were still some mercenary adventures to come with the East India Company conquering India for trade using an army of hired guns, and when Britain's colonies in America rebelled and King George, short of manpower, paid a 30,000-strong Hessian force from his native Germany to fight Washington's Continental Army. The mercenaries lost and ironically the US Army, founded by Washington, is now hiring a similar number of PMC fighters in Iraq because they're short of manpower.

Eventually the French Revolution, the unification of Italy and the amalgamation of princedoms under Prussia to form the German empire in the nineteenth century accelerated the movement away from mercenary forces and towards mass national armies. In 1792 the French came up with the notion of the nation in army. They called it the *levée en masse*. When it arrived in Britain (during the First World War) it was called variously conscription, the call-up or National Service. The Americans call it the draft. Allegiance to the flag and nation became the order of the day and patriotism the motive for fighting. Now governments could call the men of their country to arms on pain of imprisonment if they didn't show up. Generals could have all the soldiers they wanted and – guess what – they only had to pay them peanuts.

Imagine the course of the First World War, the so-called Great War, if those mule-headed, ignorant generals had been obliged to pay mercenaries to fight it. I'm pretty sure trench warfare would never have got off the ground. Years bogged down in a hole, staring at your enemy across no-man's-land then a catastrophic burst of action with countless thousands dying in each battle. Fine, as long as the generals had a stream of conscripts to waste on their nonsense but not if they had to pay for them. They'd have soon dreamt up something a bit more efficient.

To keep the conscripts coming the authorities had to play up the glories of patriotism and paint those only prepared to fight for money as real villains, rapists and looters, but throughout the ages mercenary soldiers have tended to be no worse and generally a lot better behaved than state troops. In fact it's been the great national armies which have perpetrated the worst outrages on civilians. Look no further than the mass murder carried out by the forces of Nazi Germany during the Second World War and remember, no one had to pay them any overtime.

It was during the break-up of the European overseas empires following the end of that war and the onset of the cold war that the mercenary soldier attracted fresh disdain. The world was awash with ideologies, most of them left of centre, and the idea of a soldier who fought for money was firmly linked

to colonialism. Africa became the stamping ground
of a new breed of mercenaries and their client base
was relatively straightforward: it tended to be the
leaders of newly independent states or the opposition in exile. Wars and conflagrations paid for by
'blood diamonds' ebbed and flowed across the continent and mercenaries were often employed to train
the opposing armies and sometimes lead them in
battle.

Mercenaries from many European countries
flocked to fight for the Biafrans during the Nigerian
Civil War, which lasted for three years until it ended
in a mess in 1970. British soldier Mike Hoare was
heavily involved in the Congo crisis of the 1960s and
a failed coup on the holiday islands of the Seychelles
in 1978. The former Portuguese colony of Angola
became the favourite destination of mercenaries in
the 1970s fighting for the FNLA against the MPLA
in the long-running civil war. When they were
captured white mercenaries got short shrift in Angola.
Nine were jailed for lengthy periods and four, three
Brits and a Yank, were executed. Among those
topped in a high-profile case were Costas Georgiou,
the self-styled Colonel Callan, who had served in the
British Parachute Regiment. A charismatic French
figure, Bob Denard, was also involved in numerous
plots in Africa ending in a failed coup in the Comoros
in 1995.

This was the era of the mercenary movies *The Dogs of War* and *The Wild Geese*, which has continued into the modern era with interventions by well-organised PMC forces in Sierra Leone in the 1990s. Then in August 2004 the latest African adventure ended with the arrest of former Blade officer Simon Mann in Zimbabwe, apparently hell-bent on a coup in Equatorial Guinea. Famously, Lady Thatcher's son Mark was implicated in the plot.

Meanwhile the Soviet system collapsed in Russia and the Warsaw Pact folded like the paper castle it had always, in reality, been. Millions of troops were redundant around the world and the most committed looked for work to utilise their professional skills. In Russia many became involved in organised crime and numbers of Muslims who'd been trained in the Soviet era made their expertise available to Islamic militants. In South America former intelligence agents and some special forces soldiers allied themselves to drugs cartels and narco-terrorists in a bid to make a fortune. In Britain and South Africa, both countries with well trained and highly experienced special forces, companies were sprouting up and looking for business opportunities. They were growing rapidly in the US too and the first major PMC contracts handed out by the Pentagon were to support-and-supply firms for their ill-fated incursion into Somalia and the Horn of Africa.

But the big PMC opportunity came in May 2003

when the forerunner to the Coalition Provisional Authority in Iraq, a body known as the Office of Reconstruction and Humanitarian Assistance, awarded the British company Global Risk Strategies a contract to protect its staff and assess the potential security risk. It was like turning on a tap. PMCs became official in the war zone and numbers began to rise exponentially in line with the intensifying insurgency until they levelled off at around 30,000. Practically all the protection work in the country was hived off to the private sector. This worked down from the tip of the pyramid so that everything and everyone moving across the landscape which wasn't a Coalition combat force had a PMC guard.

It's natural that with such a huge force there came concerns; these centred around the chain of command and the accountability of PMCs. This was because most private military contractors in Iraq operated in a legal vacuum. US citizens, who make up most of their number, could not be touched by American law and were more or less given carte blanche by the CPA. American lawyers even went so far as to describe PMCs working in Iraq as falling into the same legal no-man's-land as those being held at Guantanamo Bay. Certainly some of the PMC interrogators at Abu Ghraib prison involved in those notorious humiliation tortures were never prosecuted while their serving army counterparts faced courts martial.

But as time moved on and a fledgling Iraqi government began to take shape more regulation was brought in and by August 2005 the Iraqi administration was licensing PMCs and the weapons they carried. The rules of engagement still entitled PMCs to fire at Iraqi vehicles they believed to be a threat, the practice I described earlier in the book as common among the big American companies, and it took a British company to come up with a less lethal approach. Olive Security use a special shotgun cartridge called a Hatton round. These are designed to blow locks and hinges off doors during counterterrorist operations to minimise collateral damage on the inside and are made from a mixture of wax and lead powder. When a round is fired at a car radiator grille it gives it a hell of a smack and lets the driver know that a nervous man with a gun doesn't want him coming any closer. A better option than standard ammunition, I think. But glitches and complaints aside the plain fact is that PMCs are here to stay and this was recognised before the Iraq War by the British government, who published a green paper to consult on the issues.

Of course it wasn't just the moral or military issues that led to this move by the Foreign and Commonwealth Office. Even before the Iraq situation PMC companies were making shedloads of dollars and the British tradition links registration inexorably with taxation. In other words the government wanted to get a handle on every UK citizen involved in PMC work then take them for as much money as they could. So by 2005 anyone who wanted to work as a PMC had to attend a course properly approved by the Security Industry Authority, who suddenly found themselves catapulted from regulating nightclub bouncers to dealing with hard-core military types – a whole new ball game.

This is a step forward. Criticism and suspicion of the PMC industry don't address the problems; it's up to governments to provide an acceptable set of national and international regulations for any industry including the mercenary business. What's certain is that the reality of PMC power as seen in Iraq is now accepted as the future by the military and political establishment of the world's leading power, the USA. So it's not going to go away. But there's more to it than that, and to examine some of the strongest arguments for a well regulated and ethically motivated international pool of PMCs we have to go back to Africa and back into the heart of darkness.

Back to 2005. A refugee camp near Bunia in the Congo and two senior UN officials are inspecting the camp looking for evidence that soldiers in their peacekeeping force have been sexually abusing the women, girls and boys they've been charged to protect. As they walk near the perimeter fence the investigators hear a child sobbing. They approach and soon the reason for the young girl's distress is evident. Hunched over her body raping her is a UN soldier. His blue beret lies on the ground beside his victim.

I'm sure the investigators were shocked to find such graphic proof of the allegations literally under their noses, but I doubt that they were surprised. Allegations of paedophile activities and systematic rape in the Congo are legion. I know the country well. Remember the diamond mine and Bob the Builder? It's been ravaged by civil war on and off for the past forty years. War there is like the weather. Some years it's better than others. For six years it's not just been civil war; Congo has been the focus for the ambitions and rivalries of neighbouring countries. Militias from Zimbabwe, Rwanda, Angola, Namibia and Uganda have all been fighting like cats for a share of the Congo's enormous and barely tapped mineral wealth.

Diamonds are the obvious magnet but there's also coltan. This is the local name for columbite-tantalite, a rare metallic ore which few have heard about, but everyone who uses a computer or mobile phone will have some inside their equipment. It's valuable stuff, valuable enough to be a curse on the suffering people of the Congo. So you'd imagine they'd have been happy to see the sky-blue berets of the UN coming to their aid. However, the Congolese have been subject to more abuse as the 10,000 troops from fifty nations in the MONUC force have just proved yet another curse on the displaced and vulnerable of the country. Moroccan troops have apparently been at the forefront of the abuse but they're not alone. Women and children needing food, shelter and protection have found themselves having to pay for it in a currency to which the UN and international experts have given the name 'survival sex'. That's literally what it is: sex to survive.

One or two officials whose rampant excesses could not be ignored have been removed and tried but hundreds of allegations have been swept under the carpet. A terrible situation, you'll agree, but hang on, there's more. You see it's not just the Congo. For decades UN peacekeeping forces have been arriving in stricken countries where people need their help like a plague of sexual locusts.

There are around 70,000 UN troops serving in sixteen peacekeeping missions in sixteen countries around the globe. In Liberia, Sierra Leone, Ivory Coast and Burundi there are similar allegations of peacekeepers turning into sexual predators. In Cambodia during the 1990s the presence of UN peacekeepers saw an explosion in the number of

Thai brothels in the country and the arrival of HIV and AIDS. The UN's top official in Cambodia at the time, a Japanese diplomat, shrugged off the depravity with, 'Oh well, boys will be boys.' In East Timor there was a similar phenomenon with Thai prostitutes flocking into the country and bringing AIDS with them. The hookers didn't have any problems with flights into the war-torn country; they were flown in courtesy of UN pilots on transport planes meant for humanitarian relief.

In Africa the UN maxim is 'the younger the better'; after all a ten-year-old girl is less likely to be carrying the HIV virus than her mother. The legacy of personal misery this cynical abuse leaves in its wake is obvious but there's another effect that really makes me want to spit. In another corner of Africa the Sudanese government is actively encouraging and probably sponsoring militia attacks on refugee camps. This is overt ethnic cleansing carried out by Arab militias who often travel considerable distances on camels over tracts of desert to attack black refugees cowering in camps in Darfur. When the subject of a peacekeeping force to protect the camps was raised the Sudanese government threw its hands up in horror and refused on the grounds that UN soldiers would bring AIDS into the country. Well, they had a point. A propaganda victory had been handed to them on a plate as a result of the tarnished history of the United Nations.

Large-scale serious sex crimes are only one part of the UN problem. A second is the total ineffectiveness of its military capability. The examples are too many to list here but the paralysis of Dutch troops during the massacre in the Bihaj enclave in Bosnia was one of the most shocking because they were not 'gash' – useless troops. Those lads were well trained and tough. I suspect it was political dithering by their bosses in the Hague that paralysed the Dutch troops. We'll probably never know the true reason but sadly we do know the result. Rwanda was another. Half a million people murdered and the UN couldn't even muster a decent reconnaissance force to let the world know what was going on. Kofi Annan was in charge of the UN in Rwanda and at one point he advocated a desperate solution. Hire PMCs, he urged his bosses in New York. Not a chance, came the reply.

Kofi Annan is now UN general secretary and after impotently watching over the Rwanda genocide he helped set up the oil-for-food programme to Iraq – I call it oil for cash – which handed Saddam and his Ba'athists billions of dollars which are now funding the insurgency. So the people of Iraq were twice robbed. Once by the corrupt UN officials who made millions helping Saddam nick the cash and a second time when that money robbed them of the chance of peace. Nice one, Kofi.

To my mind there are fundamental problems with UN peacekeeping forces, and I have watched them closely on a number of occasions around the world.

The first is the quality of troops. This goes right across the scale from the top-quality professionals provided by countries like Britain and Norway down to the illiterate conscripts of the Moroccans in the Congo. Don't get me wrong – developing nations have some crack troops – but do you think the king of Morocco, faced with potential Islamic revolution, is going to send his best lads to the Congo? Not a chance. Look at India and Pakistan. They have some of the best soldiers on the planet – thanks, I'd suggest, to the fact that they are organised and trained along British lines. Are they likely to make these guys available for UN duties when India has Sikh separatists to worry about and the Pakistanis are chasing al Qaeda around the tribal territories? On top of that they have a tense stand-off with each other in the mountains of the Hindu Kush and Kashmir. We know what their best men are going to be doing and it isn't UN peacekeeping.

The second problem is politics. It would take a cleverer man than me to unravel the mare's nest of international collaborations, trade interests and treaties that complicate requests by the UN for troops. Countries just won't send help if it doesn't suit their interests. Sometimes they send them but seem to just want troops in a particular trouble spot to throw a spanner in the works.

The third problem I've already mentioned in the context of PMCs in Iraq, and that's accountability. Virtually no one has been brought to trial for the crimes of UN peacekeepers yet academics who object to PMCs constantly bat on about the lack of accountability of military corporations.

Back to Africa and Sierra Leone in 1995, where a rebel army was roasting innocent people alive and had begun the hand-chopping that was to be their hallmark for nearly a decade. The country's rulers were desperate to restore order and as nobody else was helping they hired the South African PMC Executive Outcomes. EO brought in 250 crack soldiers and a small wing of helicopter gunships for air support and within eleven days had pushed the rebels into the jungle away from the Koidu diamond mines and innocent civilians. As the Sierra Leone government was broke at the time they paid Executive Outcomes with a diamond mining concession, which gave the PMCs even more cash and influence.

In 1998 the PMCs were back again after another coup by rebels and Sandline, run by Tim Spicer, regained the country for the government. International dithering and a shoddy UN peacekeeping force subsequently let the rebels get a foothold again and it was left to British Paras and the SAS in the

Operation Barras attack on the West Side Boys to finally sort it out.

The point about Sierra Leone is that PMCs quickly and efficiently sorted out horrific situations and restored lawful governments to power with main force, well applied by fine troops. The UN, on the other hand, has proved time and time again that it has neither the quality of troops or the political will to be decisive. Not only that but UN forces are more expensive than PMCs largely because that lack of will means that the troops on the ground do not get the job done quickly. They are not well controlled or quartermastered and they waste and steal at an astonishing rate. When I was in Bosnia, for instance, I noticed that the main preoccupation of some UN troops seemed to be the theft and export of UN Land Rovers for resale in their home countries.

Let's go back to the Darfur genocide in Sudan. Indiscriminate rape and killings at refugee camps by the feared and hated Janjaweed Arab militia have been met with strong words of condemnation at the UN but no action. Isn't it just possible that if countries didn't have to send their own troops and instead could mandate a PMC force to do the job instead then things would happen? Once there was a UN resolution to protect the camps the big companies would tender within hours and be there within days with a complete force for the job. Moreover, PMCs wouldn't stand there guarding camp perimeters; they'd be out in the scrub hunting down the militias and would hit them so hard they wouldn't even contemplate another rape or murder of an unarmed refugee. Job done.

What stands in the way of this is the International Convention Against the Recruitment, Use, Financing and Training of Mercenaries, as passed by the General Assembly of the UN in 1989. This was a knee-jerk international reaction against the profession, whose numbers and influence on civil wars had grown steadily over the years. Some of the major powers did not sign up to it and some countries who did, like Angola and Zaire, still regularly employ mercenaries to further their aims. The British government seem to rather like the idea of a pool of registered and vetted PMCs working under strict international laws and available for UN operations. The Americans, who pay much of the UN's bills, would love it. Kofi Annan has said that if he'd had PMCs in Rwanda he could have saved hundreds of thousands of lives, so why doesn't the world just get on with it, recognise the realities and help those most at risk in the world?

Remember that mate of mine who called in an air strike on his own coordinates to stop a massacre in Kosovo? Well another mate, an ex-Blade, was working as a PMC in Ghana when he came across thirty or so children tied together by their necks with a blue nylon rope on the back of a truck. The slave trade is alive and well in Africa and he knew those kids would be working as slaves in the fields or a factory within hours. The driver was taking a piss so my mate battered the armed guard left in charge of them and drove the kids off in the truck to an aid agency down the road while his sidekick followed in their 4 x 4. Both those men now run PMC companies hiring out top guns in Iraq and they're likely to stay as management in the business for years to come. Who would you rather have fighting for the oppressed under the sky-blue UN flag: those two or some ragtag rapists from a conscript army who can't fight for shit?

14

ON THE ROAD AGAIN

MAY Day 2003. I was a prisoner of the Nigerian secret service at the moment when President George W. Bush strode across the deck of the aircraft carrier USS *Abraham Lincoln*, stood in front of a microphone and made the most controversial statement of his life – no mean feat for the man, I'll admit: 'My fellow Americans, major combat operations in Iraq have ended. In the battle of Iraq, the United States and our allies have prevailed.'

Well, that's what he said, although he was at least three years premature with his announcement. It's a shame I missed it because it's not every day you get to hear a monumental 'peace in our time' clanger being dropped but that's the way it was.

Anyway there I was banged up by the Nigerians with more than enough on my plate to worry about. It had begun when Mike Curtis asked me to lead a team out to Nigeria to review the security of a well-known opposition politician in a country where people die in quite large numbers for the sake of the party they support.

I had three ex-army types with me and an expert in electronic counter surveillance. Things had been going fine; the job was progressing well but the guys had got cheesed off with staying in the client's security compound and decided to bug out to a hotel four or five miles away. I decided to stay at the compound with the client's own Nigerian security guys. We were unarmed and they were tooled up with automatic weapons of every shape and size. Better safe than sorry; after all you never know what's around the corner in a hardball African democracy like Nigeria. If there was going to be an attack then I wanted to be near a gun and I told the others they ought to be too.

They had gone to the hotel anyway. The bugging expert, we called him Bug Man, was white and obviously stood out like a sore thumb down in the town. The three ex-army guys were black; somebody had had the bright idea that they wouldn't look conspicuous in an African environment. Wrong, dead wrong. With their Thames Estuary accents and English mannerisms marking them out as pure John Bull they were as much sore thumbs as the Bug Man.

It wasn't long before the local state governor's network got to know about their presence in town and we were arrested by a posse of security service heavies in the hotel lobby when I went to brief the boys for the next move. Bug Man and I were pushed around a bit, nothing too rough, but I witnessed a nasty bit of inverted racism when my three black mates Nev, Vince and Rich were given a battering. To be honest the six or seven blokes bashing them had a narrow escape because Nev and Vince were experts in a high-powered martial art called steel-wire kung fu. Don't ask me – I was just a champion at bog-standard karate – but I've seen them scrapping and it's devastating stuff. Anyway, Nev and Vince were showing remarkable restraint – those Nigerians might easily have been ripped limb from limb and had their guns rammed up their skinny arses.

We were taken to the local police station and put through forty-eight hours of sleep deprivation and constant questioning. It's tedious hearing the same questions over and over when you haven't had a kip. 'Who are you?' 'Why are you here?' On and on it went, but I wasn't too bothered; it was pretty standard stuff as interrogations go and if they wanted to waste their time asking me shit I was quite happy to sit there, at least for a while. Then I was taken back to the inter-view room expecting more of the same and a new face introduced himself as a captain from secret service headquarters in Lagos. He told us we were being moved.

We were put in a people carrier with three armed guards in the back carrying old US Army machine guns, Second World War grease guns. The backup car carried two more secret service men. The driver set off down a road through the bush. We didn't like it. What was going on? Were they going to take us deeper into the bush and rub us out? The guards were really tense too as the journey began and the whole business had a nasty feel about it. You could cut the atmosphere in that vehicle with a knife and I put down the mood of the guards to the fact that they may have been told to mallet us.

I wasn't having that so I began a conversation with the steel-wire guys in a Geordie accent, which I knew they'd both understand because in the army you get to know all the UK regional accents. They replied in Jamaican patois, which I just about had a handle on but only just. I was smiling as I talked to make the guards think we were just having a friendly chat, and it was obvious they didn't have the foggiest idea what was going on.

Nev, Vince and Rich didn't like the feel of things either so we agreed a strategy that was a bit radical – but then if you think there's a chance you're going to be shot like a dog, you're obviously going to think about biting back.

'If they turn off this road into the bush we take these three muppets out then deal with the driver, and then we make our way across country to the high commission in Lagos, okay?' I said.

'No problem, Johnny; we'll snap their necks,' said Nev in a very matter-of-fact voice.

'Okay, Nev,' I said in my singsong Geordie accent. 'You take the one opposite. Vince, you take the one alongside you. I'll take the one with the pencil neck and, Rich, you get the driver. Grab the weapons and we take on the backup vehicle. Do it on my word and at the same time.'

I could see Vince and Nev were itching to have a go. I think they were still a bit cross about the battering when they were arrested and I wasn't sure they were going to wait for my word before snapping the guards. One suspicious move on the part of those men would have seen them killed in the blink of an eye – I'm certain of that. I was beginning to think that we should just do it anyway to relieve the tension building up, which was turning the Japanese people carrier into a pressure cooker, when suddenly the guards looked around them as if recognising where they were, laid their guns down and started beaming with relief. The driver even started singing.

What the fuck was happening? They spoke reasonably good English so I asked the guy in charge. 'We've been through a very, very bad area. Very bad. We had to be on alert for an attack. The captain said that no harm must come to you.'

Fuck me. We'd nearly totalled those poor bastards and all they were doing was looking after us. Nev nearly pissed himself laughing at the irony of it. 'Fucking hell, John, what a laugh,' said Nev, back to Estuary English. 'Another few minutes and I wouldn't have been able to hold back. I was going to give that fucker my best move.'

The guards looked at Nev quizzically as though he was some sort of nutcase. Perhaps they thought he was laughing with the relief of knowing he was out of danger. If they'd twigged the real reason he was almost wetting himself they'd have known just who had been in danger.

We were held for another day and went through the same mind-numbing interrogation routine at their Lagos headquarters. However, Bug Man had got a text message out to Mike Curtis, who rode to the rescue in double-quick time. Mike informed the Foreign and Commonwealth Office and they were able to convince the Nigerian authorities we were doing genuine security work. During my last grilling the chief interrogator had taken a phone call. He was sort of standing to attention while he was on the phone, a sure giveaway he was talking to a superior. There was a lot of nodding and shaking of the head as he spoke then he put the phone down and smiled.

'Mr Geddes, you and your friends are free to go. Thank you for your cooperation and please make sure that you account for every piece of your personal belongings.'

I collected and signed for my kit. I was very glad to be on my way and free from the tedious interrogation. We were soon at the airport and then straight onto the first flight back to Britain. I've still got Nev's and Vince's numbers; after all you never know when you might need some steel-wire work done. Although I don't keep a diary and my perception of time had been a bit fucked around by the interrogations, I reckon it was around the time of that road journey to Lagos that President Bush was making his statement on the USS *Abraham Lincoln*.

Funny, the last world leader to make such a historic cock-up also stepped off an aircraft to address the microphones. That was in 1939 and British Prime Minister Neville Chamberlain was fresh back from talks with Hitler in Munich when he uttered the fateful words 'peace for our time' to the newsreel cameras. Fair play to George: he'd just arrived via a spectacular carrier landing on board a four-seater US Navy jet which had been stopped by a cable brake across the deck. I bet that was the newest length of cable in the US Navy and the blokes who'd laid it must have been in a real sweat. Still he didn't crash. Just his predictions.

The president's bravura announcement that the war had been won was followed by a speech. I think it's worth looking at some of his words because that speech actually heralded the creation of the environment in Iraq in which PMCs could flourish.

My fellow Americans, major combat operations in Iraq have ended. In the battle of Iraq, the United States and our allies have prevailed. And now our coalition is engaged in securing and reconstructing that country. In this battle, we have fought for the cause of liberty and for the peace of the world. Our nation and our coalition are proud of this accomplishment, yet it is you, the members of the United States military, who achieved it. Your courage, your willingness to face danger for your country and for each other made this day possible. Because of you our nation is more secure. Because of you the tyrant has fallen and Iraq is free. Operation Iraqi Freedom was carried out with a combination of precision and speed and boldness the enemy did not expect and the world had not seen before.

When Iraqi civilians looked into the faces of our service men and women, they saw strength and kindness and good will. Today we have the greater power to free a nation by breaking a dangerous and aggressive regime. With new tactics and precision weapons, we can achieve military objectives without directing violence against civilians. No device of man can remove the tragedy from war, yet it is a great advance when the guilty have far more to fear from war than the innocent. We have difficult work to do in Iraq. We're bringing order to parts of that country that remain dangerous. We're pursuing and finding leaders of the old regime who will be held to account for their crimes.

The battle of Iraq is one victory in a war on terror that began on September the 11th, 2001 and still goes on. The liberation of Iraq is a crucial advance in the campaign against terror. We have removed an ally of al Qaeda and cut off a source of terrorist funding.

Just think about what has happened since President Bush made that speech. From May 2003 to Christmas 2005 the US government spent $200 billion on the continuing war. Around 30,000 Iraqi civilians were killed by both sides and the cost of reconstruction was estimated by the World Bank at a staggering $35,819 million. Two hundred and fifty one foreign civilian workers were kidnapped, an average of about five a month, and sixty-six journalists were killed, which relatively speaking is a media bloodbath. Altogether, 2,389 Coalition troops died including ninety-eight British soldiers by December 2005, and although there are no firm figures, it's reckoned that around 300 PMCs were killed and scores more wounded.

Most of those casualties, I reckon about 60 per cent of them, can be put down to roadside IEDs and suicide bombs, with one call sign being wiped out by a bomber who had two young boys travelling with him. That's as ruthless and barbaric a camouflage to get his deadly cargo waved through checkpoints as you can imagine. PMCs rate their casualty figures as high but look at the official US estimate of the number of insurgents slotted during the same period of time: 53,470. That's a huge bloodletting by any reckoning, and although he's been subjected to a barrage of criticism I suspect that's one figure George Bush will be pleased about whatever the cost.

His critics say he was wrong to go to war against Saddam, and to be fair the facts appear to show he was mistaken on many counts. We know quite well that far from stamping out al Qaeda in Iraq the organisation's fighters and suicide bombers have flooded into the country causing mayhem and huge loss of life under the direction of Abu Musab al Zarqawi. But I have a soldier's hunch that the Pentagon and the CIA want it that way. They want al Qaeda to have a focus for their jihad and deliberately set one up. If they flock to Iraq then the CIA know where they are and in effect they've created a killing ground to suck the enemy in. Better bombs in Iraq than in the USA and it suits the Americans to fight the war against terror on the streets of Ramadi rather than the centre of New York. It also suits them to see a PMC army developing there, honing its skills and fine-tuning its organisation.

The al Qaeda activities and the actions of the Sunni insurgents allied to them have made PMCs in Iraq an essential element of the Coalition game plan. US companies in particular are well meshed into Coalition military strategy – embedded if you like with the US Army – and often travel in convoy with marines or rangers. PMCs of all nations have shown themselves with very few exceptions to be well organised, and carry out their responsibilities with integrity and due diligence to the law. In many ways they are self-regulating and it is to the credit of their managements that anyone stepping over the line is swiftly booted out with little chance of getting another job.

In December 2005 election officials in Fallujah ran out of ballot papers as the inhabitants of the City of Insurgents rushed to the polling booths to engage in the democratic process. This was seen as an indication that the Sunnis were beginning to believe they had to engage in the political process, and there were signs of a growing contempt for the activities of al Qaeda, who, when all was said and done, were killing more Iraqis than Americans.

Time will tell whether the insurgency will actually fade away or if Sunni political engagement is just a cloak for the insurgency – as Republican engagement was in Northern Ireland – but it was PMCs who had the job of supervising the delivery of ballot papers around Iraq during the elections and referendums of 2005. It was PMCs who distributed the new Iraqi currency across the country as the economy was being revived. It is PMCs who protect the lives of the thousands of contractors rebuilding the country. They are for the most part lightly armed and they do not represent a cohesive offensive force but they have accomplished these high-risk tasks with style and professionalism. If democracy and the will of the people do eventually prevail in Iraq it will be in no small part due to the presence of private military contractors in the country.

In my own small way I tried to make a difference whenever I could and I remember one day when I was with a media crew in the north of the Marsh Arab territory.

It's worth remembering that the marshes of southern Iraq were a great flood plain with reed-covered islands where wild boar ran. Between them were channels of clear water filled with fish, home to huge flocks of ducks and wading birds. All around the marshes are baking desert regions; no wonder some people thought this place was the Garden of Eden. The people, the Mahd, were unique too and lived close to nature, making fantastic reed buildings and living off the harvest of fish and wildfowl provided by their environment. They were a tribal people and deeply independent. Saddam loathed them. After the First Gulf War he killed the Marsh Arabs by the tens of thousands and then built a canal to divert the Tigris and the Euphrates and drain hundreds of square miles of marshland in one of the greatest pieces of environmental vandalism of all time.

The crew were filming in a small village not far from the Saddam Canal that had brought desolation to their land. The first thing the few Marsh Arabs who were left had done was breach the canal and let the waters take their natural course again. Channels and lagoons were beginning to reappear and one of the villagers took me out in a traditional dugout boat onto a lake. It was the most tranquil place I'd ever found in Iraq.

What usually happened in these situations was that I would get my medical kit out of the vehicle and ask if anyone needed help. Invariably children were brought to me and it was no different this time. I got talking to an old man through the interpreter. Wearing a pinstripe jacket over his long robe and the trailing Mahd turban, he treated me as an honoured guest with a meal of dates and milk.

'I had a son who should be your age,' he told me, 'but the army took him away and I never saw him again. It was when Saddam made war with our brothers from Iran. Why would my son want to fight Iran? It is a terrible thing.'

I told him about Kurt, how I had feared for my own son's life and how I was truly sorry for his loss. They brought me his granddaughter, who had a nasty gash on her leg which I cleaned and sutured. I remember her big brown eyes looking up at me –

completely trusting – and I thought of my own daughter. I felt an overwhelming wish to protect those people who'd suffered so much. I stitched another kid, gave one some eye lotion and then treated about fifteen of them for scabies. I was always sorting out scabies among village kids; I made a point of carrying a bottle of the right lotion with me.

When I left the village the old man embraced me and gave me his blessing. I took that blessing back onto the Highway. I had unfinished business there.

The two guys sitting in the car were completely comfortable with the weapons on their laps and pretty relaxed as their Iraqi driver sped them along the Highway. The relentless rock and sand of the desert spun past them as they headed towards Baghdad. They had an RV to make at about midday at a grid reference just before the gauntlet of the Fallujah bypass, but for some unfathomable reason they decided to drive past and carry on down the road. No sweat. They were on time and all was well with the world but they were a bit too relaxed for a pair of crows on their first trip into Iraq. They'd been well briefed on the lethal environment they were going into but perhaps they'd had one warning too many. Perhaps they believed nothing could be as bad as the picture that had been painted. But things were going to get a lot messier before the day was over.

It began when the amber warning light on the fuel gauge flashed on. Their driver pointed it out. They needed fuel so they asked him if he knew where there was a service station. He did, he said. Twenty minutes later and they'd gone up a bullet-pocked slip road off the Highway and turned into the suburbs of a large town. They drove straight past the signpost announcing the name of the town: Fallujah. Twinned with Hades. Still no alarm bells were ringing in their minds and yet they should have been deafened. These guys were not new to the security game. One was ex-Guards, the other a 14 Int guy who'd done a huge amount of time undercover in Northern Ireland. He was well versed in tactical awareness from his spook days but he hadn't twigged that it was all going wrong.

The driver just kept going and for some strange reason wasn't bothered about ferrying two white-eyes into the heart of bandit country. There was no evidence he was connected to the insurgency. Perhaps he was just having a thick day too. They found their garage and the two of them got out and had a stretch while the driver filled the tank. One of them lit a fag and relaxed a bit more and they both stood around in blissful ignorance as if someone had erected a force field around them. Then the 14 Int guy woke up and began to smell the roses. The same car had come round the block for the third time and his instincts were now screaming at him, That's a fucking dicker!

He was right; the sharks were circling and they'd smelt easy blood. But at that very moment his mobile began ringing and a voice snarled down the line. It was Mike Curtis. 'Where the fuck are you? You should be at the RV.'

'We're in Fallujah,' came what was now an extremely limp-dick reply.

'For fuck's sake! Stay where you are; we're on our way!' said Mike.

That call saved their bacon because it's certain the dickers were making their own call at the very same time – for the heavy brigade, their gunned-up comrades, to come and mallet the madmen queuing up for an orange boiler suit at that petrol station in Fallujah. And so it was that the two sets of opposing cavalry met on the way.

I was in a vehicle following Mike up the slip road from the Highway with a South African and a Jordanian driver on our way to stop the guys getting intimate with al Zarqawi's blade when two flatbed Toyotas suddenly pulled out of a junction at the top and attempted to block Mike's vehicle. They were trying to force his car off the top of the slip road and roll it down the embankment to the Highway.

I heard Mike on the headset: 'Front! Front! Front!'

He managed to swerve round them and keep going but the first of the Toyotas ran alongside his car, smashing into the side of it. Sparks and chunks of metal flew as Mike, who was driving, rammed them back. The window of his 4 x 4 rocked as Stu, Mike's call sign partner, opened up on the Toyota with his weapon. Two of the insurgents in the back of the cab were hit and thrown onto the road like rag dolls as the life was slammed out of them. The Toyota ran off the road as Mike screamed to a halt and leapt out to deploy across the bonnet with Stu continuing to paste the Toyota, which still had three insurgents returning rounds. Mike then began firing from beside his vehicle, hammering rounds into the second flatbed with absolute disregard for the incoming rounds chewing lumps out of the car frame around him.

Voosh!! The first Toyota burst into flames just as me and the South African deployed on the boot and bonnet of our vehicle, firing burst after burst into the second insurgent truck. They were well fucked up. How many? We didn't stop to count but I'd hit one of them as he tried a long triple jump into the ditch beside the road to escape the hail of lead. I got him in the thigh and then a second round whacked him in the torso doubling him up, midway through his jump.

Minutes later Mike rocked up at the fuel station and bollocked the two crows, labelling them 'fucking donkeys'. It was over and there was no time for long inquests as we sped off, but one thing was for sure: if we hadn't been close to hand those two would have been killed or taken hostage. We'd just happened to bump into their nemesis before they'd met at the petrol station. Simple fate really. The 14 Int guy went on to prove that his lapse had been a one-off. I doubt whether he could ever explain how he'd been so lax but he ended up as a top player. The other guy vanished after a negligent discharge – jargon for firing his weapon when he shouldn't have – and then resurfaced in Baghdad and is doing a good job.

For Mike and Stu it had been a hot action; for me it had been the contact I needed to confirm that I was as sharp as ever, no luck involved. And it had been a personal success. I was over the worst of it. I'd survived my nightmare of booze and insurgents and the never-ending stress of the Highway. What of the men we'd left dead on the road? As we drove off I looked into the ditch and saw the body of the man I'd just killed. Who was he? What was he? Bandit, Ba'athist or al Qaeda?

For sure he was some mother's son. But am I haunted by his ghost and those of the other dead men on the Highway? No, because as I glanced at his body I asked myself how he would have felt if it had been me lying lifeless in the ditch, and I knew he would have been glad.

You see, the Highway to Hell is a toll road. Someone has to pay. And, guess what? It ain't gonna be me.

IRAQ: A SURVIVAL HANDBOOK

THE air con had broken down so that my friend Joe, his Jordanian driver and a three-man TV crew were sitting in a seventy mile per hour sauna as they thundered down the Fallujah bypass in an ex-police issue GMC 4 x 4.

Usual rules. Joe's gut feelings about the trip were giving him gripe when he saw a Toyota truck kicking up plumes of grit and dust as it headed down a desert track on a collision course with their truck.

Two bandits-stroke-insurgents in the front, two in the back and one of them had a wicked RPG launcher over his shoulder pointing menacingly at the GMC. They'd obviously been patrolling the roads looking for some white-eyes and it was their lucky day because, guess what, they had all the weapons and the GMC had none.

That's because the correspondent in charge of this particular crew had little common sense and he was being a hard arse and sticking rigidly to the station policy of no weapons. Joe didn't like it but he's a man with an acute belief in his abilities and one of those was the ability to negotiate a triple fee for the job. No gun means lots of money; that's a basic principle in PMC work.

Anyway that was the situation they found themselves in and Joe told me his only fleeting moment of satisfaction in the seconds before they were forced to pull up was the correspondent's chalk-white face as the awful truth hit him.

Close up the TV journalist could see that insurgents are not people who would be easily impressed by his station's logo or his international press pass. Guns on the other hand did impress them and they had a monopoly on weapons; he was crapping himself.

They were hauled out of the vehicle within seconds of pulling over and with practised ease the leader of the insurgent team quickly ran his eye over them and worked out who was who in the group they'd captured.

Joe reckoned their leader looked pleased with his bag as he snapped out an order to one of his men; there was no mistaking what was going on even though the order had been too quick-fire for Joe's basic Arabic. It was simple, his appearance and demeanour spelt out bodyguard and he was going to be malleted. They had three prime hostages and they would keep the driver until he'd delivered the captives and the GMC then kill him. Why keep the one most likely to cause them problems in the meantime?

Sure enough Joe was grabbed roughly by the shoulder and pushed in the direction of a high bank of sand alongside the road with endless desert scrub stretching away behind it. A jab with an AK reinforced the order and Joe set off on what was meant to be his last walk.

They went over the top of the bank and that's when Joe moved. He's an ex-Blade and he knows the first rule of survival and escape after capture is a simple one – you make your move as soon as you possibly can.

The young Sunni terrorist came too close. It was enough. Joe grabbed him and spun him around like a top. Shots were fired and one badly grazed Joe's hand before he was able to drop the gunman with two blows that left him near dead. Joe was about to grab the weapon and sort the situation out once and for all but the others were coming after him and firing furiously at him so he legged it into the scrub.

One of the BSI's jumped into the driving seat of the Toyota and tore into the desert to give chase too. Joe managed to keep running parallel with the road for a while as the insurgents fired wildly after him.

But now the Jordanian driver was on the case and with heroic courage he decided he couldn't leave Joe to his fate despite knowing he was on the menu as well. He could have torn off down the Highway with the TV crew still intact but he didn't. Instead he raced down the road after him then jolted across the desert to collect Joe who leapt gratefully into the vehicle. Bullets were still whining around them as he cursed the day he'd agreed to come down the Highway without a weapon.

They thumped and bumped through the desert scrub but by now the Toyota driver had picked up his mates and they were crashing over the terrain in hot pursuit. It was only a matter of time before they would be able to get a shot off with the RPG or, more likely, rivet the GMC with their AKs.

That's when it happened. It was one of those off-the-wall, tell-the-grandchildren situations that you just couldn't make up. Remember I mentioned that the GMC was an ex-police vehicle? Well among the equipment that had been left in it was a public address system with a mike in the cab and loudspeakers back and front. It was meant for telling motorists to pull over, that sort of thing, and Joe and the driver had messed around with it a bit themselves.

For some reason the driver got it into his head that he would pray and he decided to make his prayers public so he did it over the PA system. He picked up the mike and started praying, reciting passages from the holy Koran. He quoted sections from the holy book on peace and justice and as he chanted them his voice broadcast the verses across the desert in the strange, metallic electronic voice of the loudspeakers.

And it worked. Suddenly and for no possible reason except the exhortations for peace and harmony from the Koran, the Toyota braked to a halt and the gunmen just watched Joe and his clients drive away to safety.

Needless to say Joe never travelled on a BG job without a gun again and that was his personal lesson from the incident. But I've told you the story because I believe it's a parable of modern Babylon that teaches those who want to survive in Iraq some vital lessons.

Firstly, it illustrates the central truth that underlies all conflicts, not just the one in Iraq but anywhere in the world. It's commonly known as the fog of war but I call it the 'fuck knows' factor and the main principle to bear in mind is that you should never be taken aback by what war and mayhem throws up.

All conflicts take on a life of their own. Sometimes it involves violence so intense that only fate can steer you through it; sometimes quirky things happen like those stories of Bibles and cigarette cases, tucked into soldiers' tunics, that saved them from bullets in the First World War.

In this case it was prayers on a public address system that saved our heroes' lives. The point is that they didn't stand around gawping at their good fate they grasped the opportunity and escaped.

Who knows what's going to happen when you walk into the casino called war when the only game at the tables is Russian roulette. If you don't like the game, don't go into that casino because there's no guarantees that you'll come out alive, and those that give such guarantees are liars.

The second lesson is one that Joe didn't need to read in the manual. It's simply this; the sooner you act the more likely you are to survive. With typical understatement the British military call this life or death rule 'Conduct After Capture.'

Joe knew that the edge he had when the insurgents got him out of the car would erode rapidly. In his case that was on a steep downward curve leading to a point, after a few minutes, when he would be shot dead in the sand dunes. He knew that; he knew too that he had to act and he did. In other circumstances the erosion of your initiative might take longer but it begins from the moment you are captured.

As time in captivity goes on you lose kit, even down to the bootlaces that you might be able to use to throttle a guard. Crucially you also lose the will to make a move. Joe did it when his adrenaline rush was in full drive and it was his resolve to act and some very loud prayers on a PA system that saved his life. You have to go for it.

The third lesson is an important one. Joe's contact underscores the fact that you should know something about the culture you're immersing yourself in before you go to a country ravaged by war and insurrection.

I already speak some Arabic from my days in the Regiment but I also made it my business to learn about the Muslim culture and its local and regional variants in Iraq. You simply never know when that will come in useful. It can help you to build bridges in a small but significant ways when you do business with locals. But in another situation it could also help you to make crucial, life-saving bonds with captors building an invisible shield around you if just one of them feels some sympathy for your plight.

This isn't pie in the sky. Shrinks call it Stockholm Syndrome and it's named after a bank robbery in that city which turned into a police siege. The hostages were bank staff and trapped customers. They began to empathise with their captors and even spoke out for them when they were released.

It happened at the Iranian Embassy Siege in London too, the one so famously broken by the SAS. When the Regiment stormed the place killing all but one of the terrorists the one who lived was smuggled out of the building by women secretaries who sympathised with him because he'd shown them some small kindnesses.

Obviously people at the mercy of robbers or terrorists instinctively think that being liked might save their lives but Stockholm Syndrome works both ways and when a bond has been made individual captors will sometimes go a long way to save their captives.

It nearly worked for Ken Bigley who evidently befriended one of his guards who then helped him get out of his terrorist jail. He nearly escaped but he was picked up again by the rest of the al Qaeda gang and infamously beheaded in a videoed execution. We don't know what happened to the man who showed him mercy but there's little doubt he paid with his life for his glimmer of humanity.

A US hostage called Thomas Hamill made it work for him too. I'd like to meet Tom Hamill because from everything I've heard he must be one hell of a man. Tom was a truck driver working for the giant Halliburton company when his convoy was attacked and he was taken captive by insurgents. It was April 2004 and the insurgents were on the warpath because of the assault on Fallujah by US forces following the infamous murder and mutilation of the Blackwater Four a few days earlier.

Four other people taken with him were later found murdered but Tom Hamill was a valuable prize and he was quickly taken to a remote farmhouse ninety miles north of the ambush near Tikrit.

He was there for a month and during that time Tom weaved his own peculiar brand of magic on his captors. He was a handy sort of guy and he showed them a few ways of filtering and purifying their domestic water supply; ways they were able to use back in their homes to benefit their families. They were grateful.

Tom used that advantage to create a more relaxed regime for himself and in the end persuaded them that he wouldn't try to escape. Where would he go? He was in the middle of the desert and anyway if he did happen to be seen he would be handed in again.

They didn't want to be hanging about guarding him all day and Tom was a good guy wasn't he, so they took him on his word and left him for days at a time locked in a room at the farm with water and supplies. Tom had turned the situation into one where he became his own jailer and soon found a way out. He actually tried to wave down some Coalition helicopters but they didn't spot him so he returned to his cell for the next visit by his guards.

Out again he found the main oil pipeline through the region and reasoned correctly that this would be heavily patrolled. Soon enough he was found by US troops and returned to his home in Macon, Missouri.

It was a fantastic outcome and Tom Hamill did it all on his own because when it came down to it he used the only weapons he had at his disposal; his huge personality and his humanity. Top marks for survival.

I want to mention a couple more things that I believe are vital. First, anyone going to Iraq or Afghanistan to work would be crazy not to go on a hostile environment course before they set off. You'll be put into simulations of engagements complete with live rounds and that will prepare you for the real thing better than any number of sleepless nights wondering what may lie in store. More than that, you'll learn how to act, how to help and how to give yourself the best chance of surviving.

Escape driving techniques and four-wheel driving skills should be part of the course and if someone in your security party is injured you would then be in a position to use those skills to fill a vital role while the others fight on. You should also do a battlefield first aid course. It will transform you from a parcel being delivered by a security detail into a potentially useful member of the team.

The other thing I'd like to touch on again is the question of carrying arms. I don't necessarily think that it's a great idea, it really depends on the individual because if you haven't go the resolve to use it then you shouldn't carry a weapon. Engineers and managers are happier firing away on slide rules and calculators and that's the way it should be.

But you're in Iraq and you've been ambushed on the Fallujah bypass. One of your bodyguards is dead the other wounded and you've been isolated from a second protection vehicle with your Jordanian driver.

At that moment you might decide you'd rather have a go than be shot or measured for an orange boiler suit. That's when the basic weapons knowledge you can learn on a hostile environment course might save your life. Do the course!

As I write, most journeys in Iraq undertaken by foreigners are between the Green Zone and the airport. Journalists now venture outside the security zone only if they're embedded with Coalition troops or by strict agreement with the militias who will escort them into areas like Sadr City in Baghdad or around Basra in the south. That's the Shia militia of course as no deals at all are being struck with the really evil axis of former Sadaam Ba'athists and al Qaeda types who run the Sunni insurgency.

Businessmen and engineers are travelling outside the country but that is generally in armed convoys the length of a Wild West wagon train that are being whacked the moment they show their faces, or else they travel British-style and go covert.

And that's where I come to my number one rule for surviving in Iraq. I've really taken it from the

mantra of most estate agents who reckon selling a
house is about three things – Location! Location!
Location!

Surviving in Iraq is about three things too – Low
profile! Low profile! Low profile!

Spearhead Assault

John Geddes

Blood, Guts and Glory on the Falklands Frontlines

On May 21st, 1982, nearly four hundred soldiers from the 2cd Battalion Parachute Regiment under the command of Lieutenant-Colonel Herbert 'H' Jones, landed with a British Task Force at San Carlos Bay on the Falklands. Their mission: to take the strategic position at Goose Green where military intelligence reckoned there were a couple of hundred Argentine troops guarding an airstrip.

The intelligence was wrong and when they attacked on May 27th, they were confronted by a 1,500-strong regiment of Argentine soldiers dug in with so much machine-gun ammunition they stood on the ammo boxes to keep their feet dry. It was going to be a hard and dreadful fight.

Fourteen hours later when the smoke had cleared on the most ferocious battle in post-war British history, nearly 250 Argentine soldiers were killed. Scores more were wounded and another 1,300 had been captured. Goose Green would also cost 2 Para the lives of seventeen men.

Now, John Geddes, a former 2 Para close reconnaissance corporal and SAS hero tells the uncut story of the Battle of Goose Green, the decisive battle of the Falklands War. This is a no-holds barred account of what it was really like to walk into the storm of lead the Argentines hurled at their attackers.

Century · London